The Shurangama Sutra

Volume Eight

The Shurangama Sutra

Volume Eight

with commentary by the

Venerable Master Hsuan Hua

A nine book series

First Edition, 2003
Sutra Text and Supplements, Volumes 1 to 8

English translation by the
Buddhist Text Translation Society
ISBN 0-88139-949-3

The Shurangama Sutra - Volume Eight

Published and translated by:

Buddhist Text Translation Society
1777 Murchison Drive, Burlingame, CA 94010-4504

© 2003   **Buddhist Text Translation Society**
Dharma Realm Buddhist University
Dharma Realm Buddhist Association

First edition 2003

12 11 10 09 08 07 06 05 04 03   10 9 8 7 6 5 4 3 2 1

ISBN 0-88139-948-5

Printed in Malaysia.

Addresses of the Dharma Realm Buddhist Association branches are listed at the back of this book.

Library of Congress Cataloging-in-Publication Data

Hsüan Hua, 1908-
 The Shurangama sutra with commentary / by Hsuan Hua ; English translation by the Buddhist Text Translation Society.-- 1st ed.
   p. cm.
 Sutra translated from Chinese, originally written in Sanskrit. "The Shurangama sutra/ Sutra & suppliments" (ISBN 0-88139-940-X) issued together.
  ISBN 0-88139-949-3 (set : alk. paper) -- ISBN 0-88139-941-8 (v. 1 : alk. paper) -- ISBN 0-88139-942-6 (v. 2 : alk. paper) -- ISBN 0-88139-943-4 (v. 3 : alk. paper) -- ISBN 0-88139-944-2 (v. 4 : alk. paper) -- ISBN 0-88139-945-0 (v. 5 : alk. paper) -- ISBN 0-88139-946-9 (v. 6 : alk. paper) -- ISBN 0-88139-947-7 (v. 7 : alk. paper) -- ISBN 0-88139-948-5 (v. 8 : alk. paper)
  1. Tripiṭaka. Sūtrapiṭaka. Sūraṅgamasūtra--Commentaries. I. Buddhist Text Translation Society. II. Tripiṭaka. Sūtrapiṭaka. Sūraṅgamasūtra. English. III. Title.

BQ2127.H7813 2003
294.3'85--dc21

2002151845

Contents

Introduction vi

User's Guide viii

Exhortation to Protect and Propagate ix

The Eight Guidelines. xii

Outline. xiii

Chapter 1. The Origin of Demonic States 1

Chapter 2. The Form Skandha 25

Chapter 3. The Feeling Skandha. 50

Chapter 4. The Thinking Skandha 81

Chapter 5. The Formations Skandha 171

Chapter 6. The Consciousness Skandha 233

Chapter 7. Concluding Instructions 271

Chapter 8. The Arising and Cessation of the Five Skandhas . . 281

Chapter 9. Exhortation to Propagate the Sutra 313

General Index 323

Introduction

This is Volume Eight of the *Shurangama Sutra* series, with commentaries by the Venerable Master Hsuan Hua.

The Buddha appears to be finished with the sermon as he prepares to leave, but then a compassionate afterthought makes him resume his Dharma seat. Having given Ananda and the great assembly a precise and detailed account of the methods of cultivation, the Buddha was concerned that if cultivators were not equipped with the knowledge of spotting subtle demonic states that can happen during the cultivation of samadhi, they may be swayed and turned into demonic beings themselves.

In "The Origin of Demonic States," the Buddha states clearly that samadhi is the main cause for the demons' unrest. The demons then will attempt to confuse the good cultivator. If the good cultivator recognizes the situation and remains unattached, then the cultivator has not erred. However, if the cultivator is confused by the state, he or she will then fall under the spell of the demons.

The Buddha then proceeds to list and explain the ten demonic states that can occur for each skandhic realm: "The Form Skandha," "The Feeling Skandha," "The Thinking Skandha," "The Formations Skandha" and "The Consciousness Skandha," making fifty in all. The Buddha relates exactly what the cultivator might experience at each of these fifty states, and warns them to remain unattached and unconfused.

In "Concluding Instructions," the Buddha tells that by relying on this dharma-door, Buddhas of the past have attained enlightenment. The Buddha again reiterates that if the cultivator recognizes a demonic-state and remains unconfused and unattached, then the demon will be powerless.

In "The Arising and Cessation of the Five Skandhas," Ananda requests further explanation for the arisal and cessation of the five skandhas. The Buddha then instructs that the five skandhas arise solely from false thinking alone, and will also cessate with the ending of false thinking. The cessation of false thinking can only be achieved if the six sense faculties are united and function interchangeably.

Finally, the Buddha exhorts all to propagate the teachings in "Exhortation to Propagate the Sutra," so that living beings of the present and future will derive limitless benefit.

User's Guide

to the Shurangama Sutra series

Because of the length of the *Shurangama Sutra*, and the need to provide aid to various readers, the sutra has been compiled into a series of 9 books: the "Sutra Text and Supplements," and the remaining volumes one to eight.

The "Sutra Text and Supplements" contains:

1. the entire sutra text, consisting of over 2700 paragraphs;
2. the entire outline, consisting of over 1670 entries; and
3. a master index for the eight commentarial volumes.

Volumes one to eight contain:

1. sutra text, with commentaries by Venerable Master Hua;
2. local outline entries; and
3. a local index.

Readers who wish to read, study or recite the sutra in its entirety will find the "Sutra Text and Supplements" very useful.

Those who wish to deeply delve into the sutra will find the commentaries in volumes one to eight indispensable.

Exhortation to Protect and Propagate

by Tripitaka Master Hsuan Hua

Within Buddhism, there are very many important sutras. However, the most important sutra is the *Shurangama Sutra*. If there are places which have the *Shurangama Sutra*, then the proper dharma dwells in the world. If there is no *Shurangama Sutra*, then the dharma ending age appears. Therefore, we Buddhist disciples, each and every one, must bring our strength, must bring our blood, and must bring our sweat to protect the *Shurangama Sutra*. In the *Sutra of the Ultimate Extinction of the Dharma*, it says very, very clearly that in the dharma ending age, the *Shurangama Sutra* is the first to disappear, and the rest of the sutras disappear after it. If the *Shurangama Sutra* does not disappear, then the proper dharma age is present. Because of that, we Buddhist disciples must use our lives to protect the *Shurangama Sutra*. We must use vows and resolution to protect the *Shurangama Sutra*, and cause the *Shurangama Sutra* to be known far and wide, reaching every nook and cranny, reaching into each and every dust-mote, reaching out to the exhaustion of empty space and of the dharma realm. If we can do that, then there will be a time of proper dharma radiating great light.

Why would the *Shurangama Sutra* be destroyed? It is because it is too true. The *Shurangama Sutra* is the Buddha's true body. The *Shurangama Sutra* is the Buddha's sharira. The *Shurangama Sutra* is the Buddha's true and actual stupa and shrine. Therefore, because the *Shurangama Sutra* is so true, all the demon kings use all kinds of methods to destroy the *Shurangama Sutra*. They begin by starting rumors, saying that the *Shurangama Sutra* is phony. Why do they say the *Shurangama Sutra* is phony? It is because the *Shurangama Sutra* speaks too truly, especially in the sections on the Four Decisive Deeds, the Twenty-five Sages Describing Perfect Penetration, and the States of the Fifty Skandha Demons. Those of off-center persuasions and externally-oriented ways, weird demons and strange freaks, are unable to stand it. Consequently, there are a good many senseless people who claim that the *Shurangama Sutra* is a forgery.

Now, the principles set forth in the *Shurangama Sutra* are on the one hand proper, and on the other in accord with principle, and the weird demons and strange freaks, those in various cults and sects, all cannot hide away their forms. Most senseless people, in particular the unwise scholars and garbage-collecting professors, "tread upon the holy writ." With their extremely scant and partial understanding, they are confused and unclear, lacking real erudition and true and actual wisdom. That is why they falsely criticize. We who study the Buddhadharma should very deeply be aware of these circumstances. Therefore, wherever we go, we should bring up the *Shurangama Sutra*. Wherever we go, we should propagate the *Shurangama Sutra*. Wherever we go, we should introduce the *Shurangama Sutra* to people. Why is that? It is because we wish to cause the proper dharma to dwell long in the world.

If the *Shurangama Sutra* is regarded as true, then there is no problem. To verify its truth, let me say that if the *Shurangama Sutra* were phony, then I would willingly fall into the hells forever through all eternity – for being unable to recognize the Buddhadharma – for mistaking the false for true. If the *Shurangama Sutra* is true, then life after life in every time I make the vow to propagate the great dharma of the Shurangama, that I shall in every time and every place propagate the true principles of the Shurangama.

Everyone should pay attention to the following point. How could the *Shurangama Sutra* not have been spoken by the Buddha?

No one else could have spoken the *Shurangama Sutra*. And so I hope that all those people who make senseless accusations will wake up fast and stop creating the causes for suffering in the Hell of Pulling Out Tongues. No matter who the scholar is, no matter what country students of the Buddhadharma are from, all should quickly mend their ways, admit their mistakes, and manage to change. There is no greater good than that. I can then say that all who look at the *Shurangama Sutra*, all who listen to the *Shurangama Sutra*, and all who investigate the *Shurangama Sutra*, will very quickly accomplish Buddhahood.

composed by,
Gold Mountain Shramana Tripitaka Master Hua

The Eight Guidelines

of the Buddhist Text Translation Society

1. A volunteer must free him/herself from the motives of personal fame and profit.
2. A volunteer must cultivate a respectful and sincere attitude free from arrogance and conceit.
3. A volunteer must refrain from aggrandizing his/her work and denigrating that of others.
4. A volunteer must not establish him/herself as the standard of correctness and suppress the work of others with his or her fault-finding.
5. A volunteer must take the Buddha-mind as his/her own mind.
6. A volunteer must use the wisdom of Dharma-selecting Vision to determine true principles.
7. A volunteer must request Virtuous Elders in the ten directions to certify his/her translations.
8. A volunteer must endeavour to propagate the teachings by printing Sutras, Shastra texts, and Vinaya texts when the translations are certified as being correct.

Outline

of the Shurangama Sutra

The outline for the *Shurangama Sutra*, compiled by Dharma Master Yuan Ying, categorizes the various parts of the sutra text of over 2,700 paragraphs to over 1,670 entries.

These entries are presented in the form of a tree-like structure which divides the various parts of the sutra text into sections and sub-sections.

Though the outline is not a prerequisite to reading the sutra text and the accompanying commentaries, it serves as a useful tool for students of the Way who wish to systematically study the sutra. Without this outline, students may find it difficult to refer to specific parts of the text.

Only outline entries which pertain to the sutra text contained within this volume is included.

For the outline of the entire sutra, please refer to the "Sutra Text and Supplements."

Outline of Shurangama Sutra – Volume Eight

- D2 Identifying the five demons so cultivators can recognize them and avoid failing. ... 1
  - E1 The demonic states of the five skandhas are spoken without request. ... 1
    - F1 Everyone should recognize these demonic states. ... 1
      - G1 Final true and unending compassion. ... 1
      - G2 Specific indication of the subtle demonic events. ... 2
      - G3 Exhortation to pay attention and promise to speak. ... 9
    - F2 The members of the assembly bow and listen respectfully. ... 9
    - F3 Detailed explanation of the demons' deeds. ... 10
      - G1 Telling where they come from. ... 10
        - H1 Samadhi is the reason for the demons' agitation. ... 10
          - I1 Emphasizing the significance of the dual aspects of true and false, production and destruction. ... 10
            - J1 First, explaining that our fundamental enlightenment is the same as the Buddha's. ... 10
            - J2 Next, explaining how emptiness comes from falseness. ... 12
            - J3 For the sake of comparison, describing the minuteness of the realm of space. ... 13
            - J4 Returning to the source obliterates space. ... 14
          - I2 Explaining that great samadhi causes demons to manifest. ... 14
            - J1 One's mind tallies with the minds of the sages. ... 15
            - J2 The demons come en masse to cause disturbance. ... 19
        - H2 The demons can succeed in their destructiveness through the cultivator's confusion. ... 19
          - I1 Explanation by analogy of how "the guests" cannot bring harm. ... 20
          - I2 Conclusion that the confusion is on the part of the cultivator. ... 20
          - I3 Once enlightened, one surely will transcend their disturbance. ... 23
          - I4 Confusion will certainly bring a fall. ... 23
          - I5 The prior incident in the house of prostitution brought only slight harm. ... 24
          - I6 Joining the ranks of demons would bring great harm. ... 25
      - G2 Detailed analysis of the characteristics of the demons of the five skandhas. ... 25
        - H1 The characteristics of the demons of the form skandha. ... 25
          - I1 Overview from beginning to end. ... 25
            - J1 Initial cultivation does not break though the skandhas' boundaries. ... 25
            - J2 Ultimately it breaks up and reveals its false source. ... 26

- I2 The ten states within this region. 27
  - J1 His body can transcend obstructions. 27
  - J2 Internally the light pervades and he can extract intestinal worms. 30
  - J3 His essence and souls alternately separate and unite. 32
  - J4 The state changes and Buddhas appear. 35
  - J5 Space takes on the color of precious things. 37
  - J6 He can see things in the dark. 38
  - J7 His body becomes like grass or wood. 40
  - J8 He can see everywhere without obstruction. 41
  - J9 He sees and hears distant things. 43
  - J10 False visions and false words. 44
- I3 Conclusion on the harm, and command to offer protection. 46
  - J1 Showing how the states come about from interaction. 46
  - J2 Confusion will bring harm. 47
  - J3 Command to offer protection. 49
- H2 The characteristics of demons of the feeling. 50
  - I1 Overview of the beginning and the end. 50
    - J1 In the beginning, cultivation has not yet broken out of this region. 50
      - K1 Review of the ending of the previous form skandha. 50
      - K2 Introduction to the region of the feeling skandha. 51
    - J2 Ultimately it breaks up and reveals its false source. 51
  - I2 The ten states within this region. 52
    - J1 Suppression of the self leads to sadness. 52
      - K1 The characteristics of its beginning. 52
      - K2 Giving its name and instructions to awaken. 52
      - K3 Showing how confusion will certainly bring a fall. 52
    - J2 He praises himself as being equal to the Buddhas. 54
      - K1 The characteristics of its beginning. 54
      - K2 Giving the name and instructions to awaken. 55
      - K3 Showing how confusion will certainly bring a fall. 55

Outline of Shurangama Sutra – Volume Eight

Outline of Shurangama Sutra – Volume Eight

- J3 Samadhi out of balance brings much reverie... 57
  - K1 The characteristics of its beginning... 57
  - K2 Giving the name and instructions to awaken... 59
  - K3 Showing how confusion will certainly bring a fall... 59
- J4 Wisdom out of balance brings much arrogance... 60
  - K1 The characteristics of its beginning... 60
  - K2 Giving the name and instructions to awaken... 60
  - K3 Showing how confusion will certainly bring a fall... 60
- J5 Passing through danger leads to anxiety... 62
  - K1 The characteristics of its beginning... 62
  - K2 Giving the name and instructions to awaken... 63
  - K3 Showing how confusion will certainly bring a fall... 63
- J6 Experiencing ease leads to joy... 66
  - K1 The characteristics of its beginning... 66
  - K2 Giving the name, and instructions to awaken... 67
  - K3 Showing how confusion will certainly bring a fall... 67
- J7 Seeing the sublime and becoming proud... 68
  - K1 The characteristics of its beginning... 68
  - K2 Giving the name and instructions to awaken... 69
  - K3 Showing how confusion will certainly bring a fall... 69
- J8 With wisdom comes lightness and ease, which leads to complacency... 71
  - K1 The characteristics of its beginning... 71
  - K2 Giving the name and instructions to awaken... 71
  - K3 Showing how confusion will certainly bring a fall... 72
- J9 Becoming attached to emptiness and slandering precepts... 73
  - K1 The characteristics of its beginning... 73
  - K2 Giving its name and instructions to awaken... 73
  - K3 Showing how confusion will certainly bring a fall... 74
- J10 Becoming attached to existence and indulging in lust... 76
  - K1 The characteristics of its beginning... 76

		K2	Giving its name and instructions to awaken.	76
		K3	Showing how confusion will certainly bring a fall.	77
	I3	Conclusion on the harm, and command to offer protection.		79
		J1	Showing how this happens due to interaction.	79
		J2	Confusion will bring harm.	79
		J3	Command to offer protection.	80
H3	The characteristics of the demons of the thinking skandha.			81
	I1	Overview of the beginning and end.		81
		J1	In the beginning, cultivation has not yet broken out of this region.	81
			K1 Review of the ending of the previous feeling skandha.	81
			K2 Introduction to the region of the thinking skandha.	82
		J2	Ultimately it breaks up and reveals its false source.	83
	I2	The ten states within this.		84
		J1	Greed for clever skill.	84
			K1 Samadhi leads to craving and seeking.	84
			K2 A demon dispatches a deviant force to possess a person.	86
			K3 The person who is possessed causes trouble.	92
			K4 The cultivator becomes deluded and confused.	94
			K5 The types of things he says.	94
			K6 Giving the name and pointing out the harm.	96
			K7 Instructions to be aware and not become confused.	99
		J2	Greedy for adventure.	99
			K1 Samadhi leads to craving and seeking.	99
			K2 A demon dispatches a deviant force to possess a person.	100
			K3 The person who is possessed causes trouble.	100
			K4 The cultivator becomes deluded and confused.	101
			K5 The types of things he says.	102
			K6 Giving the name and pointing out the harm.	104
			K7 Instructions to be aware and not become confused.	104
		J3	Greed for union.	105

Outline of Shurangama Sutra – Volume Eight

Outline of Shurangama Sutra – Volume Eight

- K1 Samadhi leads to craving and seeking. ... 105
- K2 A demon dispatches a deviant force to possess a person. ... 105
- K3 The person who is possessed causes trouble. ... 106
- K4 The cultivator becomes deluded and confused. ... 109
- K5 The types of things he says. ... 109
- K6 Giving the name and pointing out the harm. ... 110
- K7 Instructions to be aware and not become confused. ... 111
- J4 Greed to analyze things. ... 111
  - K1 Samadhi leads to craving and seeking. ... 111
  - K2 A demon dispatches a deviant force to possess a person. ... 112
  - K3 The person who is possessed causes trouble. ... 113
  - K4 The people become deluded and confused. ... 115
  - K5 The types of things he says. ... 116
  - K6 Giving the name, and pointing out the harm. ... 116
  - K7 Instructions to be aware and not become confused. ... 117
- J5 Greed for spiritual responses. ... 117
  - K1 Samadhi leads to craving and seeking. ... 117
  - K2 A demon dispatches a deviant force to possess a person. ... 118
  - K3 The person who is possessed causes trouble. ... 118
  - K4 The cultivator becomes deluded and confused. ... 121
  - K5 The types of things he says. ... 122
  - K6 Giving the name and pointing out the harm. ... 123
  - K7 Instructions to be aware and not become confused. ... 123
- J6 Greed for peace and quiet. ... 124
  - K1 Samadhi leads to craving and seeking. ... 124
  - K2 A demon dispatches a deviant force to possess a person. ... 124
  - K3 The demon's words and deeds that mislead others. ... 125
  - K4 Giving the name and pointing out the harm. ... 131
  - K5 Instructions to be aware and not become confused. ... 131
- J7 Greed to know past lives. ... 132

K1	Samadhi leads to craving and seeking.	132
K2	A demon dispatches a deviant force to possess a person.	133
K3	The demon's words and deeds that mislead others.	133
K4	Giving the name and pointing out the harm.	139
K5	Instructions to be aware and not become confused.	140
J8 Greed for spiritual powers.		141
K1	Samadhi leads to craving and seeking.	141
K2	A demon dispatches a deviant force to possess a person.	142
K3	The demon's words and deeds that mislead others.	142
K4	Giving the name and pointing out the harm.	144
K5	Instructions to be aware and not become confused.	145
J9 Greed for profound emptiness.		145
K1	Samadhi leads to craving and seeking.	145
K2	A demon dispatches a deviant force to possess a person.	146
K3	The demon's words and deeds that mislead others.	146
K4	Giving the name and pointing out the harm.	148
K5	Instructions to be aware and not become confused.	152
J10 Greed for immortality.		152
K1	Samadhi leads to craving and seeking.	152
K2	A demon dispatches a deviant spirit to possess a person.	153
K3	The demon's words and deeds that mislead others.	154
K4	Giving the name and pointing out the harm.	156
K5	Instructions to be aware and not become confused.	160
I3 The Buddha exhorts those in the Dharma-ending Age.		161
J1	False boasting of accomplishment to sagely fruition.	161
J2	They use lust in their teaching.	164
J3	They are beguiled by demons and fall into the hells.	165
J4	Exhortation to compassionately rescue them to repay kindness.	166
I4 Conclusion on the harm, and command to offer protection.		168
J1	Showing how the states come about from interaction.	168

Outline of Shurangama Sutra – Volume Eight

xix

Outline of Shurangama Sutra – Volume Eight

- J2 Confusion will bring harm. ... 168
- J3 Command to offer protection. ... 170
- H4 The characteristics of the demons of the formations skandha. ... 171
  - I1 Overview of the beginning and end. ... 171
    - J1 In the beginning, one cultivates but has not yet broken through this region. ... 171
      - K1 Review of the ending of the previous thinking skandha. ... 171
      - K2 Introduction to the region of the formations skandha. ... 176
    - J2 Ultimately it breaks up and reveals its false source. ... 177
  - I2 The ten speculations therein. ... 178
    - J1 Two theories on the absence of cause. ... 178
      - K1 Describes the source and shows the error. ... 178
      - K2 Detailed explanation of their appearance. ... 179
        - L1 He sees no cause for the origin of life. ... 179
          - M1 He describes the measure of his vision. ... 179
          - M2 He comes up with a wrong speculation. ... 180
          - M3 He mistakes the principle and falls for an externalist teaching. ... 180
        - L2 He sees no cause for the end of life. ... 181
          - M1 He describes the measure of his vision. ... 181
          - M2 He comes up with a wrong speculation. ... 184
          - M3 He mistakes the principle and falls for an externalist teaching. ... 187
      - K3 Concludes that it is an externalist teaching. ... 187
    - J2 Four theories regarding pervasive permanence. ... 187
      - K1 Describes their source and shows the error. ... 187
      - K2 Detailed explanation of their appearance. ... 188
        - L1 He speculates that the mind and states are permanent. ... 188
        - L2 He speculates that the four elements are permanent. ... 189
        - L3 He speculates that the eight consciousnesses are permanent. ... 189
        - L4 He speculates that the cessation of thoughts is permanent. ... 190
      - K3 Concludes that it is an externalist teaching. ... 191
    - J3 Four upside-down theories. ... 191

	K1	Describes the source and shows the error.		191
	K2	Detailed explanation of their appearance.		192
		L1	Speculation regarding self and others.	192
		L2	Speculation regarding worlds.	193
		L3	Speculation regarding his body and mind.	194
		L4	Speculation regarding neither self nor others.	195
	K3	Concludes that it is an externalist teaching.		195
J4	Four theories regarding finiteness.			196
	K1	Describes the source and shows the error.		196
	K2	Detailed explanation of their appearance.		197
		L1	Speculation regarding the three periods of time.	197
		L2	Speculation regarding what he hears and sees.	198
		L3	Speculation regarding self and others.	199
		L4	Speculation regarding production and destruction.	200
	K3	Concludes that it is an externalist teaching.		201
J5	Four kinds of sophistry.			201
	K1	Describes the source and shows the error.		201
	K2	Detailed explanation of their appearance.		204
		L1	Eight sophistries.	204
		L2	The sophistry of only "no."	206
		L3	The sophistry of only "yes."	207
		L4	The sophistry of existence and non-existence.	209
	K3	Concludes that it is an externalist teaching.		210
J6	The sixteen ways in which form can exist after death.			213
	K1	Describes the source and shows the error.		213
	K2	Detailed explanation of their appearance.		214
	K3	Concludes that it is an externalist teaching.		216
J7	Eight ideas about the non-existence of form.			216
	K1	Describes the source and shows the error.		216
	K2	Detailed explanation of their appearance.		217

Outline of Shurangama Sutra – Volume Eight

Outline of Shurangama Sutra – Volume Eight

```
      K3  Concludes that it is an externalist teaching. . . . . . . . . . . . . . . . . . . . . . . 219
   J8  Eight kinds of negation. . . . . . . . . . . . . . . . . . . . . . . . . . . . . . . . . . . . . . . . . . 220
      K1  Describes the source and shows the error. . . . . . . . . . . . . . . . . . . . . 220
      K2  Detailed explanation of their appearance. . . . . . . . . . . . . . . . . . . . . . 221
      K3  Concludes that it is an externalist teaching. . . . . . . . . . . . . . . . . . . . 222
   J9  Seven theories on the cessation of existence. . . . . . . . . . . . . . . . . . . . . . 223
      K1  Describes the source and shows the error. . . . . . . . . . . . . . . . . . . . . 223
      K2  Detailed explanation of their appearance. . . . . . . . . . . . . . . . . . . . . . 224
      K3  Concludes that it is an externalist teaching. . . . . . . . . . . . . . . . . . . . 227
   J10 Five kinds of immediate nirvana. . . . . . . . . . . . . . . . . . . . . . . . . . . . . . . . . 227
      K1  Describes the source and shows the error. . . . . . . . . . . . . . . . . . . . . 227
      K2  Detailed explanation of their appearance. . . . . . . . . . . . . . . . . . . . . . 228
      K3  Concludes that it is an externalist teaching. . . . . . . . . . . . . . . . . . . . 230
 I3  Conclusion on the harm, and command to offer protection. . . . . . . . . . . . . . 230
   J1  Showing how this happens due to interaction. . . . . . . . . . . . . . . . . . . . . 230
   J2  Confusion will bring harm. . . . . . . . . . . . . . . . . . . . . . . . . . . . . . . . . . . . . 231
   J3  Command to offer protection. . . . . . . . . . . . . . . . . . . . . . . . . . . . . . . . . . 231
H5 The characteristics of the demons of the consciousness skandha. . . . . . . . . . 233
 I1  Overview of the beginning and the end. . . . . . . . . . . . . . . . . . . . . . . . . . . . . 233
   J1  In the beginning, one cultivates but has not yet broken through this region. . 233
      K1  Review of the ending of the previous formations skandha. . . . . . . . . 233
      K2  Introduction to the region of the consciousness skandha. . . . . . . . . . 234
   J2  Ultimately it breaks up and reveals its false source. . . . . . . . . . . . . . . . . 236
 I2  Ten attachments within this. . . . . . . . . . . . . . . . . . . . . . . . . . . . . . . . . . . . . . 237
   J1  Attachment to causes and that which is caused. . . . . . . . . . . . . . . . . . . 237
      K1  When formations are gone, consciousness appears. . . . . . . . . . . . . 237
      K2  A wrong understanding leads to a mistake. . . . . . . . . . . . . . . . . . . . . 238
      K3  Giving the name and instructions to awaken. . . . . . . . . . . . . . . . . . . 241
   J2  Attachment to an ability that is not actually an ability. . . . . . . . . . . . . . . 241
      K1  When formations are gone, consciousness appears. . . . . . . . . . . . . 241
```

	K2	A wrong understanding leads to a mistake.	242
	K3	Giving its name and instructions to awaken.	244
J3		Attachment to a wrong idea of permanence.	245
	K1	When formations are gone, consciousness appears.	245
	K2	A wrong understanding leads to a mistake.	245
	K3	He gives it a name and warns us to be aware of it.	247
J4		Attachment to an awareness that is not actually awareness.	247
	K1	When formations are gone, consciousness appears.	247
	K2	A wrong understanding leads to a mistake.	248
	K3	He gives it a name and warns us to be aware of it.	249
J5		Attachment to birth that is not actually birth.	250
	K1	When formations are gone, consciousness appears.	250
	K2	A wrong understanding leads to a mistake.	251
	K3	He gives it a name and warns us to be aware of it.	253
J6		Attachment to a refuge that is not actually a refuge.	253
	K1	After formations are ended, consciousness manifests.	253
	K2	A wrong understanding leads to a mistake.	254
	K3	Giving its name and instructions to awaken.	255
J7		Attachment to an unattainable craving.	255
	K1	After formations are ended, consciousness manifests.	255
	K2	A wrong understanding leads to a mistake.	256
	K3	Giving its name and instructions to awaken.	256
J8		Attachment to truth that is not actually truth.	257
	K1	After formations are ended, consciousness manifests.	257
	K2	A wrong understanding leads to a mistake.	257
	K3	Giving its name and instructions to awaken.	259
J9		Fixed-nature hearers.	259
	K1	After formations are ended, consciousness manifests.	259
	K2	A wrong understanding leads to a mistake.	260
	K3	Giving its name and instructions to awaken.	261

Outline of Shurangama Sutra – Volume Eight

xxiii

Outline of Shurangama Sutra – Volume Eight

```
        J10 Fixed-nature pratyekas. .................................................................. 262
            K1  After formations are ended, consciousness manifests. ............ 262
            K2  A wrong understanding leads to a mistake. ............................ 262
            K3  Giving its name and instructions to awaken. .......................... 263
        I3  Conclusion on the harm and command to offer protection. ................ 264
            J1  Show how this happens due to interaction. ............................. 264
            J2  Confusion will bring harm. ...................................................... 268
            J3  Command to offer protection. ................................................. 269
    G3  Concluding instructs. ................................................................................ 271
        H1  First instructs to transcend and certify. ............................................... 271
            I1  All Buddhas' former certification. ............................................... 271
            I2  The end of consciousness is transcendence. ........................... 272
            I3  Perfect realization of the ultimate fruition. ................................. 273
        H2  He then instructs us to protect and uphold it. ..................................... 274
            I1  He first explains how it accords with the honored ones of the past. .... 274
            I2  Orders him to recognize the demonic states, and to protect and uphold the samadhi. .... 276
            I3  Advises him to revere this teaching as an example from the past. ...... 280
E2  Request for further explanation of the arising and cessation of the five skandhas. ..... 281
    F1  Ananda repeats the former teaching and makes a request. ........................ 281
    F2  The Buddha answers three questions. ........................................................ 284
        G1  He first answers that they arise from falseness. ................................. 284
            H1  He shows the reasons for false thinking. ................................. 284
                I1  Pursuing the source and finding it empty. ........................... 284
                I2  Judges the upside-down speculations to be wrong. ........... 289
                I3  Concluding with reiteration that the cause is false thinking. .... 291
            H2  Detailed examination of the fivefold false thinking. ................... 293
                I1  The false thinking of the form skandha. .............................. 293
                    J1  Explains that one's body is because of thinking. ........... 293
                    J2  Provides an analogy to explain in detail. ........................ 295
                    J3  Concludes by naming it false thinking. ........................... 297
```

- I2 The false thinking of the feeling skandha. 297
  - J1 Thinking results in feeling. 297
  - J2 Discussing its extent and concluding with the name. 298
- I3 The false thinking of the thinking skandha. 299
  - J1 Body and mind in mutual response. 299
  - J2 Discussing its extent and concluding with the name. 300
- I4 The false thinking of the formations skandha. 301
  - J1 Lack of awareness of bodily changes. 301
  - J2 Discusses its extent and concludes with the name. 303
- I5 The false thinking of the consciousness skandha. 304
  - J1 Directly destroying the duality of true and false. 304
  - J2 Uses an analogy to explain. 305
  - J3 Indicates accurately its time of cessation. 306
  - J4 Discussing its extent and concluding with the name. 306
- H3 General conclusion of what false thinking brings into being. 307
- G2 Answers about the depth of the realms of the skandhas. 307
- G3 Answers about the suddenness or gradualness of cessation. 308
- F3 Concluding exhortation to transmit this teaching. 311
- B3 Propagation section. 313
  - C1 Compares to blessings of offering to Buddhas. 313
  - C3 Praising the merit of extinguishing evil. 315
  - C4 Brings up the supremacy of two benefits. 317
  - C5 Concludes with the dharma bliss experienced by the great assembly. 320

Outline of Shurangama Sutra – Volume Eight

Namo Original Teacher Shakyamuni Buddha

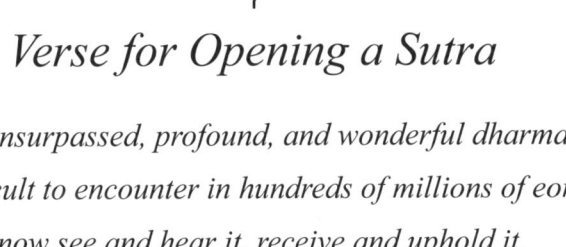

Verse for Opening a Sutra

*The unsurpassed, profound, and wonderful dharma,
Is difficult to encounter in hundreds of millions of eons,
I now see and hear it, receive and uphold it,
And I vow to fathom the Tathagata's true meaning.*

CHAPTER 1

The Origin of Demonic States

D2 Identifying the five demons so cultivators can recognize them and avoid failing.
E1 The demonic states of the five skandhas are spoken without request.
F1 Everyone should recognize these demonic states.
G1 Final true and unending compassion.

Sutra:

At that time, the Tathagata was preparing to leave the dharma seat. From the lion throne, he extended his hand and placed it on a small table wrought of the seven precious things. But then he turned his body, which was the color of purple golden mountains, and leaned back, saying to everyone in the assembly and to Ananda: "Those of you with more to learn, those enlightened by conditions, and those who are soundhearers have now turned your minds to pursue the attainment of supreme bodhi, the unsurpassed, wonderful enlightenment. I have already taught you the true method of cultivation.

Commentary:

At that time, the Tathagata was preparing to leave the dharma seat, since he had almost finished speaking the *Shurangama Sutra*. **From the lion throne, he reached his hand out and placed it on a small table wrought of the seven precious things.** The Buddha was on his dharma seat, the lion throne. The

Buddha's speaking of the dharma is like a lion's roar. When a lion roars, all the animals are frightened. That's why the Buddha's dharma seat is called the lion throne. The small table in front of the Buddha was made of and adorned with the seven precious things.

But then he turned his body, which was the color of purple golden mountains, and leaned back. The Buddha's body is like a purple golden mountain; its brightness shines everywhere. He leaned on the small table again to speak the dharma, **saying to everyone in the assembly and to Ananda: Those of you with more to learn.** Before certifying to the fourth stage of arhatship, one is in the position of having more to learn. **Those enlightened by conditions and those who are sound-hearers** – those who become enlightened through cultivating the twelve links of conditioned causation and those sound-hearers who become enlightened through cultivating the dharma of the four noble truths – **have now turned your minds to pursue the attainment of supreme bodhi – the unsurpassed, wonderful enlightenment.** You have now turned from the small to go towards the great. You of the two vehicles have brought forth the great vehicle resolve and seek to attain great enlightenment; there is no enlightenment higher than this. **I have already taught you the true method of cultivation.** I have already explained the real method of cultivation for you.

G2 Specific indication of the subtle demonic events.

Sutra:

"**You are still not aware of the subtle demonic events that can occur when you cultivate shamatha and vipashyana. If you cannot recognize a demonic state when it appears, it is because the cleansing of your mind has not been proper. You will then be engulfed by deviant views.**

Commentary:

You are still not aware. Earlier, Ananda asked the Buddha how to cultivate. He had requested the dharma on behalf of living beings of the future. But, although he now understands the principle of cultivation, he doesn't have any actual experience. He understands the theory, but since he lacks experience, he doesn't know what can occur in cultivation. So the Buddha said, "You are still not aware **of the subtle demonic events that can occur when you cultivate shamatha and vipashyana.**" In cultivating *shamatha*, which refers to the great Shurangama Samadhi, and in cultivating *vipashyana*, a method of subtle contemplation, subtle demonic states can arise. In the process of cultivation, many demonic states can arise which are not very obvious, but, rather, extremely obscure.

If you cannot recognize a demonic state when it appears. When you are cultivating the Way and practicing the skill of "directing the hearing inward to listen to the inherent nature," a demonic state may appear. If you do not recognize the demon and do not know what demons are, **it is because the cleansing of your mind has not been proper**. You have been cleansing your mind, but what you have done is slightly incorrect – not in accord with proper knowledge and views. For that reason, **you will then be engulfed by deviant views**. If your knowledge and views are the slightest bit improper, you will be caught up in deviant views.

Sutra:
   "You may be troubled by a demon from your own skandhas or a demon from the heavens. Or you may be possessed by a ghost or spirit, or you may encounter a li ghost or a mei ghost. If your mind is not clear, you will mistake a thief for your own son.

Commentary:
   You may be troubled by a demon from your own skandhas; that is, a demon produced from your own mind, or one of the ten kinds of demons produced from the form skandha, which is also of your own making. **Or** it may be **a demon from the heavens**. Why should a demon from the heavens come to disturb you? It's because you have cultivated to the point that you have some samadhi. Having samadhi is no problem in itself, but what happens is that the demon king's palace starts to shake. It seems just like an

earthquake. Since the demon king has spiritual powers, as soon as the shaking starts, he investigates, "Why is my palace shaking for no apparent reason? Why is it breaking apart? Aha!" He discovers that someone in the world is about to accomplish the Way and that the strength of that person's samadhi is shattering his palace. The demon king thinks, "So you want to destroy me? Well, I'm going to destroy your samadhi first!" Then he comes to wipe out your samadhi power.

Or you may be possessed by a ghost or spirit. When the ghosts and spirits see that you are about to realize the fruition in your cultivation, they become jealous. They think, "Oh, so you are going to realize the fruition? We're going to destroy your cultivation first!" Then they enter your mind or possess your body, making it impossible for you to perfect your samadhi power. They cause you to "catch on fire" and become possessed. Didn't the preceding passage of text talk about being possessed by a demon? This is very important. Why do you become possessed by a demon? Because "the cleansing of your mind has not been proper," and because your motivation is improper. With even the slightest deviant thought, you get caught by a demon. This is known as "catching on fire and entering a demonic state."

Or you may encounter a li ghost or a mei ghost or a *wang liang*. Those are types of ghosts and goblins. **If your mind is not clear, you will mistake a thief for your own son.** If you encounter such a state and fail to recognize or understand it, you will end up "mistaking a thief for your son." Think about it: How can they not rob or steal your possessions? If you invite a thief into your home, then all the priceless treasures in your house will be stolen. What are your priceless treasures? I will tell you frankly, and be sure to remember this! You should believe what I say. Whatever you do, don't fail to believe what I say. Why? Because it is important to your future and to your life. What are your treasures? They are your very own treasury of the Tathagata. Can your treasury of the Tathagata be stolen? Didn't I mention essence, energy and spirit before? If you want to regain your treasury of the Tathagata, you first have to protect your essence, energy, and spirit. If you fail to guard these three, you are allowing your wealth to be robbed from you. So be careful!

[January 1983]

All people like money. They think, "What heaven has conferred is called money; accordance with nature is called money. Money may not be left for an instant. If it could be left, it would not be money." Ordinary worldly people have this problem. That is, they cannot see through the matter of money, so they can't put it down. It wouldn't be so bad if you were the only one poisoned by money. But you also want to poison your children and grandchildren, so you leave money for your sons and daughters. Your children then leave money for their children, and they in turn leave money for their children. Passing the money back and forth, people are so poisoned by this toxic substance that they can't even catch their breath. This is really frightening. Therefore, here we tell everyone that money has poison on it. You still don't believe it though, and you always want to be very close to money. You've been poisoned by it, and the harmful effects will poison your children and grandchildren as well in all the generations to come.

In the past I've said this many times: people think saving up money is a good thing. But people who cultivate the Way should not take money so seriously; they need not save money. We don't need to think "Money may not be left for an instant." We should change the phrase around to say, "What heaven has conferred is called the dharma; accordance with nature is called the dharma. The dharma may not be left for an instant. If it could be left, it would not be the dharma." What is meant by "the dharma?" You say, "I know. It's the dharma of the Buddha, the Dharma, and the Sangha." You don't really understand yet. If you really understood, you wouldn't lose your dharma.

Ultimately, what is the dharma? It is just our energy, our vital energy which penetrates heaven and earth to the point that all Buddhas and Bodhisattvas are of the same substance as us because our energy is connected. This energy is like our breath; it can be detected. That which is within the energy and controls it is the dharma. Therefore, it is essential that we nurture our energy; we should not lose our temper. You should cultivate your energy, as in the saying, "Foster the ground of your mind, and nurture the sky of your nature." This is nurturing your energy. If you want to nurture your energy, then don't lose your dharma. I will tell you a most important and essential dharma-door. If you listen, fine. If you don't listen, that's okay, too, but I'll tell you anyway. What is it? If you want to nurture your energy, then don't talk so much.

Don't talk so much in the kitchen. Today it's a little better. But in the last two days, when I went to the kitchen and dining hall, it sounded like a marketplace. Everyone was shouting. One person was selling carrots, another was selling cabbage, another was selling potatoes, and someone else was selling sweet potatoes. What did they think they were doing, shouting and yelling like that? They'd forgotten completely about the Buddha, the Dharma, and the Sangha. There's no need to make such a racket in the kitchen. That is not how cultivators should behave. Later I found out that the dormitory was also like a marketplace. People were quarreling, chattering, and making noise everywhere. No one knows what they were talking about.

A person who cannot limit his speech will not be able to cultivate. If you cannot nurture your energy, then you do not have the dharma. Therefore, "The dharma may not be left for an instant." You can very easily and carelessly squander this dharma by talking all the time. I do not like to interfere in other people's business, but this is really too much! If this continues, these people who argue all day long will be the villains of the City of Ten Thousand Buddhas. No wonder the Buddhas don't want to stay here anymore, and the bodhisattvas also stay far away; they don't want to listen to these people who do nothing but gossip and chatter. I don't mean to say that people shouldn't talk to each other at the City of Ten Thousand Buddhas. People should certainly discuss important matters, but they should not be chatting idly all the time.

You say, "Oh, nothing's happening around here. I'm so lonely, I've gotta find someone to talk to."

That might be all right, but after you've had your chat, you will have lost all dharma whatsoever. If you lose the dharma, how can you cultivate the Way?

Sutra:

"It is also possible to feel satisfied after a small accomplishment, like the unlearned bhikshu who reached the fourth dhyana and claimed that he had realized sagehood. When his celestial reward ended and the signs of decay appeared, he slandered arhatship as being subject to birth and death, and thus he fell into the Avichi Hell.

Commentary:

It is also possible to feel satisfied after a small accomplishment. In cultivation, even if you do not become possessed by a demon, you must still have genuine wisdom and dharma-selecting vision. If you recognize the Buddhadharma, you yourself should know what level you have reached. Don't obtain only a little bit and feel satisfied, **like the unlearned bhikshu who reached the fourth dhyana and claimed that he had realized sagehood.** He was called the unlearned bhikshu because he didn't have much sense. He knew little about the principles of Buddhism. In what way was he unlearned? Basically, the four fruitions of arhatship are all beyond the four dhyana heavens. The Buddha explained that one who has realized the fourth fruition of arhatship no longer undergoes birth and death. A sage who has realized the second fruition is called a "once returner." He is born once in the heavens and once in the human realm; he has one more round of birth and death to undergo. A sage of the first fruition has seven more rounds of birth and death to undergo. All of these states surpass the four dhyana heavens. The unlearned bhikshu had only reached the level of the fourth dhyana heaven in his cultivation, but he thought he had already realized the fourth fruition of arhatship. In fact, at the level of the fourth dhyana heaven, one has not realized any fruition and is still an ordinary person.

But the unlearned bhikshu claimed that he had attained the fourth fruition of arhatship. Now, however, people think that the level of a fourth stage arhat is still too low for them, and they brazenly claim that they themselves are Buddhas. But a Buddha has three bodies, four wisdoms, five eyes, and six spiritual powers. You can ask those people who claim to be Buddhas how many spiritual powers they have. Ghosts have five of the six spiritual powers; they lack the spiritual power of freedom from outflows. At the fruition of Buddhahood, one has all six spiritual powers. I believe that anyone who claimed to be a Buddha would not have even one spiritual power, let alone five or six. Only someone lacking spiritual powers would claim to be a Buddha. Anyone with even one spiritual power wouldn't tell such a great lie.

When his celestial reward ended, when his life in the heavens came to an end **and the signs of decay appeared...** Do you remember the five signs of decay[1]? When the life of a heavenly being comes to an end and he is about to die, these five signs appear.

He slandered arhatship as being subject to birth and death, and thus he fell into the Avichi Hell. When his blessings in the heavens ran out, the five signs of decay appeared and his life in the heavens came to an end, the unlearned bhikshu got angry. What was he angry about? He said, "I've been deceived by the Buddha! The Buddha is a charlatan. He said that when you realize the fourth fruition of arhatship, you don't have to undergo birth and death ever again. Why is my life coming to an end now? Why do I have to be reborn? Why do I have to undergo transmigration again? The Buddha is a liar!" Guess what happened when he slandered the Buddha like that. He fell into the Avichi Hell.

---

[1]. The five signs of decay are: i) The flowers on the gods' crowns wilt; ii) their clothes become dirty; iii) their armpits sweat; iv) their bodies become smelly and filthy; and v) they cannot sit still.

The Avichi Hell is also called the Relentless Hell. Basically he had not realized the fourth fruition of arhatship at all, but he claimed that he had. When he used up his celestial blessings and reached the end of his life, he fell into the lower realms. He did not realize his mistake and said that the Buddha had spoken the dharma incorrectly. In fact the Buddha had said, "You have not realized the fourth fruition of arhatship. If you had, naturally there would be no more birth and death for you. How could the five signs of decay appear?" Upon slandering the Buddha, the unlearned bhikshu immediately fell into the Relentless Hell – the Avichi Hell. Where do you suppose those people who claim to be Buddhas go? I don't know where they end up.

G3 Exhortation to pay attention and promise to speak.

Sutra:

"You should pay attention. I will now explain this for you in detail."

Commentary:

You should pay attention. Ananda, you should pay special attention. Listen carefully. **I will now explain this for you,** Ananda, and for everyone else, **in** great **detail,** so don't disappoint me.

F2 The members of the assembly bow and listen respectfully.

Sutra:

Ananda stood up and, with the others in the assembly who had more to learn, bowed joyfully. They quieted themselves in order to listen to the compassionate instruction.

Commentary:

Ananda stood up immediately **and, with the others in the assembly** – the great bodhisattvas, the great arhats, the great bhikshus, and those **who had more to learn,** people at the first, second, and third fruitions – **bowed joyfully.** Since the Buddha was about to explain the matter in detail, everyone was happy, and together they joyfully paid homage and bowed to the Buddha. **They quieted themselves in order to listen to the compassionate instruction.** They subdued their minds and had no more extraneous thoughts, so they could listen with full attention to the dharma the Buddha was about to speak.

F3　Detailed explanation of the demons' deeds.
G1　Telling where they come from.
H1　Samadhi is the reason for the demons' agitation.
I1　Emphasizing the significance of the dual aspects of true and false, production and destruction.
J1　First, explaining that our fundamental enlightenment is the same as the Buddha's.

Sutra:

The Buddha told Ananda and the whole assembly, "You should know that the twelve categories of beings in this world of outflows are endowed with a wonderfully bright, fundamental enlightenment – the enlightened, perfect substance of the mind which is not different from that of the Buddhas of the ten directions.

Commentary:

The Buddha told Ananda and everyone in **the whole assembly:** All of **you** people who are now present **should know that the twelve categories of beings in this world of outflows are endowed with a wonderfully bright, fundamental enlightenment** – an inherent, enlightened nature, the wonderfully bright, true mind – **the enlightened, perfect substance of the mind, which is not different from that of the Buddhas of the ten directions.** It is the same. There is no difference. The Buddhas of the ten directions are endowed with it, and the twelve categories of beings are also endowed with this enlightened nature, which is also called the treasury of the Tathagata.

J2　Next, explaining how emptiness comes from falseness.

Sutra:

"Due to the fault of false thinking and confusion about the truth, infatuation arises and makes your confusion all

pervasive. Consequently, an emptiness appears. Worlds come into being as that confusion is ceaselessly transformed. Therefore, the lands that are not without outflows, as numerous as motes of dust throughout the ten directions, are all created as a result of confusion, dullness, and false thinking.

Commentary:

Due to the fault of false thinking and confusion about the truth. Hey, Ananda! Your inherent nature and the inherent nature of the twelve categories of beings are not different from the Buddhas'; they are one and the same. However, because you create falseness out of the truth and then become confused about what is the genuine truth, faults arise and errors are made.

Infatuation arises. What is the biggest fault? Infatuation (literally, "obsessed love"). You could say obsession and love are two things; you can also explain them as one: infatuation. Your ignorance prevents you from understanding, and love is all you know about. You think about love, from morning to night. You can't put down love and lust for a moment. If you investigated the Buddhadharma as attentively as you pursue lust and love, you would become a Buddha very soon. What a pity you cannot transform your fondness for the opposite sex into fondness for the Buddhadharma instead! The more you study the Buddhadharma, the more boring you think it is. You say, "I have many faults, and the Buddhadharma points them all out to me. I don't want to study it anymore. The Buddhadharma wants me to change my habits, and how can I do that?" That's one example of obsession about love. Above, the text said, "Due to the fault of false thinking and confusion about the truth..." Now, I could say that mistakes are made due to obsession about love.

You make mistakes based on infatuation. Infatuation arises **and makes your confusion all pervasive**. Your infatuation produces an all-pervading confusion. You become confused about everything. It all starts with infatuation. Once you become infatuated, you don't understand anything. Nothing matters to you. You figure, "If I fall into the hells, so be it! Why should I worry?" You no longer care about anything.

Consequently, an emptiness appears. Because you make mistakes based on infatuation – because men think about women from morning to night, and women think about men all day long – a false emptiness arises. **Worlds come into being as that confusion is ceaselessly transformed.** The confusion multiplies so that one confusion becomes two confusions, and two confusions turn into three confusions. The confusion evolves without end. Intelligent people should take note of this! You should pay attention to this passage of sutra text. Its message really penetrates to the bone. It points out all of your faults!

Then the world comes into being. **Therefore, the lands that are not without outflows, as numerous as motes of dust throughout the ten directions, are all created as a result of confusion, dullness, and false thinking.** The worlds throughout the ten directions are not indestructible; they are not without outflows, because they have no basic substance of their own. They are all mere creations of false thinking. Confusion refers to lack of understanding; dullness refers to being obstinate and unyielding. The world is created by your false thinking. Did you know that?

J3 For the sake of comparison, describing the minuteness of the realm of space.

Sutra:

"You should know that the space created in your mind is like a wisp of cloud that dots the vast sky. How much smaller must all the worlds within that space be!

Commentary:

"Ananda, don't sleep! You should know that when I say don't sleep, that means don't be confused. Don't be infatuated anymore. Don't be confused about the truth anymore." The Buddha told Ananda not to sleep, and now I'm telling you all not to sleep!

Right now, what's important is that **you should know that the space created in your mind is like a wisp of cloud that dots the**

vast sky. All of space, which is created from your mind, is like a wisp of cloud in the sky when compared to your mind. A wisp of cloud in the sky is tiny, and the sky, representing your mind, is vast. Earlier the sutra said:

> The space created within great enlightenment
> Is like a single bubble in all the sea.

And now it says, "The space created in your mind is like a wisp of cloud that dots the vast sky." All of space being that small, how vast your mind must be! And **how much smaller must all the worlds within that space be!** All the worlds within that empty space must be minute. If they were in your mind, they would be even smaller. So this describes how our enlightened nature pervades all places.

J4 Returning to the source obliterates space.

Sutra:

"If even one person among you finds the truth and returns to the source, then all of space in the ten directions is obliterated. How could the worlds within that space fail to be destroyed as well?

Commentary:

If even one person among you finds the truth and returns to the source. Finding the truth and returning to the source means becoming a Buddha. Realizing the fourth fruition of arhatship can also be called finding the truth and returning to the source. Ananda, if one person among you becomes a Buddha, **then all of space in the ten directions is obliterated. How could the worlds within that space fail to be destroyed as well?** Even space is gone, so how can the worlds still exist? The worlds are all gone, too.

Someone says, "If so many Buddhas have accomplished Buddhahood and becoming a Buddha is supposed to obliterate space, then why hasn't space disappeared yet?"

From the point of view of living beings, space exists; but from the point of view of the Buddhas, there is nothing at all. There are different points of view, and so you can't make generalizations. For instance, people who have opened the five eyes can see what is happening in this country and in other countries that are tens of thousands of miles away. Can you who haven't opened the buddha eye see such things? No. By the same token, one cannot say, "I can see it, therefore it must exist." You may see it as existing, but from the Buddhas' perspective, there is nothing at all, not even space.

I2   Explaining that great samadhi causes demons to manifest.
J1   One's mind tallies with the minds of the sages.

Sutra:

"When you cultivate dhyana and attain samadhi, your mind tallies with the minds of the bodhisattvas and the great arhats of the ten directions who are free of outflows, and you abide in a state of profound purity.

Commentary:

When you cultivate dhyana concentration **and attain samadhi**, the essence of **your mind tallies** and unites **with the minds of** all **the bodhisattvas and** all **the great arhats of the ten directions who are free of outflows, and you abide in a state of profound purity.** You don't have to seek elsewhere for this pure, fundamental tranquillity. It is right where you are. Right here is the pure, inherently tranquil treasury of the Tathagata, which pervades the dharma realm.

Why do the minds of the bodhisattvas, the great arhats, and the cultivators of samadhi tally in this way? Because they cultivate the same samadhi. They direct the hearing inward to listen to the inherent nature, until the inherent nature accomplishes the Unsurpassed Way. They all cultivate the great Shurangama Samadhi, and so they are all the same; they become unified. Their minds are connected as if there were an electric current running between them.

This connection, however, doesn't occur only at the level of Buddhas, bodhisattvas, and arhats. It also occurs among ordinary people. For example, when you think about a person, your thought will reach his mind, just like a telegram. "Does the other person know?" you ask. His inherent nature knows, even though his conscious mind may be unaware of it. At the level of that nature, we all know one another.

"Well, if I think about someone from morning to night, then that person will also think about me, right?"

You could think till you die, and it still wouldn't be any use. It is like the infatuation we talked about before. If a person is infatuated, he will think about the object of his affection all day long, unable to put the thought down. He is always thinking and thinking, until he thinks himself to death! How does he die? He thinks about her until they come together and get married. Once married, he becomes muddled. After being muddled for a time, he dies. Being married is equivalent to being muddled – not knowing anything at all. In Chinese, you can deduce that meaning from the character for "marriage" *hun* (婚), which contains the word for "muddled" *hun* (昏); I don't know if this interpretation exists in English.

J2 The demons come en masse to cause disturbance.

Sutra:

"All the kings of demons, the ghosts and spirits, and the ordinary gods see their palaces collapse for no apparent reason. The earth quakes, and all the creatures in the water, on the land, and in the air, without exception, are frightened. Yet ordinary people who are sunk in dim confusion remain unaware of these changes.

Commentary:

When one obtains the great Shurangama Samadhi, the true samadhi, the demon kings shudder. **All the kings of demons, the ghosts and spirits, and the ordinary gods** of the six desire heavens and four dhyana heavens **see their palaces collapse for no apparent reason.** The situation is really out of control. For no apparent reason, their palaces start falling apart.

Have I ever told you about a young disciple I had in Manchuria? He was about fourteen years old, and although he was young, his spiritual powers certainly weren't insignificant. He could ascend to the heavens and enter the earth. He had opened the five eyes, but had not obtained the six spiritual powers. He had five of the spiritual powers, but lacked the power of freedom from outflows. When a person attains this power, he becomes an arhat.

One day he ascended to the heavens to amuse himself. When he got there, the demon king took a liking to him and trapped him in his palace. It was an exquisite palace, made of transparent crystal-like material, but he was trapped in it. Since he had opened his five eyes, he could see his dharma body being held captive there by the demon king. So he came and told me, "Teacher, I went to the heavens, and now I can't come back."

"So you're stuck in the heavens, huh?" I said, "Well, who told you to go there in the first place?"

"I thought that it would be lots of fun, so I went there to take a look. But now that person up in the heavens won't let me come back."

I said, "If you want to have fun, don't go there to play. Those demons in the six desire heavens are always looking for an opportunity to destroy the samadhi power of cultivators." Then I said, "Don't be scared; I'll get you back."

I tried to get him back, but the demon king refused to let him go. At that point he became really frightened and said, "He won't let me come back! What should I do?"

I said, "Don't worry. I'll bring you back now." Then I used the Shurangama Mantra, the section which I've told you destroys demons, the "Mantra of the Five Great Hearts." Ah! The demon palace immediately shattered, and he came back that time. This is a true story.

Now the palaces of the demon kings have fallen apart and collapsed, and **the earth quakes** and cracks open in many places, **and all the creatures in the water, on the land, and in the air,**

without exception, are frightened. All the creatures in the water and on the land go flying through the air, scared out of their wits and frightened beyond control. **Yet ordinary people who are sunk in dim confusion remain unaware of these changes.** Ordinary people do not have such sharp perception, and they do not realize the earth is undergoing all these changes. They are not sensitive enough to perceive the six kinds of quaking occurring in the earth.

Sutra:

"**All these beings have five kinds of spiritual powers; they lack only freedom from outflows, because they are still attached to worldly passions. How could they allow you to destroy their palaces? That is why the ghosts, spirits, celestial demons, sprites, and goblins come to disturb you when you are in samadhi.**

Commentary:

Now do you understand? Why do the demons come? It is just because **all these** celestial **beings**, ghosts, and spirits **have five kinds of spiritual powers**, which are the celestial eye, the celestial ear, the knowledge of others' thoughts, the knowledge of previous lives, and the complete spirit. But they don't have the power of freedom from outflows. If they obtained that power, they wouldn't trouble you anymore. But since they haven't obtained it, they still want to be evil and come to destroy you.

They lack only freedom from outflows. It is not easy to attain the power of freedom from outflows. What does this mean? I will be very frank about it. What we call "outflows" are the daily, random thoughts that men and women have about one another. If you have not put an end to such thoughts, then you have not rid yourself of outflows.

Now I'll discuss this more in depth, and I'll be very frank with you. If I didn't tell you the truth, then you would never know what is really being referred to. Being rid of outflows simply means retaining your essence. If your essence escapes, that's an outflow. Now I have told you the secret of heaven and earth. If you retain your essence, then you won't have outflows. Furthermore, if you cannot only prevent your essence from escaping, but can also be without lustful thoughts, even on the subtlest level, then you have truly rid yourself of outflows. Now do you understand? Why haven't the celestial demons achieved freedom from outflows? Because they still have thoughts of lust, as do ghosts and spirits.

Because they are still attached to worldly passions. Worldly passions are simply a form of lust. That's what they indulge in. **How could they allow you to destroy their palaces?** Since they are attached to lust, they do not want to see you renounce it. They want you to be greedy for it, too. "The two of us are good friends," they will say. "I haven't put this down, so you can't just run away and renounce it." That's why they come. They cannot bear to see you transcend the world. **That is why the ghosts, spirits, celestial demons, sprites, and goblins come to disturb you when you are in samadhi.** When I mentioned goblins in the past, you didn't know what they were, so now I will explain. Do you see how the Chinese character for "goblin" (妖 *yao*) is written? It is the character for "woman" (女 *nu*) beside the character for a short life – for death before thirty years of age (夭 *hun*). You can figure out the meaning from there; I don't have to say too much. In general, people who die young will become goblins.

When you are in samadhi, they all come en masse to bother you. Their aim, as it's said, is "to devour the flesh of the monk from Tang." The monk from Tang was Great Master Xuan Zang. Many goblins would have liked to eat his flesh; that is, they wanted to disturb his samadhi. If you cultivate to the point that you have samadhi, the goblins, ghosts, and monsters will want to devour your flesh as well. Actually, they do not really eat your flesh. I will be more honest with you. I will bring it all out into the open and not hold anything back. What is really happening? When your essence, energy, and spirit are all full, because you have no thoughts of lust, these demons and ghosts want to steal your treasures. That's why they come to disturb you. If you have a girlfriend or boyfriend, she or he is also stealing your treasures. What else did you think was happening?

"The Buddhadharma teaches us to practice giving, so I'm giving away my treasures to others," you say.

Well then, you're going to end up as a poor ghost who falls into the hells. When that happens, the person who stole your treasures isn't going to say, "Here, I'll give you back some of your treasures so that you can get out of there." No one will help you then. You think it over.

H2 The demons can succeed in their destructiveness through the cultivator's confusion.
I1 Explanation by analogy of how "the guests" cannot bring harm.

Sutra:

"Although these demons possess tremendous enmity, they are in the grip of their worldly passions, while you are within wonderful enlightenment. They cannot affect you any more than a blowing wind can affect light or a knife can cut through water. You are like boiling water, while the demons are like solid ice which, in the presence of heat, soon melts away. Since they rely exclusively on spiritual powers, they are like mere guests.

Commentary:

When you achieve some samadhi power in your cultivation, the demon kings will be afraid and so they come to destroy it. They do not want you to have samadhi. **Although these demons** come to give you trouble, and although they **possess tremendous enmity**, much wrath, **they are in the grip of their worldly passions**. They are controlled by their defiled sense experiences, **while you are within wonderful enlightenment. They cannot affect you any more than a blowing wind can affect light or a knife can cut through water.** They cannot do anything to you, just as, blowing wind could not make light move; and just as a knife, however many times it is slashed through water, could not harm the water.

You are like boiling water. In this analogy, the samadhi power from your cultivation is compared to hot water, **while the demons are like solid ice.** The demon kings can be compared to the solid ice of winter, **which, in the presence of heat, soon melts away.** As hard as the ice is, the heat of boiling water gradually causes it to melt. **Since they rely exclusively on spiritual powers, they are like mere guests.** All they have going for themselves is their spiritual powers, so they can never be the "host" or "master." They are merely "guests" [they cannot stay long], and they cannot succeed in their efforts to disturb you.

---

12   Conclusion that the confusion is on the part of the cultivator.

Sutra:

"They can succeed in their destructiveness through your mind, which is the host of the five skandhas. If the host becomes confused, the guests will be able to do as they please.

Commentary:

They can succeed in their destructiveness through your mind, which is the host of the five skandhas. Basically, they cannot succeed in their destructiveness. However, **if the host becomes confused** – if your mind, which is the master of the five skandhas, is deluded – **the guests will be able to do as they please.** The guests will be able to take advantage of you. As long as you, the host, are not confused, they cannot do anything to you. Who is the host? It is your inherent nature. If your inherent nature is confused, then the demons can have their way with you. But if your inherent nature is not confused, then they are powerless to do anything.

---

13   Once enlightened, one surely will transcend their disturbance.

Sutra:

"When you are in dhyana, awakened, aware, and free of delusion, their demonic deeds can do nothing to you. As the skandhas dissolve, you enter the light. All those deviant hordes depend upon dark energy. Since light can destroy darkness,

they would be destroyed if they drew near you. How could they dare linger and try to disrupt your dhyana-samadhi?

Commentary:

When you are in dhyana, when you have stilled your thoughts and attained the proper concentration of samadhi, you are **awakened, aware, and free of delusion. Their demonic deeds can do nothing to you**. The demons won't be able to trouble you with their tactics. **As the skandhas dissolve, you enter the light.** Demons belong to the darkness (*yin*), and the darkness can be dispelled. It is as if the demons were ice and you were hot water. The darkness is dispelled like ice dissolving in hot water. The fire of your wisdom is bright, so you enter the light.

All those deviant hordes of demons, externalists, goblins, ghosts, and monsters **depend upon dark energy**. All their tactics depend on a dark, dismal energy. **Since light can destroy darkness**, if you have true samadhi and wisdom, your wisdom light will shine forth and dispel the darkness.

They would be destroyed if they drew near you. How could they dare linger and try to disrupt your dhyana-samadhi? If they came near you, they would do themselves in, so they dare not disturb you.

[January 1983]

Skandha-demons are not limited to fifty kinds; there may be five hundred, five thousand, fifty thousand, or even five hundred thousand kinds. Each kind can further be divided into ten kinds. If analyzed in detail, there are thousands upon tens of thousands of kinds. In general, what is a skandha-demon? Basically it's nothing but a mass of *yin* energy, which comes from our *yin* thoughts. *Yin* thoughts include thoughts of greed, anger, and stupidity. They give rise to the skandhas of form, feeling, thought, formations, and consciousness; and in each of these skandhas, all kinds of *yin* phenomena are produced. These *yin* phenomena naturally appear when your skill reaches a certain level. If your skill hasn't reached that level, then you won't encounter these skandha-demons, even if you want to. They manifest only when your skill has reached that level. Don't worry when they appear. There's no need to fear being possessed by demons.

When these *yin* phenomena appear, you should remain calm, as if they didn't exist. See them as if not seeing them; hear them as if not hearing them; and smell them without perceiving their smell. If you don't enter into sights, sounds, smells, tastes, tangible objects, and mental constructs, then the skandha-demons will not be able to do anything to you. If you are without greed, anger, and stupidity, then you will subdue these skandha-demons. If you do not have the faults of being selfish, wanting personal profit, seeking, being greedy, or contending, then no demon will be able to do anything to you.

Now as we are investigating the skandha-demons, we should not be afraid of demons. There's no need for fear. What is this mass of energy like? There's a rough analogy: When water boils and gives off steam, the rising of the steam indicates that the water is boiling.

The demons that you encounter in cultivation are illusory transformations produced from the *yin* thoughts and *yin* energy in your own nature. If you can remain unmoved by these illusory transformations, then there's no problem. For example, there's nothing strange about boiling water and letting the steam rise. After the steam has risen, you can drink the water.

When a person manifests demonic energy, it's like gold being smelted. All the dross is smelted away, leaving only pure gold. Cultivation is like smelting gold. It is said, "True gold does not fear the fire of the furnace." You must smelt the pure gold and forge your vajra-indestructible body. To obtain the vajra-indestructible body, you must apply effort in cultivation at all times, in thought after thought. No matter what level you reach in your cultivation, do not become happy or afraid. This is a most essential and basic way for cultivators to resolve demonic obstacles.

I4 Confusion will certainly bring a fall.

Sutra:

"If you were not clear and aware, but were confused by the skandhas, then you, Ananda, would surely become one of the demons; you would turn into a demonic being.

Commentary:

If you were not clear and aware, if you did not understand and wake up, **but were confused by the** demons of the five **skandhas, then you, Ananda, would surely become one of the demons; you would turn into a demonic being.** You would join the retinue of demons.

I5 The prior incident in the house of prostitution brought only slight harm.

Sutra:

"Your encounter with Matangi's daughter was a minor incident. She cast a spell on you to make you break the Buddha's moral precepts. Still, among the eighty thousand modes of conduct, you violated only one precept. Because your mind was pure, all was not lost.

Commentary:

Your encounter with Matangi's daughter was a minor incident. It was a relatively insignificant, commonplace demonic event. **She cast a spell on you to make you break the Buddha's moral precepts**. She used a mantra of the ancient Brahma Heaven to confuse you and tried to make you break the Buddha's rules. **Still, among the eighty thousand modes of conduct, you violated only one precept. Because your mind was pure, all was not lost**. Because you had already attained the first stage of arhatship, you were not totally confused by her, and you did not fall.

I6　Joining the ranks of demons would bring great harm.

Sutra:

"**This would be an attempt to completely destroy your precious enlightenment. Were it to succeed, you would become like the family of a senior government official who is suddenly exiled; his family wanders, bereft and alone, with no one to pity or rescue them.**

Commentary:

This would be an attempt to completely destroy your precious enlightenment. That kind of behavior was an attempt to make you fall. **Were it to succeed, you would become like the family of a senior government official who is suddenly exiled**. A high official is banished, and his family's property is abruptly confiscated by the emperor, so **his family wanders, bereft and alone, with no one to pity or rescue them**. You would be standing all alone, with no place to seek for help, no one to turn to for sympathy or aid.

CHAPTER 2

The Form Skandha

G2 Detailed analysis of the characteristics of the demons of the five skandhas.
H1 The characteristics of the demons of the form skandha.
I1 Overview from beginning to end.
J1 Initial cultivation does not break though the skandhas' boundaries.

Sutra:

"Ananda, you should know that as a cultivator sits in the bodhimanda, he is doing away with all thoughts. When his thoughts come to an end, there will be nothing on his mind. This state of pure clarity will stay the same whether in movement or stillness, in remembrance or forgetfulness.

Commentary:

Ananda, you should know that as a cultivator sits in the bodhimanda, he is doing away with all thoughts. Ananda, you should know that you are simply cultivating the skill of "turning back your hearing to listen to your inherent nature." In that way you obliterate all thoughts. **When his thoughts come to an end, there will be nothing on his mind. This state of pure clarity**, this wisdom and samadhi power, **will stay the same whether in movement or stillness, in remembrance or forgetfulness**. Your mind does not change whether you are moving or still. Whether you are mindful or absent-minded, your state is the same. It is non-dual.

Sutra:

"When he dwells in this place and enters samadhi, he is like a person with clear vision who finds himself in total darkness. Although his nature is wonderfully pure, his mind is not yet illuminated. This is the region of the form skandha.

Commentary:

When he dwells in this place and enters samadhi. Ananda! When he cultivates samadhi power and resides in a state of purity that remains the same whether he is moving or still, mindful or forgetful, **he is like a person with clear vision who finds himself in total darkness.** He is like a person with good eyes who is living in a dark house. **Although his nature is wonderfully pure, his mind is not yet illuminated.** Although his nature is pure, bright, and wondrous, his mind has not yet attained the light of genuine wisdom. **This is the region of the form skandha.**

J2 Ultimately it breaks up and reveals its false source.

Sutra:

"If his eyes become clear, he will then experience the ten directions as an open expanse, and the darkness will be gone. This is the end of the form skandha. He will then be able to transcend the turbidity of kalpas. Contemplating the cause of the form skandha, one sees that false thoughts of solidity are its source.

Commentary:

If his eyes become clear, he will then experience the ten directions as an open expanse, and the darkness will be gone. What is this state called? **This is the end of the form skandha.** Of the five skandhas: form, feeling, thinking, formations, and consciousness, the form skandha is gone. He will then be able to transcend the turbidity of kalpas. **Contemplating the cause of the form skandha, one sees that false thoughts of solidity are its source.** When the person goes beyond the turbidity of kalpas, his actions will be based on false thoughts of solidity.

[December 2, 1993]

Disciple: When the form skandha comes to an end, this person can then transcend the turbidity of kalpas. Contemplating the cause of the form skandha, he sees that false thoughts of solidity are its source.

Venerable Master: He still has false thoughts. They are "solid" because he is too deeply attached to that state.

Disciple: Are false thoughts of solidity the source of the form skandha?

Venerable Master: That's how it is when he reaches that state. It is not a matter of whether or not something is the source. There's no way to get to the root of it. This is all false. Form, feeling, thinking, formations, and consciousness are all like this. "The five skandhas, like floating clouds, emptily come and go. The three poisons, like air bubbles in water, rise and disappear." They are unreal. Every state is false.

Disciple: It's just like a dream; you can't make any sense out of dreams.

Venerable Master: Yes, "In a dream, the six destinies clearly exist. After awakening, everything is empty and the universe is gone."

I2 The ten states within this region.
J1 His body can transcend obstructions.

Sutra:

"Ananda, at this point, as the person intently investigates that wondrous brightness, the four elements will no longer function together, and soon the body will be able to transcend obstructions. This state is called 'the pure brightness merging into the environment.' It is a temporary state in the course of cultivation and does not indicate sagehood. If he does not think he has become a sage, then this will be a good state. But if he considers himself a sage, then he will be vulnerable to the demons' influence.

Commentary:

We are now discussing the demons associated with the five skandhas: form, feeling, thinking, formations, and consciousness. There are ten kinds of demons for each of the skandhas, making a total of fifty. Cultivators should have a clear understanding of these fifty types of demons. If you are not clear about these states, you could easily end up in the demon king's retinue, and you won't even know how you got there. That's why you have to be especially careful.

Ananda, at this point, as the person intently investigates that wondrous brightness. When the form skandha is about to end, he experiences the ten directions opening up and perceives a kind of brightness. As he investigates that state of subtle wonder and brightness, **the four elements will no longer function together, and soon the body will be able to transcend obstructions.** The four elements will cease to function (normally), and very soon after that the body will become free of obstructions, just like empty space. This is known as the "body produced by intent." It is another body that can leave the physical body. Earlier I mentioned my disciple who went to the heavens in his dharma body, which is also the "body produced by intent." The intent refers to the mind, one of the six sense faculties. Such a body, being a creation of the mind, is able to transcend obstructions.

This state is called "the pure brightness merging into the environment." The pure light flows into the surrounding environment.

[December 2, 1993]

Disciple: "This state is called the pure brightness merging into the environment." How is this sentence explained?

Venerable Master: This means that the person is too smart. He has false intelligence and worldly wisdom. He's simply too clever!

Disciple: What does "the environment" refer to?

Venerable Master: It refers to the state mentioned earlier.

Disciple: Is it the state that occurs when he is working at cultivation?

Venerable Master: It's simply the state he attained previously.

It is a temporary state in the course of cultivation. This kind of skill is temporary; it will not last. It is different from being able to come and go wherever you please. With that kind of complete freedom, one can:

> Let it go, and it fills the six directions;
> Roll it up, and it secretly hides away.

If one lets it go, it fills the universe. And yet one can gather it back in at any time. If you cannot do this whenever you want, then yours is only a temporary skill. It's a state that you may encounter when you reach a certain level in your cultivation. However, this state is temporary. You won't always have a body that transcends obstructions. **And so it does not indicate sagehood.** You have not reached the fruition of a sage. This isn't what it's like when a sage realizes the fruition.

If he does not think he has become a sage, then this will be a good state. That is, you don't say, "Oh, I truly have some skill in my cultivation! I can actually send a body out through the top of my head!" If you become arrogant like that, what happens? It's all over for you. However, if you don't interpret this state as proof that you have attained to sagehood, then this state is no great hindrance; there is nothing particularly wrong with it.

But if he considers himself a sage, then he will be vulnerable to the demons' influence. You might say, "Oh! My skill is extraordinary. I'm fantastic! I am a sage who has transcended the world! I'm an arhat!" If you think that way, the demons will descend upon you. Once the demons come, you are headed for a fall into the hells.

J2 Internally the light pervades and he can extract intestinal worms.

Sutra:

"Further, Ananda, as the person uses his mind to intently investigate that wondrous light, the light will pervade his body. Suddenly he will be able to extract intestinal worms from his own body, yet his body will remain intact and unharmed. This state is called 'the pure light surging through one's physical body.' It is a temporary state in the course of intense practice, and does not indicate sagehood. If he does not think he has become a sage, then this will be a good state. But if he considers himself a sage, then he will be vulnerable to the demons' influence.

Commentary:

This is the second demonic state of the form skandha. These demonic states are brought about by your vigorous effort in cultivation. If you were not working hard, you could not attract such demonic states even if you wanted to. The demons would pay no attention to you. In their eyes, you would be just another poor person, and they would obtain no advantage in coming after you. But now since you've been cultivating, you've amassed some treasures, and that's what the demons are after.

What should you do when they come? You have to remain in a state of unmoving suchness and clear understanding. Do not become attached to appearances. Have no attachments at all. Do not think, "What a fine state! I'd like to experience it again!" Don't welcome it, and don't reject it. Just act as if nothing were happening. If you do not consider yourself a sage, then it is a good state. But if you think you are a sage, and you say, "Wow! I'm incredible! I can pull parasites out of my body," if you decide you've obtained spiritual powers and self-mastery, then you've made a mistake. With that one thought of arrogance, the demons come. Riding on that thought of arrogance, they bore into your mind and take over. They manipulate you until you have no samadhi power left.

Therefore, you have to truly understand the principles of cultivation! Only then can you keep from falling into a trap or going down the wrong road. If you don't understand the Buddhadharma, it is very easy to go astray. There is no problem if you do not have any real skill. But when you gain some skill, the demon kings will have their eyes on you every moment, and the first opportunity they see, they will come to disturb you.

Further, Ananda, as the person uses his mind to intently investigate that wondrous brightness, the light will pervade his body. If you persist in your cultivation, you will eventually be able to see everything inside your own body. It's one thing if you are always able to see like that; but if you only have this ability once in a while, then it is merely a state of the form skandha.

Suddenly he will be able to extract intestinal worms from his own body, yet his body will remain intact and unharmed. In this state, suddenly you can pull worms out of your own abdomen. There are long worms and short ones, big ones and small ones. You can just reach your hand in and pluck them out. The extracted worms are real, and yet there is no injury to the abdomen. How do you suppose they came out? If you reach your hand into the abdomen to pull out the worms, the abdomen should be injured, but there is no rupture at all. "His body will remain intact" could be explained in two ways. One way would be to change the translation to read "their bodies will remain intact" and say that the worms' bodies' are still intact, not in the least damaged; they are whole and complete, alive and healthy. You could also say that your own abdomen is intact and uninjured.

This state is called "the pure light surging through one's physical body." An extremely pure and brilliant light penetrates your body. You do not actually put your hand in the abdomen and pluck the worms out; they issue forth of themselves. **It is a temporary state in the course of intense practice and does not indicate sagehood**. This state is not something that happens all the time. If this were a perpetual state, the situation would be different. This is not the state of a sage.

If he does not think he has become a sage, then this will be a good state. It is fine; it won't cause any great trouble. **But if he considers himself a sage, then he will be vulnerable to the demons' influence.** If you say, "I've attained sagehood. I can take things out of my stomach. Isn't it wonderful? *You* don't have such a state." If you become arrogant and attached to your state, you are in for trouble. You will be dragged off by the demon king to become part of his retinue.

J3 His essence and souls alternately separate and unite.

Sutra:

"Further, as the person uses his mind to intently investigate inside and outside, his physical and spiritual souls, intellect, will, essence, and spirit will be able to interact with one another without affecting his body. They will take turns as host and guests. Then he may suddenly hear the dharma being spoken in space, or perhaps he will hear esoteric truths being pronounced simultaneously throughout the ten directions. This state is called 'the essence and souls alternately separating and uniting, and the planting of good seeds.' It is a temporary state and does not indicate sagehood. If he does not think he has become a sage, then this will be a good state. But if he considers himself a sage, then he will be vulnerable to the demons' influence.

Commentary:

Further, as the person uses his mind to intently investigate the wondrous brightness **inside and outside**, striving to exceed excellence, incessantly trying to refine that process, **his spiritual and physical souls** undergo a change. There are three spiritual and seven physical souls residing in the human body. I have mentioned these ten "brothers" before. Some of them have only ears or only eyes. Some have merely a nose, but no lips, eyes, or ears. Each of them possesses only one sense organ and lacks the other five, so they cannot function on their own. They must work cooperatively as a team. Those with ears help out those lacking ears; those with eyes help out those lacking eyes. They depend on and help one another.

[December 2, 1993]

Venerable Master: Our three souls and seven spirits are like children. But they each have only one sense faculty, not many. Because they control our bodies, we are able to speak and perform actions. They are gathered together, and when your cultivation is accomplished, they become what is known as a Buddha in Buddhism or an immortal in Taoism. Some have only eyes and some have only ears, so they help each other. The child who has ears and can hear will help the one who can see. They are interconnected. So when you achieve the interchangeable functioning of the six sense faculties, your ears will be able to eat and talk. There are many states such as these that you cannot even conceive of.

Disciple: Venerable Master, you mentioned that you had a young disciple who went to the heavens to play and was captured by a demon king. He cried, "What can I do? I can't come back!" Did some of his souls and spirits go there?

Venerable Master: Among his three souls and seven spirits, maybe only one went, or maybe two went, or maybe three or four went. It's not for sure. Once they got there, they aggregated together. They were not seven or three separate entities. Once they go out, they unite into one. That's how wonderful and mysterious it is. It's a mass of efficacious energy!

Disciple: Is it because of different levels of cultivation that some people can send out more spirits than others?

Venerable Master: It's better not to send spirits out. If they always go out to play, they risk being caught by the demons. When the souls and spirits are captured, one becomes dumb. Retarded people and people who are "vegetables" are that way because their souls and spirits have been seized by demons. Souls are ghosts, but with some cultivation, they can become spirits, which are *yang* in nature. With more cultivation, they can become immortals.

Cultivated to the ultimate, they become Buddhas. All these states of cultivation are achieved by the same individual soul.

Disciple: If a person is in a "vegetable," or comatose state, or has lost some of his three souls and seven spirits, although his physical body is still intact, will the spirits and souls which have left him become another person?

Venerable Master: They don't become another person; they simply go with the demons. That's why the person is sometimes lucid, but sometimes very muddled.

Disciple: What if a cultivator who has sent out some of his three souls and seven spirits encounters Buddhas or bodhisattvas?

Venerable Master: If a person is truly cultivating, there will be dharma protectors invisibly surrounding him. I have met a lot of strange people who can send spirits out of their bodies. Since you haven't encountered such states, you wouldn't recognize or understand them. For instance, the experience of those who act as mediums in Taiwan is described in the fifty skandha-demon states.

Disciple: Have they reached that level in their cultivation?

Venerable Master: They are advancing in their cultivation and creating merit. Like all people, some learn to be good and others learn to be bad. Those who learn to be bad join the retinue of the demon kings.

These ten souls, together with the **intellect, will, essence, and spirit will be able to interact with one another without affecting his body. They will take turns as host and guests.** They trade off roles and assist each other. They take turns playing the roles of the host and the guests.

Then he may suddenly hear the dharma being spoken in space. Someone is lecturing on the sutras in space! Who is it? He can hear a voice, but he can't see the person. In fact it is just his own spiritual and physical souls, his intellect will, essence and spirit taking turns as host and guests to lecture. **Or perhaps he will hear esoteric truths being pronounced simultaneously throughout**

the ten directions. Maybe you hear the sutras and the dharma being spoken in space! Why? Because in your cultivation in previous lives, you heard the sutras and the dharma being spoken, and your spiritual and physical souls, intellect, will, essence and spirit have not forgotten that. Thus, in this life, when the pressure in your cultivation reaches a peak, these past experiences come forth.

This state is called "the essence and souls alternately separating and uniting and the planting of good seeds." They cooperate with one another, coming together as one party or forming groups. They may speak the dharma to enable you to understand what you didn't understand before, so that you can plant the seeds for future good roots.

It is a temporary, not a permanent, **state and does not indicate sagehood**. Don't get the idea that this state is extraordinary and say, "Look at me. I don't need to go to the sutra lectures. I can hear the dharma being spoken in space anytime I want." You may hear dharma being spoken, but that doesn't mean you have realized sagehood. **If he does not think he has become a sage**, if you don't become arrogant and think yourself extraordinary, if you don't try to deceive others, **then this will be a good state**. Suppose you say, "Wow! I can hear the dharma even when no one is lecturing the sutras. Has that ever happened to you?"

"No."

"Well, it's happened to me!"

But if you advertise your state to get people to believe in you, what will happen? **If he considers himself a sage, then he will be vulnerable to the demons' influence**. As soon as you become self-satisfied and attached, thinking you're really great, the demons will possess you and make you fall.

J4   The state changes and Buddhas appear.

Sutra:

"Further, when the person's mind becomes clear, unveiled, bright, and penetrating, an internal light will shine forth and

turn everything in the ten directions into the color of Jambu River gold. All the various species of beings will be transformed into Tathagatas. Suddenly he will see Vairochana Buddha seated upon a platform of celestial light, surrounded by a thousand Buddhas, who simultaneously appear upon lotus blossoms in a hundred million lands. This state is called 'the mind and soul being instilled with spiritual awareness.' When he has investigated to the point of clarity, the light of his mind will shine upon all worlds. This is a temporary state and does not indicate sagehood. If he does not think he has become a sage, then this will be a good state. But if he considers himself a sage, then he will be vulnerable to the demons' influence.

Commentary:

Further, when the person's mind becomes clear and pure, **unveiled** and manifest, **bright, and penetrating, an internal light will shine forth, and turn everything in the ten directions into the color of Jambu River gold.** A bright light will emanate from within, and then the worlds of the ten directions will all take on the hue of Jambu River gold. **All the various species of beings** – beings born from wombs, from eggs, from moisture, or by transformation, or any other kinds of beings – **will be transformed into Tathagatas.**

Suddenly, at this point, **he will see Vairochana Buddha.** Vairochana means "pervading everywhere" and is the name of the Buddha. He is not located anywhere, and yet there is no place where he is not present; his body is everywhere. This person suddenly sees Vairochana, the All-Pervasive Buddha, **seated on a platform of celestial light**, manifesting his ten-thousand-foot-tall body. Vairochana Buddha will be **surrounded by a thousand Buddhas, who simultaneously appear** seated **upon** blue, yellow, red, and white **lotus blossoms in a hundred million lands.**

This state is called "the mind and soul being instilled with spiritual awareness." You should not think that this is real. Your mind and your physical soul are being influenced by a state of spiritual response and awakening. However, it is not real. **When he**

has investigated to the point of clarity, the light of his mind will shine upon all worlds. When your mind comes to the point of understanding, it will illuminate all worlds.

This is a temporary state and does not indicate sagehood. What is happening will not last a long time. You have not become a sage. If he does not think he has become a sage, then this will be a good state. But if he considers himself a sage, then he will be vulnerable to the demons' influence. If you say, "Incredible! I've seen Vairochana Buddha. Have you seen him? Your skill is not as profound as mine. I've made it!" Once you have such a thought, the demon kings will come and drag you off to the hells.

J5 Space takes on the color of precious things.

Sutra:

"Further, as the person uses his mind to intently investigate that wondrous light, he will contemplate without pause, restraining and subduing his mind so that it does not go to extremes. Suddenly the space in the ten directions may take on the colors of the seven precious things or the colors of a hundred precious things, which simultaneously pervade everywhere without hindering one another. The blues, yellows, reds, and whites will each be clearly apparent. This state is called 'excessively subduing the mind.' It is a temporary state and does not indicate sagehood. If he does not think he has become a sage, then this will be a good state. But if he considers himself a sage, then he will be vulnerable to the demons' influence.

Commentary:

Further, as the person uses his mind to intently investigate that wondrous light, he will contemplate without pause, restraining and subduing his mind so that it does not go to extremes. He tries to curb his mind so that it does not become overzealous.

Suddenly the space in the ten directions may take on the colors of the seven precious things, or the colors of a hundred precious things, which will simultaneously pervade everywhere throughout space **without hindering one another.** They will be mutually unobstructing.

The blues, yellows, reds, and whites, the various colors, **will each be clearly apparent.** Each will display its own color. **This state is called "excessively subduing the mind."** You are cultivating to restrain your mind, not letting it engage in false thinking, not allowing it to have random thoughts. After the restraint occurs for a long time, it becomes excessive. You go beyond the proper measure. **It is a temporary state and does not indicate sagehood.** You will only temporarily be able to see the colors of the seven precious things in space, so this state does not mean you have attained sagehood.

If he does not think he has become a sage, then this will be a good state. It will be all right; it will not be a bad state. **But if he considers himself a sage, then he will be vulnerable to the demons' influence.** You will be surrounded by deviant influences, and you will fall.

J6 He can see things in the dark.

Sutra:

"Further, as the person uses his mind to investigate with clear discernment until the pure light no longer disperses, he will suddenly be able to see various things appear in a dark room at night, just as if it were daytime, while the objects that were already in the room do not disappear. This state is called 'refining the mind and purifying the vision until one is able to see in the dark.' It is a temporary state and does not indicate sagehood. If he does not think he has become a sage, then this will be a good state. But if he considers himself a sage, then he will be vulnerable to the demons' influence.

Commentary:

Further, as the person uses his mind to investigate with clear discernment until the pure light no longer disperses. Again, this person uses his mind in samadhi to observe states, until the pure light of his discerning mind becomes very focused and he is endowed with samadhi power. **He will suddenly be able to see various things appear in a dark room** in a house which is not lighted **at night, just as if it were daytime, while the objects that were already in the room do not disappear.** Not only will he be able to see things that are inside the house, he will also be able to see things that are outside the house. Not only will he see what is already in the house, he will also see, with great clarity, the things that come into the house from outside.

This state is called "refining the mind and purifying the vision until one is able to see in the dark." Your mind is refined to the utmost extent and your vision is purified to the extreme point. With such pure vision, you will be able to see even in dark places. But **it is a temporary state and does not indicate sagehood.** You shouldn't think that this is the fruition of sagehood, because it certainly isn't!

If he does not think he has become a sage, then this will be a good state. But if he considers himself a sage, then he will be vulnerable to the demons' influence. If you become conceited and think that you have achieved great skill in cultivation, you will attract demonic obstructions.

When some cultivators reach the state of ultimate purity and all-pervading light, they will suddenly see all kinds of things. That is because they have opened the buddha eye. However, not every person is able to open his buddha eye, and even if one does, it may not stay open forever. In the state described here, the buddha eye opens temporarily, enabling one to see the objects in a dark house as if there were light. I also mentioned that you would be able to see things coming to the house from outside. What sort of things might these be? For example, you might see a spirit, a ghost, a bodhisattva, or a Buddha coming into the dark house from outside. It's not for certain that you will experience these states.

Not everyone experiences such states, but some people might. These are states that may occur at some point in your cultivation. But don't think that all cultivators go through the same experiences, because that's not the case.

Some people open the buddha eye permanently. That is known as "a spiritual power that comes as a reward." Such people industriously cultivated the dharma of the thousand hands and thousand eyes in previous lives, and as a result, they can open the buddha eye in life after life. Other people may only be able to open the buddha eye temporarily, because their minds are not in a perpetual state of purity. If their minds were constantly pure, and they had cultivated the dharma of great compassion in their previous lives, they would be able to open the buddha eye permanently. There are a variety of differing circumstances in cultivation.

J7 His body becomes like grass or wood.

Sutra:

"Further, when his mind completely merges with emptiness, his four limbs will suddenly become like grass or wood, devoid of sensation even when burned by fire or cut with a knife. The burning of fire will not make his limbs hot, and even when his flesh is cut, it will be like wood being whittled. This state is called 'the merging of external states and the blending of the four elements into a uniform substance.' It is a temporary state and does not indicate sagehood. If he does not think he has become a sage, then this will be a good state. But if he considers himself a sage, then he will be vulnerable to the demons' influence.

Commentary:

Further, when his mind completely merges with emptiness, you may say that the mind exists, yet it doesn't; you may say it doesn't exist, yet it does. **His four limbs will suddenly become**

like grass or wood, devoid of sensation even when burned by fire or cut with a knife.** If you cut his arms or legs with a knife or burn them with fire, he will not feel any pain or discomfort. **The burning of fire will not make his limbs hot.** When you try to burn them, they won't even become hot. **And even when his flesh is cut, it will be like wood being whittled.** If you slice off the flesh from his arms and legs, it will be just like shaving wood. He will feel no pain or irritation.

This state is called "the merging of external states and the blending of the four elements into a uniform substance." Defiled external states will come together, and the natures of earth, water, fire, and air will become a single substance. However, **it is a temporary state**, an occasional experience, **and does not indicate sagehood**. Do not think you have realized sagehood.

If he does not think he has become a sage, then this will be a good state. But if he considers himself a sage and becomes self-satisfied and haughty, **then he will be vulnerable to the demons' influence**. You will be attacked and surrounded by hordes of deviant beings.

J8　He can see everywhere without obstruction.

Sutra:

"Further, when his mind accomplishes such purity that his skill in purifying the mind has reached its ultimate, he will suddenly see the earth, the mountains, and the rivers in the ten directions turn into Buddhalands replete with the seven precious things, their light shining everywhere. He will also see Buddhas, Tathagatas, as many as the sands of the Ganges, filling all of space. He will also see pavilions and palaces that are resplendent and beautiful. He will see the hells below and the celestial palaces above, all without obstruction. This state is called 'the gradual transformation of concentrated thoughts of fondness and loathing.' It does not indicate sagehood. If he does not think he has become a sage, then this will be a good state.

But if he considers himself a sage, then he will be vulnerable to the demons' influence.

Commentary:

Further, when his mind accomplishes such purity that his skill in purifying the mind has reached its ultimate. Applying his mind to cultivation of the Way and to the practice of samadhi, he achieves a state of extreme purity. At that point, **he will suddenly see the earth, the mountains, and the rivers in the ten directions turn into Buddhalands replete with the seven precious things, their light shining everywhere.** Every place will be adorned with the seven precious things: gold, silver, lapis lazuli, mother-of-pearl, red pearls, carnelian and coral. These precious things will illumine the ten directions. **He will also see Buddhas, Tathagatas, as many as the sands of the Ganges** River, **filling all of space. He will also see** tower-**pavilions and** jeweled **palaces that are resplendent and beautiful. He will see the hells below**. Looking downwards, he will see all the hells. **And** looking upwards, he will see what is happening in **the celestial palaces above, all without** the least bit of **obstruction**. He is able to see any place he wishes to see.

This state is called "the gradual transformation of concentrated thoughts of fondness and loathing." Why is he able to see these things? It's because he ordinarily has likes and dislikes. He would like to go to the heavens and the Buddhalands, and he would detest going to the hells. He concentrates on such thoughts, being as attentive as a hen sitting on her eggs, as a cat waiting for a mouse, or as a dragon nurturing its pearl. He does not think about anything else, but only about how fine it is in the Buddhalands, and how much suffering there is in the hells. His mind favors happy places and loathes the places of suffering and misery. Eventually, his concentrated thoughts create these kinds of states.

It does not indicate sagehood. He should not think that he has attained sagehood and achieved great spiritual skill. **If he does not think he has become a sage, then this will be a good state**. It's not a bad one. **But if he considers himself a sage** and says, "What a terrific state! I'm living with the Buddhas. In fact, I'm a Buddha myself!" **then he will be vulnerable to the demons' influence.** If he thinks like that, the demons and the externalists will all go to keep him company. "You say you're living with the Buddhas? Well, we'll be your friends and join you," they say.

J9 He sees and hears distant things.

Sutra:

"Further, as the person uses his mind to investigate what is profound and far away, he will suddenly be able to see distant places in the middle of the night. He will see city markets and community wells, streets and alleys, and relatives and friends, and he may hear their conversations. This state is called 'having been suppressed to the utmost, the mind flies out and sees much that had been blocked from view.' It does not indicate sagehood. If he does not think he has become a sage, then this will be a good state. But if he considers himself a sage, then he will be vulnerable to the demons' influence.

Commentary:

Further, as the person uses his mind to investigate what is profound and far away, he will suddenly be able to see various situations in **distant places in the middle of the night. He will see city markets** where things are sold on the street **and community wells** where people draw water, large **streets and** small **alleys**. He may see his **relatives and friends**, his associates, **and he may hear their conversations**; he will be able to listen to them talking.

This state is called "having been suppressed to the utmost, the mind flies out and sees much that had been blocked from view." In his cultivation, he restrained the mind from indulging in idle thinking. Having stifled the mind to the extreme, he experiences a sensation of flying out and seeing things no matter how far away they are. Usually he tries not to look at things, but now all of a sudden his mind breaks loose and he can see everything.

It does not indicate sagehood. He should not think that this is a good state. **If he does not think he has become a sage, then this will be a good,** passable **state. But if he considers himself a sage, then he will be vulnerable to the demons' influence.** If he claims to have realized sagehood when he hasn't, or if he claims to have attained what he hasn't, he will find himself surrounded by demons.

J10 False visions and false words.

Sutra:

"**Further, as the person uses his mind to investigate to the utmost point, he may see a good and wise advisor whose body undergoes changes. Within a brief interval, various transformations will occur which cannot be explained. This state is called 'having an improper mind which is possessed by a li-ghost, a mei-ghost, or a celestial demon, and without reason speaking dharma that fathoms wondrous truths.' It does not indicate sagehood. If he does not think he has become a sage, then the demonic formations will subside. But if he considers himself a sage, then he will be vulnerable to the demons' influence.**

Commentary:

This is the tenth demonic state of the form skandha, called "false visions and false words."

Further, as the person uses his mind to investigate to the utmost point, he may see a good and wise advisor with whom he studied the dharma in the past, **whose body undergoes changes**. Right before his eyes, the good and wise advisor suddenly turns into an old man; in the next moment he becomes a middle-aged person; and, in another instant he turns into a young person. Then, if the good and wise advisor is a man, for example, he suddenly changes into a woman, and the person thinks, "Oh! Probably in his previous life he was a woman." Actually, what he is seeing is not real. These changes are the result of his false thinking.

Within a brief interval, various transformations will occur which cannot be explained. Everything changes and becomes different from normal. This is similar to what people who take LSD experience. To them, everything becomes brightly colored, and they cannot see clearly. They paint some bizarre paintings which no one can figure out, because they just recklessly splash on the colors. After they finish painting, some people say, "Wow! What a masterpiece!" People actually praise them. You see? That's the way it goes.

"Is it the case that this cultivator has taken a drug?" you ask.

No. This experience is caused by the demon king. When you take LSD, the demons are also at work, making you experience changes.

[January 1983]

Venerable Master: "In our investigation of the fifty skandha-demon states, everyone is welcome to bring up an opinion. We want to use everyone's wisdom to investigate the principles. In the Dharma-ending Age, everyone is greedy for quick results and shortcuts. They think they can get a lucky break, just like people who gamble and win at the first try. So some people go running around to a lot of different places. They study esoteric practices and various other teachings. They hear this place has something to offer, so they go there. Then they hear that place has something, so they run over there. Running here and there, they waste all their time on the road; but in the end, they don't understand anything. We should all recognize this kind of state. If we don't, it will be very easy for us to go astray."

Disciple: "It's like taking drugs, which is a serious problem in Western society. You could say that hallucinogenic drugs are transformation bodies of demons. The demons come up with a new form of drug and everyone becomes addicted to it. Even though people don't really need to take the drug, a demonic energy combined with their own habits causes them to get hooked. Nowadays there are many deviant teachers who, without the help of drugs, hypnotize people and cause them to see lights and various things. This happens because the drugs in people's bodies are acting up."

These states in the form skandha may change for the better and for the worse. If the person has enough good roots, the changes will be for the better. But people whose good roots are insufficient will change for the worse. There are all sorts of transformations.

This state is called "having an improper and deviant mind which is possessed by a li-ghost, a mei-ghost, or a celestial demon, and without reason speaking dharma that fathoms wondrous truths." When a ghost or a demon from the heavens enters your mind, you may act like those people who claim they know how to lecture the sutras or speak the dharma, or who call themselves enlightened, elder masters. Such people start speaking the dharma for no reason, with no idea what they are talking about. They say they have fathomed wondrous truths, but they have not really done so. They are not really speaking the dharma either. They take what is wrong to be right and claim that their teaching is the most wonderful. Praising themselves and putting others down, they call themselves the foremost elder masters.

It does not indicate sagehood. This state is not a good one. **If he does not think he has become a sage, then the demonic formations will subside.** They will disappear. **But if he considers himself a sage, then he will be vulnerable to the demons' influence.** If he thinks he has attained the fruition of a sage, he will soon find himself in the hells. He will attain the fruition of the hells.

I3   Conclusion on the harm, and command to offer protection.
J1   Showing how the states come about from interaction.

Sutra:

"Ananda, these ten states may occur in dhyana as one's mental effort interacts with the form skandha.

Commentary:

Ananda, these ten states described above **may occur in** the still contemplation of **dhyana as one's mental effort interacts**

with the form skandha. These states involve the form skandha. When the mind interacts with and investigates the form skandha to the ultimate, one may experience such states.

J2 Confusion will bring harm.

Sutra:

"Dull and confused living beings do not evaluate themselves. Encountering such situations, in their confusion they fail to recognize them and say that they have become sages, thereby uttering a great lie. They will fall into the Relentless Hells.

Commentary:

Dull and confused living beings do not evaluate themselves. Living beings are stubborn and intractable, and they do not wake up from their delusion. They do not take stock of themselves to see what level they are at. **Encountering such situations**, such demonic states, **in their** muddled **confusion they fail to recognize them and say that they have become sages**. They claim, "Oh, I am a Buddha! I am enlightened; I've attained sagehood," **thereby uttering a great lie**. They are really telling the greatest lie. **They will** surely **fall into the Relentless Hells**.

[January 1983]

We have to be very cautious in all aspects. As it's said, "If you're off by a hairsbreadth in the beginning, you'll miss by a thousand miles in the end." We keep studying the Buddhadharma, but we end up falling into the hells. Why? Because we haven't really been able to follow the teachings. We haven't really been able to refrain from lying, stealing, sexual misconduct, taking intoxicants, and killing. If you can't even hold the five precepts, how can you think of accomplishing Buddhahood?

First of all, you must not kill. That doesn't simply mean eating vegetarian food.

"I haven't killed any creature with my own hands," you may say.

That doesn't necessarily mean you haven't violated the precept of not killing. Holding this precept means you must not even harbor anger toward people in your heart. That is not easy to do. As I said earlier, "I also have a strong urge to kill. But I want to stop killing; I want to liberate creatures instead of killing them. If I wanted to kill creatures, all the fine hairs on my body could turn into flying swords, sharp knives, lances, and spears to stab people to death. That's how fierce my fine hairs could be. That's how powerful the urge to kill is, but I'm not going to kill. Why not? Because I realize that killing living beings is equivalent to killing bodhisattvas, killing arhats, breaking up the harmonious sangha, and shedding the Buddha's blood. That's why I don't kill."

Not stealing. Gaining something by improper means or taking something that does not belong to you without informing the owner is considered stealing. If you take something from its place without anyone knowing about it, you are stealing. The causes, conditions, methods, and karma of stealing are explained very clearly in the *Brahma Net Sutra*. The causes, conditions, methods and karma of killing are also explained clearly in that text.

Not engaging in sexual misconduct is also like that. It only counts if you don't have thoughts of lust in your mind and your own nature. To hold the precept against lying, you shouldn't lie under any circumstances. Nor should you take intoxicants. The stimulating effect of alcohol causes you to be unable to function normally. It also makes you lose your wisdom, and once that happens, you do stupid things.

These are the precepts of not killing, not stealing, not engaging in sexual misconduct, not lying, and not taking intoxicants. Buddhists should pay close attention to these five precepts and avoid committing the slightest transgression; only then are they qualified to be called Buddhists. Some of you casually entertain thoughts of killing, stealing, engaging in sexual misconduct, and deceiving people with lies, and you casually take intoxicants. You are greedy for everything. Being greedy for food is equivalent to taking intoxicants. If you are so greedy for food that you eat until you're fat as can be, you are also taking intoxicants. We who study Buddhism should constantly examine ourselves on this point. We must be very attentive, without making the slightest mistake or being sloppy at any moment.

On the other hand, we should not be too rigid; we should apply the precepts in a flexible way.

"Then I can be a little more expedient; I can still kill, steal, engage in sexual misconduct, lie, and take intoxicants," you say.

That's not what flexibility means. It means we should not bind ourselves up with the five precepts so tightly that we have no room to turn around. When we receive the five precepts, we are not being bound up by the five precepts. We should look into this well. A certain person in Canada used my name to cheat his disciples, alleging that I certified him. People who tell great lies like that are bound to fall into the Hell of Ripping Out Tongues.

J3 Command to offer protection.

Sutra:

"In the Dharma-ending Age, after the Tathagata enters nirvana, all of you should rely on and proclaim this teaching. Do not let the demons of the heavens have their way. Offer protection so all can realize the Unsurpassed Way.

Commentary:

In the Dharma-ending Age, after the Tathagata enters nirvana, all of you should rely on and proclaim this teaching. Ananda, you all should follow and practice the dharma that I have explained for you. In the future Dharma-ending Age, after I have entered nirvana, you must propagate these teachings. **Do not let the demons of the heavens have their way. Offer protection so all can realize the Unsurpassed Way**. Maintain and support the true and orthodox Buddhadharma so that you will be able to attain the supreme fruition of the Way.

CHAPTER 3

The Feeling Skandha

H2 The characteristics of demons of the feeling.
I1 Overview of the beginning and the end.
J1 In the beginning, cultivation has not yet broken out of this region.
K1 Review of the ending of the previous form skandha.

Sutra:

"Ananda, when the good person who is cultivating samadhi and shamatha has put an end to the form skandha, he can see the mind of all Buddhas as if seeing an image reflected in a clear mirror.

Commentary:

Ananda, when the good person who is cultivating samadhi, who cultivates the skill of directing the hearing inward to hear his own nature, who cultivates perfect understanding through the faculty of hearing, **and shamatha**, the quieting of thoughts, the practice of "stopping" so that contemplation is possible, **has put an end to the form skandha, he can see the mind of all Buddhas as if seeing an image reflected in a clear mirror**. What happens when he puts an end to the form skandha? He can see the dharma-door of the mind seal of all Buddhas, just as if he were seeing his own reflection in a mirror.

K2 Introduction to the region of the feeling skandha.

Sutra:

"He seems to have obtained something, but he cannot use it. In this he resembles a paralyzed person. His hands and feet are intact, his seeing and hearing are not distorted, and yet his mind has come under a deviant influence, so that he is unable to move. This is the region of the feeling skandha.

Commentary:

He seems to have obtained something, but he cannot use it. In this he resembles a paralyzed person. I talked before about the kumbhanda ghost (paralysis ghost). When a person falls under the influence of such a ghost, **his hands and feet are intact**, not missing, **his seeing and hearing are not distorted** or confused, **and yet his mind has come under a deviant influence, so that he is unable to move. This is the region of the feeling skandha.** This state falls within the realm of the feeling skandha.

J2 Ultimately it breaks up and reveals its false source.

Sutra:

"Once the problem of paralysis subsides, his mind can then leave his body and look back upon his face. It can go or stay as it pleases without further hindrance. This is the end of the feeling skandha. This person can then transcend the turbidity of views. Contemplating the cause of the feeling skandha, one sees that false thoughts of illusory clarity are its source.

Commentary:

Once the problem of being immobilized by the **paralysis ghost subsides, his mind can then leave his body and look back upon his face.** When you are within the feeling skandha, it is like being paralyzed by a kumbhanda ghost, so you cannot get free. If this situation disappears and the feeling skandha is broken through, your mind can leave your body and you can see your own face. **It can go or stay as it pleases.** You may go or not go as you wish. You are completely unfettered and **without further hindrance. This is**

the end of the feeling skandha. The feeling skandha is gone. **This person can then transcend the turbidity of views**, which is one of the turbidities of "the evil world of the five turbidities." **Contemplating the cause of the feeling skandha, one sees that false thoughts of illusory clarity are its source.** Once the feeling skandha is broken through, its source is also done away with.

I2 The ten states within this region.
J1 Suppression of the self leads to sadness.
K1 The characteristics of its beginning.

Sutra:

"**Ananda, in this situation the good person experiences a brilliant light. As a result of the excessive internal pressure in his mind, he is suddenly overwhelmed with such boundless sadness that he looks upon even mosquitoes and gadflies as newborn children. He is filled with pity and unconsciously bursts into tears.**

Commentary:

Ananda, in this situation the good person experiences a dazzling, **brilliant light. As a result of the excessive internal pressure in his mind**, a kind of feeling arises spontaneously. He has continually been controlling his own thoughts and has overdone it. When the inner suppression becomes excessive, **he is suddenly overwhelmed with such boundless sadness** and compassion for living beings **that he looks upon** and cherishes tiny creatures, **even mosquitoes and gadflies, as** if they were his own **newborn children.** The Chinese word for newborn means "red," referring to the red color of infant children's skin. **He is filled with pity and unconsciously bursts into tears**. Without knowing it, he starts to cry.

K2 Giving its name and instructions to awaken.
K3 Showing how confusion will certainly bring a fall.

Sutra:

"**This is called 'overexertion in suppressing the mind in the course of cultivation.' If he understands, then there is no error.**

This experience does not indicate sagehood. If he realizes that and remains unconfused, then after a time it will disappear.

"**But if he considers himself a sage, then a demon of sadness will enter his mind. Then, as soon as he sees someone, he will feel sad and cry uncontrollably. Lacking proper samadhi, he will certainly fall.**

Commentary:

This is called "overexertion in suppressing the mind in the course of cultivation." This situation may arise in the course of cultivation. It happens because you have been suppressing your thoughts too hard. **If he understands, then there is no error.** If you understand and say to yourself, "Why have I started crying for no reason? I should change this state," then there will not be any problem. **This experience does not indicate sagehood.** It does not mean you have attained the "great compassion of oneness with all." Don't think that caring for mosquitoes and other small creatures as if they were your own children is genuine "great compassion of oneness with all." **If he realizes that and remains unconfused,** then after a time it will disappear. The state will go away.

But if he considers himself a sage – if he says, "Oh! Now I have the 'great compassion of oneness with all'! My cultivation has really succeeded!" – then a demon of sadness that is an expert at crying will come. It cries no matter whom it meets. This demon will enter his mind and take possession of him. **Then, as soon as he sees someone, he will feel sad and cry uncontrollably,** without knowing why he is so sad.

When I was in Manchuria I knew a woman named Liu Jintong who was like that. Whenever she met someone, she would start crying and say, "In the past, you were my son, and now you've come back. You've found your mother!" With her tears, she managed to confuse the other person into believing that he had actually met his mother. In fact, he'd encountered a demon.

Lacking proper samadhi, proper concentration, **he will certainly fall.** If you follow a demon, you will fall into the hells.

[December 2, 1993]

In the past Liu Jintong was possessed by the demons described in the fifty skandha-demon states, and now there are two others, one of whom is especially powerful because she knows a device for summoning spirits. A woman from San Jose who took refuge with me later went to study under her and contracted cancer upon her return. It was that person's doing. The San Jose woman came back to see me, but I paid no attention to her. Even if I were to do something to help her, I wouldn't let other people know.

J2 He praises himself as being equal to the Buddhas.
K1 The characteristics of its beginning.

Sutra:

"**Further, Ananda, in this state of samadhi, the good person sees the disintegration of the form skandha and understands the feeling skandha. At that time he has a sublime vision and is overwhelmed with gratitude. In this situation, he suddenly evinces tremendous courage. His mind is bold and keen. He resolves to equal all Buddhas and says he can transcend three asamkhyeyas of eons in a single thought.**

Commentary:

Further, Ananda, in this state of samadhi, the good person, which includes all good people who are cultivating the Way, **sees the disintegration of the form skandha and understands the feeling skandha**. Among the five skandhas, he knows that the form skandha is gone, and he is quite clear about the feeling skandha. **At that time he has a sublime vision and is overwhelmed with gratitude**. A very special and rare vision appears in his mind, and he feels excessively grateful for it. However, excess is as bad as insufficiency. There is little difference between going too far and not going far enough. Neither is in accord with the Middle Way. For example, while traveling, if you go beyond your destination, it is the same as if you had not arrived at all.

In this situation, in this state of samadhi, **he suddenly evinces tremendous courage. His mind is bold and keen**, fearlessly vigorous. **He resolves to equal all Buddhas,** saying, "The Buddha and I are the same." **And** he **says he can transcend three asamkhyeyas** (limitless numbers) **of eons in a single thought.** He says that he can transcend the first, second, and third asamkhyeyas of eons in the space of a single thought. Therefore, he says he is a Buddha. Not only does he say he is a Buddha, he says everyone is a Buddha. Such a person has fallen prey to wrong knowledge and views. It's true that everyone is potentially a Buddha, but one has to cultivate in order to realize Buddhahood. Even when one cultivates, it is not possible to become a Buddha in a single thought. It takes a long time. Although the time can be shortened if one understands the Buddhadharma and practices according to it, one still cannot attain Buddhahood in a single thought. This person cultivates, but he lacks wisdom and does not have a good and wise advisor to instruct him. Although he works hard at cultivation, he develops wrong views along the way. Seeing that such a long time has passed without his becoming a Buddha, he simply states that he *is* a Buddha. This is the experience of "praising oneself as the equal of the Buddhas" that occurs during the breakdown of the feeling skandha. He says he is the same as all Buddhas. Actually, with that one mistaken thought, he is already possessed by a demon.

K2 Giving the name and instructions to awaken.
K3 Showing how confusion will certainly bring a fall.

Sutra:

"**This is called 'being too anxious to excel in cultivation.' If he understands, then there is no error. This experience does not indicate sagehood.**

"**If he realizes that and remains unconfused, then after a time it will disappear. But if he considers himself a sage, then a demon of insanity will enter his mind. As soon as he sees someone, he will boast about himself. He will become extraordinarily haughty, to the point that he recognizes no Buddha above him and no people below him. Lacking proper samadhi, he will certainly fall.**

Commentary:

In the lecture on the *Shurangama Sutra*, we have now reached the very important section on the fifty kinds of deviant states caused by the five skandhas. If people who cultivate do not understand these fifty skandha demons, they will easily go astray in their cultivation. If you can recognize the states of these skandha demons, then you will not get carried away with reckless boasting and assume that you are an extraordinary individual. Therefore, I invite you to encourage your relatives and friends to come listen to this section on the fifty skandha demons, so they will know about the states which occur in cultivation.

This is called "being too anxious to excel in cultivation." This state occurs as a result of your efforts in cultivation. Because of this overexertion resulting from transformations within your own nature, you become courageous. There is nothing wrong with courage and vigor if you use them to advance in your cultivation of the Buddhadharma. But you must not become conceited and say, "Oh! I'm a Buddha myself." So you're a Buddha? The Buddha spoke the three treasuries and the twelve divisions of the canon. How many treasuries and divisions have you spoken? You don't even understand them, yet you say you are a Buddha. Isn't that absurd? The Buddha spoke the entire canon, and you haven't spoken even a single treasury or division of the canon, so how can you claim that you have become a Buddha? Even if you could explain the treasuries and divisions and understand their principles, at best you could call yourself a disciple of the Buddha, not a Buddha. But this person, feeling that everyone in the world reveres the Buddha, wants to be a Buddha, too, so that after he dies, people will make offerings to him. Actually, after death he will be buried in the ground. He will turn to dust and nothing will be left of him.

If he understands, then there is no error. It is all right to have such courage, as long as you understand that it is merely a state and does not mean you have become a sage. **This experience does not indicate sagehood. If he realizes that and remains unconfused then after a time it will disappear.**

But if he considers himself a sage, saying, "Oh, this means I've become a Buddha!" **then a demon of insanity will enter his mind**. So you see, if you do not even recognize the fifty skandha demons, how can you become a Buddha? This demon is one of arrogance, pride, and conceit. It bores into his mind and takes possession of him, driving out his soul. The demon king takes over and acts as his soul. **As soon as he sees someone**, no matter who the person is, **he will boast about himself** and how he is right and everyone else is wrong. He denigrates others to exalt himself. They are all in the wrong, and he alone is honored; he thinks he has become a Buddha!

He will become extraordinarily haughty toward everyone, **to the point that he recognizes no Buddha above him**. There are no Buddhas above. Why? Because he's a Buddha himself. **And** he sees **no people below him**. Then what does he see? He says that everyone is a Buddha, that he himself is a Buddha, and that there is no Buddha above him. He himself is Buddha, and in the future everyone will become a Buddha along with him. That is why he sees no people below. **Lacking** the **proper** state of **samadhi, he will certainly fall**.

J3 Samadhi out of balance brings much reverie.
K1 The characteristics of its beginning.

Sutra:

"Further, in this state of samadhi the good person sees the disintegration of the form skandha and understands the feeling skandha. With no new realization immediately ahead of him, and having lost his former status as well, his power of wisdom weakens, and he enters an impasse in which he sees nothing to anticipate. Suddenly a feeling of tremendous monotony and thirst arises in his mind. At all times he is fixated in memories that do not disperse. He mistakes this for a sign of diligence and vigor.

Commentary:

Further, in this state of samadhi the good person who cultivates the Way **sees the disintegration of the form skandha and understands the feeling skandha. With no new realization immediately ahead of him, and having lost his former status as well, his power of wisdom weakens.** Going forward, there is nothing new to attain; and behind him, the state where he dwelled before is also gone. His wisdom is inadequate now, and he isn't as bold and keen as before. This is a case of suddenly advancing and then suddenly retreating in one's skill. **And he enters an impasse, a place where he is about to fall, in which he sees nothing to anticipate.** He does not feel or see anything.

Suddenly a feeling of tremendous monotony and thirst arises in his mind. His feeling is one of enormous monotony, dryness, and thirst. He feels everything is meaningless and boring, and he is thirsty because he needs to be moistened by the water of the Buddhadharma. He feels he is drying up and withering away because, for him, there is nothing at all. This is similar to the way ordinary people who do not cultivate start to feel lonely and bored. This loneliness and boredom are sure to lead to trouble – the same old trouble. I did not intend to bring this up, but because I'm afraid people might not understand, I will still talk about it. It is as when a woman thinks about a man. She keeps thinking about him until she feels incredibly anxious and restless. When men think about women, they also have this feeling of restlessness. They are lonely and bored, as if they have lost something which they cannot find.

At all times he is fixated in memories that do not disperse. It is the way a man and a woman who are lovesick for each other keep thinking and thinking about each other and never forget. **He mistakes this for a sign of diligence and vigor.** This state of fixation on thoughts that don't disperse appears to him to indicate vigor.

K2	Giving the name and instructions to awaken.
K3	Showing how confusion will certainly bring a fall.

Sutra:

"This is called 'cultivating the mind but losing oneself due to a lack of wisdom.' If he understands, then there is no error. This experience does not indicate sagehood.

"But if he considers himself a sage, then a demon of memory will enter his mind. Day and night it will hold his mind suspended in one place. Lacking proper samadhi, he will certainly fall.

Commentary:

Within the states of the feeling skandha, **this is called "cultivating the mind but losing oneself due to a lack of wisdom."** You don't have any wisdom. But don't worry about having no wisdom, for **if he understands, then there is no error**. If you realize that it's only a state, then there is no problem. But if you don't understand, and you are always getting attached to emptiness and caught up in stillness, if you are always lost in reverie, then you will wither away without any accomplishment. **This experience does not indicate sagehood**. This does not mean you have attained something or have realized sagehood. Do not "mistake a thief for your son."

But if he considers himself a sage, then a demon of memory will enter his mind. Did you hear that! This is truly dangerous! If you consider it a fine state, a demon of memory will come and help you remember things. So you can't remember something? It will help you to think. It sees how much you would like to remember, so it comes to help you and enters into your mind. **Day and night it will hold his mind suspended in one place**. Your mind will be preoccupied and kept in one spot. **Lacking proper samadhi**, unable to attain samadhi, **he will certainly fall** into the hells in the future.

J4 Wisdom out of balance brings much arrogance.
K1 The characteristics of its beginning.

Sutra:

"**Further, in this state of samadhi, the good person sees the disintegration of the form skandha and understands the feeling skandha. His wisdom becomes stronger than his samadhi, and he mistakenly becomes impetuous. Cherishing the supremacy of his nature, he imagines that he is a Nishyanda (Buddha) and rests content with his minor achievement.**

Commentary:

Further, in this state of samadhi, the good person sees the disintegration of the form skandha and understands the feeling skandha. His wisdom becomes stronger than his samadhi. His wisdom power exceeds his samadhi power.

And he mistakenly becomes impetuous. He experiences a feeling of rash vigor. **Cherishing the supremacy of his nature, he imagines that he is a Nishyanda (Buddha).** In this state, he considers his nature to be supreme and extraordinary, and he is always thinking about it. Cherishing this thought of supremacy, he suspects himself to be a Nishyanda Buddha. "Nishyanda" is Sanskrit and means "light shining everywhere." He thinks he is already a Nishyanda Buddha **and rests content with his minor achievement**. He has made a little progress, and he becomes satisfied. His samadhi power falls way short of the Buddha's, and yet he claims he has become a Nishyanda Buddha.

K2 Giving the name and instructions to awaken.
K3 Showing how confusion will certainly bring a fall.

Sutra:

"**This is called 'applying the mind, but straying away from constant examination and becoming preoccupied with ideas and opinions.' If he understands, then there is no error. This experience does not indicate sagehood.**

"But if he considers himself a sage, then a lowly demon that is easily satisfied will enter his mind. As soon as he sees someone, he will announce, 'I have realized the unsurpassed absolute truth.' Lacking proper samadhi, he will certainly fall.

Commentary:

This is called "applying the mind, but straying away from constant examination – he is not skilled at constantly examining himself – and becoming preoccupied with ideas and opinions." Unable to clearly distinguish what he knows and thinks, he gets caught up and stuck in his own ideas and opinions. **If he understands, then there is no error.** There will not be any problem. **This experience does not indicate sagehood.**

But if he considers himself a sage and thinks that he has realized some supreme state, **then a lowly demon**, a most vile and worthless sort of demon **that is easily satisfied** with any situation, **will enter his mind.** It will bore into his mind and take possession of him, driving out his soul. All that will be left is a false shell of a person, but he will not realize that. **As soon as he sees someone, he will announce,** "Hey! Do you know? **I have realized the unsurpassed**, the highest, **absolute truth.**"

Now there is a character who stands on Grant Avenue in Chinatown, in the heart of the San Francisco business district, dressed in a flashy and colorful costume. He tells people, "I lived in the mountains for five years and became enlightened. Now I have such-and-such spiritual powers." Earlier he took me as his teacher and became my disciple. But he did not follow what I taught him. Before I came to America, guess what he did? He carried a big gourd on his back with a sign painted on it that proclaimed he was my disciple and that he had learned many skills from me. Further, he claimed he could solve any problem people might bring him. He used my name to swindle others before I arrived in this country. Now that I am here in America, he is still cheating people, but he no longer uses my name. This is the very kind of demon the sutra is talking about here. He claimed to have attained the absolute truth.

Lacking proper samadhi, he will certainly fall. He has lost the proper state of concentration, and he doesn't follow what I taught him, either. Since I arrived here, he has never come to listen to the sutra lectures or dharma talks, but just says he has attained the Way, is enlightened, and has spiritual powers. Ultimately what are his spiritual powers? You would never guess. They are money, money, money! He swindles people. I don't know why he wants so much money! Therefore, he will certainly fall.

J5 Passing through danger leads to anxiety.
K1 The characteristics of its beginning.

Sutra:

"**Further, in this state of samadhi the good person sees the disintegration of the form skandha and understands the feeling skandha. He has not yet obtained any results, and his prior state of mind has already disappeared. Surveying the two extremes, he feels that he is in great danger. Suddenly he becomes greatly distraught, as if he were seated on the iron bed, or as if he has taken poison. He has no wish to go on living, and he is always asking people to take his life so he can be released sooner.**

Commentary:

Further, in this state of samadhi, the good person, the cultivator, now with somewhat deeper power in samadhi, **sees the disintegration of the form skandha and understands the feeling skandha. He has not yet obtained any** of the **results** that he should obtain from his cultivation of the Way, **and** so **his prior state of mind has already disappeared. Surveying the two extremes**, past and future, he finds both are gone, and **he feels he is in great danger**. He thinks, "Oh no, this is really dangerous! It's too terrible!" **Suddenly he becomes greatly distraught.** He feels worried and afflicted about everything. The worries lead to afflictions, and what is it like to have afflictions? It's **as if he were seated on the iron bed**. From morning to night he thinks to himself, "Oh, I'm in the hells sitting on the iron bed! What can I do? To have this body is to suffer." **Or** he feels **as if he has taken poison** and is about to die. **He has no wish to go on living**. All day long he thinks, "I'd be better off dead. I'd be better off dead." In China, there is a saying "I'd be better off dead. I'd be better off dead. It would save on pants and coats." This person probably thinks that way, so he says, "I'd be better off dead. I'd be better off dead."

Ghosts are involved in most suicide cases. The ghost bows to the person and then recites a mantra, but the person does not hear the ghost reciting. The meaning of the mantra is, "You'd be better off dead! You'd be better off dead! Hurry up and die. The sooner you die the better." Even though the person contemplating suicide cannot hear it with his ears, subconsciously it penetrates his mind. Since ghosts have the spiritual power of knowing others' thoughts, they can use their demonic energy to get into your mind and persuade you to want to die. Your mind hears the ghost and believes what it says. Then you may take poison, hang yourself, cast yourself into the ocean, or jump off the Golden Gate Bridge. That's how you die! There are lots of ghosts around the Golden Gate Bridge. They dare not bother you if you are full of *yang* energy. But if someone comes along whose *yang* energy is weak, who is lacking in essence, energy, and spirit, the ghosts say, "You'd be better off dead. You'd be better off dead," and get the person to jump off the Golden Gate Bridge. Most suicides are caused by demonic ghosts that provoke people into taking their own lives. **And he**, the person who experiences tremendous anxiety, **is always asking people to take his life so he can be released sooner**. He is always saying to people, "Kill me! If you have a way to do me in, that would be great! I'll be free!"

K2 Giving the name and instructions to awaken.
K3 Showing how confusion will certainly bring a fall.

Sutra:

"This is called 'cultivating, but not understanding expedients.' If he understands, then there is no error. This experience does not indicate sagehood.

"But if he considers himself a sage, then a demon of chronic depression will enter his mind. He may take up knives and swords and cut his own flesh, happily giving up his life. Or else, driven by constant anxiety, he may flee into the wilderness and be unwilling to see people. Lacking proper samadhi, he will certainly fall."

Commentary:

This is called "cultivating, but not understanding expedients." Since the person does not understand the dharma doors of expedient means, he develops this attachment. After developing it **if he understands, then there is no error**, no problem. **This experience does not indicate sagehood**. This does not mean he has become a sage.

Having heard these principles in the sutra, you should be extremely careful not to casually indulge in random thoughts. Do not start thinking that you want to die, or that you cannot get what you want. If you keep thinking like that, you will attract this kind of demon. There are a great many of them in the world, so you should not indulge in random thoughts or speak carelessly. If you do, this demon may possess you. When that happens, you will not be able to endure it. You will not be free, and even if you do not want to die, there will be no way to avoid it.

But if he considers himself a sage, then there will be **a demon of chronic depression**. So you think you're depressed? Depression also involves demons. Why are you depressed or angry? If you have opened the buddha eye, you see that when a person is not angry, there is no ghost but as soon as he gets angry, a ghost comes to goad him on, saying, "Get angrier, get madder! Make more trouble!" Behind the scenes, it urges you to lose your temper. Even if you don't believe me, what I am saying is true. If you do not believe it, just take your time and try it out.

The demon **will enter his mind** and possess his body. **He may take up knives and swords and cut his own flesh**. Did I not tell you about Filial Son Wang (Great Master Chang Ren), who practiced filiality beside his parents' graves? Once, while in samadhi, Filial Son Wang saw that bandits had captured his nephew and were about to shoot him. Filial Son Wang was about five miles away. But just as the bandit was about to pull the trigger, from within samadhi he used his hand to ward off the gun so that the shot missed his nephew, who was able to escape. Behind this incident there was a ghost that wanted the nephew's life, and it had caused the bandits to tie the boy up and try to kill him. Those were the causes and effects involved. When Filial Son Wang thwarted the ghost in its efforts to kill his nephew, the ghost went after Filial Son Wang, but could not do anything to him. Then it went to find his younger brother, Wang Erye, and possessed him instead. Taking a knife, the brother went to find Filial Son Wang at the graveside, intending to commit suicide in front of him.

The ghost wanted to kill the younger brother, but strangely, as it held the knife poised, ready to behead the younger brother, it could not bring the hand down. Meanwhile, Filial Son Wang was reciting the *Vajra Sutra* and holding a vow of silence. As he recited it silently, my teacher (Great Master Chang Ti), who had not yet left the home-life, felt very agitated, as if there were some crisis. He felt trepidation and could not put his mind at ease. He wondered, "Is there something going on with the Filial Son by the grave?" He rushed over there immediately to take a look, and sure enough, Wang Erye was holding a knife about to behead himself. Filial Son Wang wrote a few words telling my teacher, "Buy some paper for burning. (There is a Chinese custom of burning paper money for the dead.) I will recite sutras for the ghost and liberate it. There is a ghost involved here, and it wants to do such-and-such." After Filial Son Wang recited sutras and liberated the ghost, there were no more problems.

On the one hand this is an example of the demon under discussion. But in this case the ghost came because it wanted someone's life, not because of cultivation. But you could also say it is from cultivation. Because Filial Son Wang cultivated and got too involved in someone else's business, he ended up with this kind of demon trying to kill his younger brother. The ghost couldn't kill Filial Son Wang because he had samadhi power and did not have any false thinking. The ghost couldn't do anything to him, so it went after his younger brother.

Happily giving up his life, he may wish to die. **Or else**, he may be **driven by constant** incredible **anxiety**. Now that you've heard this passage, take care not to be unhappy all the time. Do not always cry and feel melancholy. If you keep feeling worried and depressed, this demon will take possession of you. That is based half on the demon's power and half on your own. The demon avails itself of your energy. If your thoughts are proper, there will be no problems. But if your thinking is improper, you will be influenced by the demon. If it tells you, "Worry," you worry, and you become more and more worried, until you flee into the mountains, refusing to see people. **And, unable to tolerate people, he may flee into the mountain forests. Lacking proper samadhi, he will certainly fall**. Such a person will fall into the hells in the future.

J6 Experiencing ease leads to joy.
K1 The characteristics of its beginning.

Sutra:

"Further, in this state of samadhi, the good person sees the disintegration of the form skandha and understands the feeling skandha. As he dwells in this purity, his mind is tranquil and at ease. Suddenly a feeling of boundless joy wells up in him. There is such bliss in his mind that he cannot contain it.

Commentary:

Further, in this state of samadhi, the good person sees the disintegration of the form skandha and understands the feeling skandha. As he dwells in this purity of samadhi, **his mind is tranquil and at ease**. His mind is exceptionally calm and settled, without any scattered thoughts. Right at that point, the feeling skandha produces another effect in him. **Suddenly a feeling of boundless joy wells up in him**. He feels a happiness that knows no bounds. **There is such** extreme **bliss in his mind that** its extent cannot be known, and **he cannot contain it**. Even if he wants to stop the joy, he cannot.

K2 Giving the name, and instructions to awaken.

Sutra:

"This is called, 'experiencing lightness and ease, but lacking the wisdom to control it.' If he understands, then there is no error. This experience does not indicate sagehood.

Commentary:

This is called, "experiencing lightness and ease, but lacking the wisdom to control it." He does not have the wisdom to control his own happiness. **If he understands, then there is no error**. If you realize what it is, then there is no problem. **This experience does not indicate sagehood**. This does not mean that you have become a sage.

K3 Showing how confusion will certainly bring a fall.

Sutra:

"But if he considers himself a sage, then a demon that likes happiness will enter his mind. As soon as he sees someone, he will laugh. He will sing and dance in the streets. He will say that he has already attained unobstructed liberation. Lacking proper samadhi, he will certainly fall.

Commentary:

But if he considers himself a sage – if you say, "Oh, now I've entered the ground of happiness! I'm a bodhisattva of the ground of happiness!" – **then a demon that likes happiness will enter his mind. As soon as he sees someone, he will laugh** uproariously. **He will sing and dance in the streets**. Like a hippie, he gets totally carried away, waving his arms and stamping his feet, singing and dancing, making all kinds of music. **He will say that he has already attained unobstructed liberation. Lacking proper samadhi, he will certainly fall**. He loses his proper concentration, his proper knowledge and views, and his powers of reasoning; and eventually, he will fall into the hells.

J7 Seeing the sublime and becoming proud.
K1 The characteristics of its beginning.

Sutra:

"**Further, in this state of samadhi, the good person sees the disintegration of the form skandha and understands the feeling skandha. He says he is already satisfied. Suddenly, a feeling of unreasonable, intense self-satisfaction may arise in him. It may include pride, outrageous pride, haughty pride, overweening pride, and pride based on inferiority, all of which occur at once. In his mind, he even looks down on the Tathagatas of the ten directions, how much the more so on the lesser positions of sound-hearers and those enlightened by conditions.**

Commentary:

Further, in this state of samadhi, the good person sees the disintegration of the form skandha and understands the feeling skandha. He says he is already satisfied. He feels he already has enough of everything; he's already realized the fruition, become enlightened, and become a Buddha. **Suddenly, a feeling of unreasonable, intense self-satisfaction may arise in him.** Self-satisfaction is a form of haughtiness. He respects no one. He looks down on everyone and thinks no one is as good as he is. **It may include pride** – arrogance; **outrageous pride**, which is extreme arrogance; **haughty pride** – there is no greater arrogance than this; **overweening pride** – pride added to pride; **and pride based on inferiority** – feeling that everyone is inferior to him and looking down on everyone. These are different kinds of pride, **all of which occur at once.**

In his mind, he even looks down on the Tathagatas of the ten directions. To what extent does his pride go? Not only is he arrogant toward people, he is arrogant toward the Buddhas, so he regards even the Tathagatas of the ten directions with contempt, feeling they are not as good as he is. How serious would you say this pride is? It's really difficult to deal with! **How much the more so on the lesser positions of sound-hearers and those enlightened by conditions.** He looks down on them even more. His attitude is, "You're nothing but an arhat of the lesser vehicle! What's so special about you?" He thinks he's higher than the Buddha, but he hasn't come up with another name yet.

K2 Giving the name and instructions to awaken.

Sutra:

"This is called 'viewing oneself as supreme, but lacking the wisdom to save oneself.' If he understands, then there is no error. This experience does not indicate sagehood."

Commentary:

This is called **"viewing oneself as supreme."** It is an occasional state that occurs in the feeling skandha. **But it involves lacking the wisdom to save oneself.** The person doesn't have the wisdom to save himself. **If he understands, then there is no error.** If he understands that this is an error, then the demon will not have its way with him. As it is said, "If you understand, then you won't be confused; but when you are confused, you lack understanding." If you understand, it is like taking a sword of wisdom and hacking through the confusion. **This experience does not indicate sagehood.** It does not mean you have realized sagehood.

K3 Showing how confusion will certainly bring a fall.

Sutra:

"But if he considers himself a sage, then a demon of intense arrogance will enter his mind. He will not bow to stupas or in temples. He will destroy sutras and images. He will say to the danapatis, 'These are gold, bronze, clay, or wood. The sutras are just leaves or cloth. The flesh body is what is real and eternal, but you don't revere it; instead you venerate clay and wood. That is totally absurd.' Those who have deep faith in him will follow him to destroy the images or bury them. He will mislead living beings so that they fall into the Relentless Hells. Lacking proper samadhi, he will certainly fall.

Commentary:

But if he considers himself a sage, if you say that this is a good state, **then a demon of intense arrogance**, an extremely haughty demon, **will enter his mind** and possess him. **He will not bow to stupas or in temples**. He will not bow to Buddhas or stupas when he sees them. Nor will he make obeisance when he goes into temples. **He will destroy sutras and images**. He will burn sutras and break images of the Buddhas. Destroying sutras and images are offenses that lead to the hells. But he will say, "These things are all false."

He will say to the danapatis. He has his own disciples, and he tells his disciples these things. *Dana* means giving and *pati* means to transcend, so in Buddhism, one who makes offerings to the Triple Jewel is called a danapati. He says to his own danapatis and followers, "**These are gold, bronze, clay, or wood. The sutras are just leaves or cloth.**" Buddha images are made of gold, or of bronze; or they may be constructed of clay or wood. Sutras are written out on leaves, or on silk or cotton cloth. "What's the use of worshipping them? They have no consciousness. **The flesh body is what is real and eternal.** This flesh body of mine is real, **but you don't revere it**, you don't revere me; **instead you venerate clay and wood**. You'd rather bow to idols of clay and wood, what's the use of that? It would be better for you to bow to me than to them. **That is totally absurd**. What awareness do those pieces of wood have? It's ridiculous for you to bow to them!"

Those followers **who have deep faith in him**, who deeply believe in him, **will follow him to destroy the** Buddha **images** and burn the sutras, **or** to **bury them** in the ground. Through such behavior, **he will mislead living beings so that** they will not believe in Buddhism, but will have doubts instead. He will hinder them like that, and **they** will definitely **fall into the Relentless Hells. Lacking proper samadhi, he will certainly fall.**

J8 With wisdom comes lightness and ease, which leads to complacency.
K1 The characteristics of its beginning.

Sutra:

"**Further, in this state of samadhi, the good person sees the disintegration of the form skandha and understands the feeling skandha. In his refined understanding, he awakens completely to subtle principles. Everything is in accord with his wishes. He may suddenly experience limitless lightness and ease in his mind. He may say that he has become a sage and attained great self-mastery.**

K2 Giving the name and instructions to awaken.

"**This is called 'attaining lightness and clarity due to wisdom.' If he understands, then there is no error. This experience does not indicate sagehood.**

Commentary:

Further, in this state of samadhi, the good person sees the disintegration of the form skandha and understands the feeling skandha. In his refined understanding – his understanding becomes even more refined than before – **he awakens completely to subtle principles.** At this time, he gains a thorough understanding of very fine and subtle principles. **Everything is in accord with his wishes. He may suddenly experience** a state of **limitless lightness and ease in his mind. He may say that he has become a sage,** a Buddha, **and obtained great self-mastery,** the greatest happiness and ease.

This is called "attaining lightness and clarity due to wisdom." Having uncovered a little wisdom, you obtain a state of lightness and purity, and that's all – it certainly does not count as an extraordinary state. **If he understands, then there is no error**, no problem. **This experience does not indicate sagehood.** You should not think this state is the realization of sagehood, for it is not.

| K3 | Showing how confusion will certainly bring a fall. |

Sutra:

"But if he considers himself a sage, then a demon that likes lightness and clarity will enter his mind. Claiming that he is already satisfied, he will not strive to make further progress. For the most part, such cultivators will become like the unlearned bhikshu. He will mislead living beings so that they will fall into the Avichi Hell. Lacking proper samadhi, he will certainly fall.

Commentary:

But if he considers himself a sage – if, upon having this state of light ease, he thinks he has already been certified to the fruition of sagehood – **then a demon that likes lightness and clarity will enter his mind.** This demon, who also experiences the state of light ease and sublime clarity, will possess the person. **Claiming that he is already satisfied,** that he has perfected everything, **he will not strive to make further progress.** Above there is no Buddhahood to accomplish, and below there are no living beings to save. He does not need to become a Buddha, for he has already become one. Nor does he need to save living beings, for he has already finished saving them. He has already accomplished the Buddhahood he was supposed to accomplish, and he has saved the living beings he was meant to save. Therefore, he does not seek further progress.

For the most part, such cultivators will become like the unlearned bhikshu mentioned earlier. Lacking wisdom, he thought the fourth dhyana was the fourth fruition of arhatship. **He will mislead living beings**, so they do not know the proper path and do not recognize the Buddhadharma. He confuses and hinders living beings, **so that they will fall into the Avichi Hell**. In the future, this sort of person will fall into the Relentless Hells. Why? **Lacking proper samadhi, he will certainly fall**. Since he has lost his proper samadhi, he is bound to fall into the Relentless Hells.

J9 Becoming attached to emptiness and slandering precepts.
K1 The characteristics of its beginning.
K2 Giving its name and instructions to awaken.

Sutra:

"**Further in this state of samadhi, the good person sees the disintegration of the form skandha and understands the feeling skandha. In that clear awakening, he experiences an illusory clarity. Within that, suddenly he may veer towards the view of eternal extinction, deny cause and effect, and take everything as empty. The thought of emptiness so predominates that he comes to believe that there is eternal extinction after death.**

"[This is called 'the mental state of samadhi dissolving so that one loses sight of what is right.'] If he understands, then there is no error. This experience does not indicate sagehood."

Commentary:

Further in this state of samadhi, the good person sees the disintegration of the form skandha and understands the feeling skandha. At that time, **in that clear awakening**, when he seems to understand but does not truly understand, **he experiences an illusory clarity**, which is not real. **Within that** illusory clarity, **suddenly** a change occurs. What is it? **He may veer towards the view of eternal extinction, deny cause and effect, and take everything as empty.** He says, "When a person dies, he is gone and dead forever. Therefore, to talk in terms of cause and effect is incorrect. There is no cause and effect. When people die, they no longer exist, so how could there be cause and effect? Everything is empty. Committing offenses is empty and so is creating blessings. It is all empty!" **The thought of emptiness so predominates that he comes to believe that there is eternal extinction after death.** The more he thinks, the more he feels he's right. "Oh! It *is* empty. Once you die, it is all over. Everything is empty." At that point, he becomes convinced that people are gone forever after they die.

The text reads: "If he understands, then there is no error. It is not an indication of sagehood." One sentence must have been left out of the text when it was originally copied. We can insert it here: **This is called "the mental state of samadhi dissolving so that one loses sight of what is right."** At this point, his samadhi is gone, so he develops the thought of emptiness and loses his sense of what is right. **If he understands, then there is no error. This experience does not indicate sagehood.** This is not the state of realizing sagehood.

K3 Showing how confusion will certainly bring a fall.

Sutra:

"But if he considers himself a sage, then a demon of emptiness will enter his mind. He will slander the holding of precepts, calling it a 'practice for the initial vehicle.' He will say, 'Since bodhisattvas have awakened to emptiness, what is there to hold or violate?' This person, in the presence of his faithful danapatis, will often drink wine, eat meat, and engage in wanton lust. The power of the demon will keep his followers from doubting or denouncing him. After the ghost has possessed him for a long time, he may consume excrement and urine, or meat and wine, claiming that all such things are empty. He will break the Buddha's moral precepts and mislead people into committing offenses. Lacking proper samadhi, he will certainly fall.

Commentary:

But if he considers himself a sage, if he views this as certifying to the fruition of sagehood, **then a demon of emptiness will enter his mind**. It will enter and possess his body. **He will slander the holding of precepts, calling it a "practice for the initial vehicle."** He will say, "Don't observe the precepts. That's a teaching for the Theravada. Great vehicle bodhisattvas do not have so many bothersome restrictions. You don't have to pay attention to them. As it is said, 'The great elephant does not travel along the rabbit's path. The great awakening is not confined by petty details.' Once you are greatly enlightened, nothing matters anymore. Everything is empty. 'Wine and meat pass through the intestines;

the Buddha dwells in the mind.' To the Buddha, everything is made from the mind alone. The mind is just the Buddha, and the Buddha is just the mind!" That's what he says. He even slanders the holding of precepts, saying, "Only adherents of the Theravada observe precepts. Followers of the great vehicle do not need this."

Actually, the precepts for the great vehicle are even more explicit and even less should one violate them. He just fools these uninformed people, who have never studied the Buddhadharma and do not understand any of the principles explained by the Buddha. That's why, no matter what he says, they take it as an order to be followed, believing that what he says is right. Why do they believe him? Just because they have never heard the Buddhadharma and don't even know what the Buddhadharma is.

He will say, "Since great vehicle **bodhisattvas have** already **awakened to** the **emptiness** of all phenomena, **what is there to hold or violate?** How can there still be a holding of precepts or a violating of precepts? There's no such thing." **This person** who is possessed by the demon, **in the presence of his faithful danapatis**, in the homes of dharma protectors who believe in him, **will often drink wine, eat meat, and engage in wanton lust**. The phrase "engage in wanton lust" is very important. Buddhism teaches people not to have lust and desire, yet his desire is excessive. He engages in defiled practices of lust, yet people still believe in him because he has a demonic power. **The power of the demon will keep his followers from doubting or denouncing him**. They have tremendous faith in him.

After the ghost has possessed him for a long time, he may consume excrement and urine, or meat and wine, claiming that all such things are empty. Because he is possessed by a ghost, he will not think of excrement as something unclean, and he will also casually drink urine. He will say that eating excrement and drinking urine are "neither defiled nor pure," using the phrase from the *Heart Sutra*. That's how he will distort the sutra's meaning. This demon will behave in a way which shows that he doesn't care whether something is clean or dirty. He will say that eating meat and drinking wine are empty, and that eating excrement and drinking urine are empty. In general, everything is empty. **He will break the Buddha's moral precepts and mislead people into committing offenses.** Then, **lacking proper samadhi, he will certainly fall.** He deserves to fall into the hells.

J10 Becoming attached to existence and indulging in lust.
K1 The characteristics of its beginning.
K2 Giving its name and instructions to awaken.

Sutra:

"**Further, in this state of samadhi, the good person sees the disintegration of the form skandha and understands the feeling skandha. He savors the state of illusory clarity, and it deeply enters his mind and bones. Boundless love may suddenly well forth from his mind. When that love becomes extreme, he goes insane with greed and lust.**

"**This is called 'when an agreeable state of samadhi enters one's mind, lacking the wisdom to control oneself and mistakenly engaging in lustful behavior.' If he understands, then there is no error. This experience does not indicate sagehood.**

Commentary:

Further, in this state of samadhi, when the cultivator has attained the samadhi of the feeling skandha, **the good person sees the disintegration of the form skandha** – the form skandha is gone – **and he understands the feeling skandha**, being clear about it. **He savors the state of illusory clarity** which he has already attained, **and** now **it deeply enters his mind and bones**. A mental transformation may suddenly occur. What transformation? A **boundless**, immeasurable **love may suddenly well forth from his mind**. This is like a certain person who says he loves everyone. He has the kind of temperament being discussed. **When that love** and desire in his mind build up and **become extreme, he goes insane with greed and lust**. He cannot control his emotions. When he goes crazy, he is just like the woman Liu Jintong I mentioned earlier. Seeing a man, she would hug him, and cry, and make all sorts of seductive gestures. She was an example of this type of demon. How could the average man remain unmoved by such tricks? After she had confused him, she would tell him, "Take this amount of money and buy me that piece of jewelry," and he would say, "Okay, okay." Then she would say, "Take that amount of money and buy me that other thing," and he would agree to do it. Why? Simply because she engaged in lust with the man, and he was taken in by her demonic power. Here, when the love becomes extreme, the person goes insane with greed and lust. Lust arises from greed.

This is called "when an agreeable state of samadhi enters one's mind, lacking the wisdom to control oneself and mistakenly engaging in lustful behavior." A state of samadhi, with light ease and compliance, comes into his mind, but he lacks the wisdom to control his emotions and desire, and ends up indulging in all manner of lust. **If he understands, then there is no error.** This is only a temporary and occasional state. He should understand that **this experience** is a demonic state and **does not indicate sagehood**. If you understand, then it's all right. It is just to be feared that you do not recognize the state when you are in it, and you fall into an inescapable maze of confusion.

K3 Showing how confusion will certainly bring a fall.

Sutra:

"But if he considers himself a sage, then a demon of desire will enter his mind. He will become an outspoken advocate of lust, calling it the way to bodhi. He will teach his lay followers to indiscriminately engage in acts of lust, calling those who commit acts of lust heirs to his teachings. The power of spirits and ghosts in the ending age will enable him to attract a following of ordinary, naive people numbering one hundred, two hundred, five or six hundred, or as many as one thousand or ten thousand. When the demon becomes bored, it will leave the person's body. Once the person's charisma is gone, he will run afoul of the law. He will mislead living beings, so that they fall into the Relentless Hells. Lacking proper samadhi, he will certainly fall.

Commentary:

But if he considers himself a sage, if he views this as the realization of sagehood, **then** because his views are mistaken, **a demon of** lust and **desire will enter his mind** and possess him. **He will become an outspoken advocate of lust, calling it the way to bodhi.** He will talk of nothing but lust. It is like a certain religion in America that promotes polygamy. They say, "The more wives you have, the better." They are just like this demon, who promotes lust and appeals to people's desires by saying, "It's all right to have more wives; it doesn't matter. That's the way of bodhi, so the more wives you have the better!"

He will teach his lay followers to indiscriminately engage in acts of lust. He says, "Don't discriminate between one another. Let's all get together and have an orgy!" Not caring whether it is their own wife or someone else's, they just do as they please. In America, there's a wife-swapping fad where everybody exchanges wives. This is similar to the kind of activity that this type of demon engages in, **calling those who commit acts of lust heirs to his teachings.** These people who engage in lustful conduct with him will be his "heirs to his teachings" who carry on his message; they will receive a transmission of the teachings. **The power of** demonic ghosts, deviant **spirits and** deviant **ghosts in the** time of the Dharma-**ending Age, will enable him to attract** and confuse a following of **ordinary, naive,** ignorant **people, numbering one hundred, two hundred, five or six hundred, or as many as one thousand or ten thousand.** Eventually, **when the demon king becomes bored,** what happens? **It will leave the person's body.** What do you suppose happens when it leaves his body? He will no longer have spiritual powers.

Once the person's charisma is gone, he will run afoul of the law. His charisma came from his spiritual powers. The demon king had spiritual powers, but now the demon king has left, so he no longer has spiritual powers. What do you suppose happens? He will violate the laws of the country. Before, when he had spiritual powers, the demon could help him escape the authorities. But when the demon leaves, and this ordinary person carries on as before, he will immediately break the law. People will find out that he is a crooked teacher who has been duping his followers and deluding them with strange incantations. Since he has broken the law, he will be arrested and executed. **He will mislead living beings, so that they** will not find the proper path and will **fall into the Relentless Hells. Lacking proper samadhi, he will certainly fall** in the Avichi Hell as well.

I3 Conclusion on the harm, and command to offer protection.
J1 Showing how this happens due to interaction.
J2 Confusion will bring harm.

Sutra:

"**Ananda, all ten of these states may occur in dhyana as one's mental effort interacts with the feeling skandha.**

"**Dull and confused living beings do not evaluate themselves. Encountering such situations, in their confusion they fail to recognize them and say that they have become sages, thereby uttering a great lie. They will fall into the Relentless Hells.**

Commentary:

Ananda, all ten of these states may occur in dhyana as one's mental effort interacts with the feeling skandha. Ananda! States like these which manifest in dhyana, "the stilling of thought," are all within the feeling skandha, interacting with one's mental effort. These events are a result of the various interactions that happen as one works hard at his cultivation.

Dull and confused living beings do not evaluate themselves. They do not reflect within and take stock of themselves. **Encountering such situations, in their confusion they fail to recognize them.** They do not recognize who they are, **and** they **say that they have** already **become sages.** They say that they have attained what they have not attained and have been certified to what they have not been certified to. They claim they have already attained the Way and become certified as sages when they have not, **thereby uttering a great lie. They will** certainly **fall into the Relentless Hells.**

J3 Command to offer protection.

Sutra:

"**In the Dharma-ending Age, after my nirvana, all of you should pass on the Tathagata's teachings, so that all living beings can awaken to their meaning. Do not let the demons of the heavens have their way. Offer protection so that all can realize the Unsurpassed Way.**

Commentary:

Ananda, **in the Dharma-ending Age, after my nirvana, all of you should pass on the Tathagata's teachings.** Take these words which the Buddha has spoken, and pass them on, **so that all living beings can awaken to their meaning.** Let them all hear these principles, understand them, and awaken to them. **Do not let the demons of the heavens have their way.** Do not give them an opportunity to disturb those people. **Offer protection so that all** these living beings **can realize the Unsurpassed Way.**

CHAPTER 4

The Thinking Skandha

H3 The characteristics of the demons of the thinking skandha.
I1 Overview of the beginning and end.
J1 In the beginning, cultivation has not yet broken out of this region.
K1 Review of the ending of the previous feeling skandha.

Sutra:

"Ananda, when the good person who is cultivating samadhi has put an end to the feeling skandha, although he has not achieved freedom from outflows, his mind can leave his body the way a bird escapes from a cage. From within his ordinary body, he already has the potential for ascending through the bodhisattvas' sixty levels of sagehood. He attains the 'body produced by intent' and can roam freely without obstruction.

Commentary:

Ananda, when the good person who is cultivating the power of **samadhi has put an end to the feeling skandha,** when the feeling skandha is already gone, **although he has not achieved** the spiritual power of **freedom from outflows,** he already has other spiritual powers and **his** true **mind can leave his body the way a bird escapes from a cage.** Before one puts an end to the feeling skandha, one is trapped in one's body, just like a bird trapped in its cage. Just as the bird can now escape from the cage, **from within**

his ordinary body, he already, by means of spiritual powers, **has the potential for ascending through the bodhisattvas' sixty levels of sagehood.** Right in this ordinary body, he can become a bodhisattva and attain the sixty levels of bodhisattvahood. **He attains the 'body produced by intent' and can roam freely without obstruction.** He has to formulate the intent before he can have the spiritual power of the "body produced by intent." With such a body, he can go wherever he wants. What are the sixty levels of bodhisattvahood? They are the fifty-five stages of a bodhisattva discussed before; the three gradual stages and the stage of dry wisdom, making four kinds; and wonderful enlightenment, which makes sixty levels altogether.

K2   Introduction to the region of the thinking skandha.

Sutra:

"This is like someone talking in his sleep. Although he does not know he is doing it, his words are clear, and his voice and inflection are all in order, so those who are awake can understand what he is saying. This is the region of the thinking skandha."

Commentary:

This is like someone talking in his sleep. This is an analogy comparing the region of the thinking skandha to someone talking in his dream. While asleep, he starts saying what he wants to say. **Although he does not know he is doing it, his words are clear, and his voice and inflection are all in order.** Although he doesn't know he is talking in his dream, what he says is intelligible. Everything he says follows in logical order and makes sense, but he himself is not aware of it. **So those who are awake can understand what he is saying.**

For instance, he says, "I wanted to eat *tofu* (soybean cake) today, so I went to the store and bought ten pieces of tofu. When I got back, I cooked them and ate them."

He is not aware of what he is saying, but other people who are awake know, "Oh! He ate tofu today." Why did he say what he said? Because he has not forgotten what he ate. He keeps thinking about it and he will talk about it even in his dream. **This is the region of the thinking skandha.** That is what the region of the thinking skandha is like. But don't take this too literally and think, "The thinking skandha is just talking in a dream." That would be wrong. It is just an analogy.

J2 Ultimately it breaks up and reveals its false source.

Sutra:

"If he puts an end to his stirring thoughts and rids himself of superfluous thinking, it is as if he has purged defilement from the enlightened, understanding mind. Then he is perfectly clear about the births and deaths of all categories of beings from beginning to end. This is the end of the thinking skandha. He can then transcend the turbidity of afflictions. Contemplating the cause of the thinking skandha, one sees that interconnected false thoughts are its source.

Commentary:

If he puts an end to his stirring thoughts, the extremely subtle thoughts in the sixth consciousness, **and rids himself of superfluous thinking.** Since those very fine thoughts in the sixth consciousness have stopped, superfluous thinking is also eliminated. **It is as if he has purged defilement from the enlightened, understanding mind.** This enlightened, clear mind is the eighth consciousness. Now, it appears that the eighth consciousness has been purged of defilement. **Then he is perfectly clear about the births and deaths of all categories of beings from beginning to end.** There are twelve categories of beings, from those born from wombs and those born from eggs up to and including those not entirely lacking thought. He knows the preceding causes and subsequent effects of every kind of being.

This is the end of the thinking skandha. At that time the person obtains the spiritual power of knowing past lives. **He can**

then transcend the turbidity of afflictions. Contemplating the cause of the thinking skandha,** contemplating the reasons behind his actions and deeds, **one sees that interconnected false thoughts are its source.** At that point, the false thoughts become interpenetrating, and such thoughts become its source.

```
I2    The ten states within this.
J1    Greed for clever skill.
K1    Samadhi leads to craving and seeking.
```

Sutra:

"**Ananda, in the unhindered clarity and wonder that ensues after the feeling skandha is gone, this good person is untroubled by any deviant mental state and experiences perfect, bright concentration. Within samadhi, his mind craves its perfect brightness, so he sharpens his concentrated thought as he greedily seeks for cleverness and skill.**

Commentary:

Ananda, in the unhindered clarity and wonder that ensues after the feeling skandha is gone, this good person is untroubled by any deviant mental state. No deviant thoughts can disturb him.

[January 1983]

"In the unhindered clarity and wonder that ensues after the feeling skandha is gone, this good person is untroubled by any deviant mental state." At this point, the feeling skandha is over, and he is in the thinking skandha, which is subtle and wondrous. What is wonderful is that when you have no faults, you will not be troubled by deviant mental states, that is, by feelings of worry and fear. What is meant by worry and fear? It's like the man of Qi, who worried that the sky would fall down. He had a deviant mental state. Now the cultivator is no longer troubled by deviant mental states. He doesn't have them in himself. However, he is not strong enough to resist troubles that come from outside, because love, greed, and seeking are still present in his mind. Since selfish and self-benefiting thoughts are still concealed inside, he is vulnerable to states from the external environment. "Deviant mental states" refer not only to thoughts, but also to feelings of worry and fear. When you are afraid of something, then you have a deviant mental state. When others oppress you and you're afraid to speak out about it, that's also a deviant mental state.

[January 1983, another day]

While we are investigating the fifty skandha-demon states, five hundred kinds of skandha demons may come, so you should open your doors to them and invite them to come make trouble. Although they are demons, they help your cultivation from the reverse; they test you to see how firmly resolved you are. If you have true determination, then a thousand demons will not make you waver, ten thousand demons will not make you retreat and you will not be afraid of anything, because you are not seeking anything. As it is said,

> When you reach the place of seeking nothing,
> You will have no more worries.

Since you seek nothing, you will not fear anything. What is there to be afraid of? Some people are afraid of ghosts because of their grotesque appearance. They know that some people turn into ghosts after they die. No one is afraid of spirits, despite the fierce appearance of those spirits clad in golden armor. Confucius said, "One should respect ghosts and spirits, but keep them at a distance." You should be very respectful toward ghosts and spirits, but don't draw near to them. You should fear neither ghosts nor spirits.

You need not fear demons; they are just testing you out, trying out your skill in cultivation. If you're afraid, then they will come even if you don't want them to. If you are not afraid, then they will not be able to come even if they want to. The secret is to not be afraid. If you're not afraid, then you are "proper" and you can subdue anything, because the deviant cannot overcome the proper. Demons fear those who are proper, great and bright. If you can be that way, then the demons will behave themselves and will even bow to you.

And he experiences perfect, bright concentration. Within samadhi, his mind craves its perfect brightness, so he sharpens his concentrated thought as he greedily seeks for cleverness and skill. "To sharpen" means to refine his intense reflection, which is that perfect brightness. He greedily seeks to have skill-in-means to teach and transform living beings. That is what he is greedy for.

[May 21, 1989]

Venerable Master: Here, being "clever and skillful" doesn't refer to ordinary expedient means. Expedient means are very casual. These "clever and skillful" methods which he uses are very ingenious and subtle, and you can't detect any flaws in them, because he applies them very well. You cannot tell that they are expedients.

Disciple: Is he seeking cleverness and skill so he can teach and transform people?

Venerable Master: Not only in teaching, but in all aspects, he has this kind of clever and skillful wisdom. Regular expedient methods can be recognized as such by people. But the kind of cleverness and skill spoken of here cannot immediately be detected by others, because the person speaks very reasonably and ingeniously. You can't find any faults with what he says.

K2 A demon dispatches a deviant force to possess a person.

Sutra:

"At that time a demon from the heavens seizes the opportunity it has been waiting for. Its spirit possesses another person and uses him as a mouthpiece to expound the sutras and the teachings.

Commentary:

At that time a demon from the sixth desire **heavens seizes the opportunity it has been waiting for.** Seeing that the cultivator's samadhi power is about to be perfected, it waits for a chance to get at him. It watches for some flaw in his character which will provide an opening. The existence of an opening indicates that his samadhi power is not yet solid. Occasionally he will have an extraneous false thought. Once he has that false thought, his samadhi power is no longer firm, and the demon will take advantage of him. Thus it says the demon "seizes the opportunity it has been waiting for."

[January 1983]

The demon "seizes the opportunity it has been waiting for." That is, he seizes the opportunity provided by the cultivator's greed and opens up the door. It's not easy to understand what the sutra means; you may be off by just that little bit in your interpretation.

Its spirit possesses another person and uses him as a mouthpiece to expound the sutras and the teachings. The demon from the heavens commands one of its followers, "Go to that place and destroy that person's samadhi power." Before the form skandha and the feeling skandha were ended, the demon could possess the cultivator himself and confuse him. But after the form skandha and feeling skandha are gone and the cultivator reaches the thinking skandha, the demon cannot possess him. It has to take possession of another person and then explains the teachings for the cultivator through that person. That person lectures on the sutras, but the dharma he speaks is deviant, and you should recognize it for what it is.

[May 21, 1989]

"Its spirit possesses another person, and uses him as a mouthpiece to expound the sutras and the teachings." There are two ways to explain this. You could say the demon possesses another person, who then comes to explain the teachings for the first person. You could also say that the demon possesses the cultivator of samadhi himself. Either of these interpretations can apply; there is more than one meaning.

When a cultivator is at the level of the thinking skandha, the demon's spirit cannot possess him and confuse his mind directly. For example, right now there is a cultivator who involuntarily does *tai ji quan* and shouts, but he realizes what is going on and knows that it is wrong. The demon is unable to confuse his mind. On the other hand, if a person has not cultivated at all, then once the demon confuses him, he will not understand anything at all; he will not realize that a demon has come or the things it has done. Most people who don't cultivate are this way. The demon possesses the person and speaks through him. Then after the demon has left, you ask the person what happened and he has no idea. That's because his mind was thoroughly confused. Someone who is not confused by the demon will be able to keep a clear mind during the experience. There are various interpretations, not just one. If you interpret the text as saying only that the demon possesses another person, your interpretation is incomplete. There are many possibilities, and the situation could develop in one of several directions, so it is not fixed.

While the text may be explained in any way that makes sense, the translation of the sutra should not be limited to a particular explanation. The sutra is like an ocean, while explanations of it are like rivers. Rivers can flow into the ocean in many different ways, and so you cannot use a particular river to represent the entire ocean.

[December 2, 1993]

Do not become too attached to what the sutra says. The sutra gives a general idea of what might happen, but each particular situation may be different. There are not only fifty, but perhaps five hundred, five thousand, or even fifty thousand kinds of states. There are so many states that we could never finish speaking of them. These [fifty states] are just a general summary, and you shouldn't think of them as profound and esoteric. Regard them as if they were spoken by an ordinary person, and don't always be splitting hairs.

My explanations of sutras are called "simple explanations"; I don't give profound explanations. When I explain a sutra, my only aim is for everyone to understand what I mean and for me to understand what everyone else means. Don't think too deeply.

Anyone who thinks too deeply will never be able to finish explaining it. Don't beat your head against the wall trying to figure out exactly what it means. After all, this sutra is a translation; it is not so rigidly fixed that you cannot add or omit a word. It does not correspond exactly to the original Sanskrit. Just try to convey the general meaning; don't spend too much time pursuing the fine details of literary interpretation.

Disciple: At the level of the thinking skandha, the demons from the heavens can no longer disturb the cultivator's mind directly. A demon has to possess another person in order to disturb the cultivator's samadhi.

Venerable Master: For example, a cultivator may frequently encounter people who are possessed by ghosts, who come to speak teachings for him, or who come to challenge him to see who is on top.

At the City of Ten Thousand Buddhas, there's a student from the University of California at Berkeley who has many snakes following him. You may not have seen them, but Guo Zhen saw those snakes get into a contest with me at Gold Mountain Monastery. They are really ferocious! His presence there gave the snakes a chance to fight with me. They have been fighting me for over ten years now. When he went to the City of Ten Thousand Buddhas, he would gradually get better, but as soon as he went back to school in Berkeley, he would get sick again. He realizes that there are many snakes on him. He killed these snakes in the past, and now they've come to get revenge. I've been using wholesome methods to try to make peace with them. That's how I treat them, regardless of whether or not they pay any heed. It's a slow process. Over the last ten years or so, many of the snakes have left him, but there are still a few left. There used to be a whole bunch of them. This case is similar to the state described in the sutra.

Disciple: When a person comes to the City of Ten Thousand Buddhas, are those beings afraid to come and seek him out?

Venerable Master: No, they still come. When it [the snake] came to challenge my dharma, it was terribly fierce. At first he [the student possessed by the snake] knelt down, but then he stood up and waved his hands and glared at me. His heavy breathing sounded worse than a screeching and hissing cat.

Disciple: Master, what did you do? Did you give it a good scolding?

Venerable Master: No, I just pretended nothing was happening. People saw me acting as if nothing were going on, but actually, I had converted it. It was hostile to me, but I wasn't hostile to it. I used to use the function of subduing, but not anymore. Now I use the function of averting disasters.

Disciple: When the form skandha has come to an end, deviant demons can no longer possess a cultivator. They have to possess another person. But is there another interpretation in which the demon can directly possess the cultivator?

Venerable Master: There are endless possibilities. The demon can even possess a cat. It all depends on whether or not you recognize it. It can also possess other animals. There's no fixed rule.

Disciple: Can it possess the cultivator himself?

Venerable Master: No, it can't get to him.

Disciple: But when the Venerable Master explained the fifty skandha demons in the past, you said it could possess the cultivator himself.

Venerable Master: As I said, none of this is fixed. The text gives one example, but that's not the only way it can be. There are many variations. Each case encompasses many possibilities.

Disciple: But didn't the Venerable Master just say that the demons can't get to the cultivator himself?

Venerable Master: If he truly cultivates, then the demons can't get to him, because there are dharma-protecting spirits protecting him.

Disciple: If the cultivator starts entertaining false thoughts, then...

Venerable Master: Then they'll get to him.

Disciple: It's just like living at the City of Ten Thousand Buddhas. If we follow the rules set down by the Master, then those beings cannot bother us. If we don't follow the rules, then they can come.

Venerable Master: Many people who come here have a lot of deviant demons of external ways, goblins, ghosts, and strange spirits attached to them. Yet the bodhisattvas who guard the dharma don't try to keep them out. We practice kindness and compassion here. Thus we haven't fortified our place or set up any defense against them.

Disciple: If someone truly cultivates, then the demons can't get to him. But if he's not cultivating and he starts indulging in false thoughts, then they can come.

Venerable Master: Right, it's a case of the deviant attracting the deviant.

Disciple: If the demons can't get to him now, it doesn't necessarily mean that they can't get to him ever. For instance, when National Master Wuda entertained a thought of arrogance...

Venerable Master: Right! That's a very clear illustration!

Disciple: The ghost hadn't been able to get to him for ten lives, but with that one improper thought, it was able to get in.

Venerable Master: It came to demand his life!

Disciple: So would you say that the demons can get to the cultivator or not? It's not fixed. If he truly cultivates, then they can't get to him, but if he doesn't, then they can.

Venerable Master: Right, it's not fixed. Whatever can be put into words loses its real meaning. Once you understand this principle, you shouldn't pursue the details too intently. As I just said, there are infinite variations and possibilities. These fifty states can be transformed into five hundred, five thousand, or fifty thousand states. Don't spend too much time on these examples. You should understand that there are other cases that are variations of these. In general, whatever can be said has no real meaning. You could say all the sutras are false, but you must find the true principles within this falseness. Any sutra that makes sense can be believed. If it doesn't make sense, if it's incorrect, then don't believe it.

K3 The person who is possessed causes trouble.

Sutra:

"This person, unaware that he is possessed by a demon, claims he has reached unsurpassed nirvana. When he comes to see that good person who seeks cleverness and skill, he arranges a seat and explains the teachings. In an instant, he may appear to be a bhikshu, enabling that person to see him as such, or he may appear as Shakra, as a woman, or as a bhikshuni; or his body may emit light as he sleeps in a dark room.

Commentary:

You can see how formidable these demonic states are. **This person, unaware that he is possessed by a demon,** has no idea a demon is helping him. He **claims** that **he has reached unsurpassed nirvana.** He claims to have obtained the truth of nirvana, the wonderful fruition of nirvana.

[January 1983]

Yesterday someone mentioned a certain person who recited the Buddha's name and then suddenly started jumping around, as if dancing. He was possessed by a demonic spirit. He didn't know what was happening, and he thought, "Wow! I've entered samadhi." He was like a rambunctious kid; he hopped about like a bunny.

When he comes to see that good person, the cultivator **who seeks cleverness and skill, he arranges a seat and explains the teachings** for that good person who seeks to be clever and skillful.

In an instant, very briefly, he may appear to be a bhikshu, enabling that person who seeks clever skill **to see him as such. Or he may appear as Shakra – Lord God – as a woman, or as a bhikshuni.** When the person seeking cleverness and skill sees him going through such transformations, he thinks, "He must be Guan Yin Bodhisattva!" He has no idea that it is a demon. That's why you shouldn't get carried away by any state you see, no matter what it is.

Or his body may emit light as he sleeps in a dark room. When people who do not understand the Buddhadharma see that, they marvel "Wow! His body emits light! If he isn't a Buddha, he must be at least a bodhisattva or an arhat!" They do not realize that the person is possessed by a demon king that is manifesting spiritual powers in order to delude the cultivator.

Therefore, as ordinary people who do not truly understand the Buddhadharma, we should not be turned by the things we see, no matter what they are. Don't become moved and run off after those states. How should you treat them? Look upon them as if they didn't exist. Seeing those things should be the same as not seeing them. Be neither elated nor disgusted. If you become elated when you see a demon, then you have been turned by the demon's state. If you get disgusted, then you have also been turned by the demon's state. How should you act? Just maintain the middle way, neither liking nor disliking it. See as if you haven't seen, and hear as if you haven't heard. You shouldn't say, "That was a fine state! I'd like to see that again!" If you have that thought, you have made a mistake.

[January 1983]

Demons are very smart. They see what you're greedy for and use that to tempt you. Therefore, cultivators don't need to recite any particular mantra or practice any particular dharma. Just be honest and true; don't contend, don't be greedy, don't seek, don't be selfish, and don't pursue personal gain. If you put your shoulder to the grindstone and cultivate diligently, no demon can bother you. But as soon as you become greedy or you start scheming for advantages and shortcuts, it's easy for demons to possess you. Demons are very wise; they can see what level of cultivation you've reached and know what methods should be used to lure you. As for choosing a person to possess, that's not a problem, because the person is only a false front for them. They use the person, and they use various methods to entice and delude you. If a cultivator is unselfish and doesn't think about benefiting himself, he will not be afraid of any demon.

K4 The cultivator becomes deluded and confused.

Sutra:

"The good person is beguiled and fooled into thinking that the other is a bodhisattva. He believes the other's teachings and his mind is swayed. He breaks the Buddha's moral precepts and covertly indulges his greedy desires."

Commentary:

The good person who cultivates samadhi **is beguiled and fooled** at this point **into thinking that the other is a bodhisattva.** When he sees how the person can appear as a bhikshu, as Shakra, as a lay woman, and as a bhikshuni, suddenly changing from one appearance to another, he thinks the person must be a bodhisattva.

He then deeply **believes the other's teachings and his mind is swayed. He breaks the Buddha's moral precepts.** What should you examine in a cultivator? See whether or not he keeps the Buddha's precepts. If he doesn't, then he is certainly a demon. If he strictly adheres to the precepts without violating them, then he is a genuine Buddhist. However, someone may claim to be a Buddhist, call himself a venerable elder, and assume other titles as well, **and** yet **he covertly indulges his greedy desires.** He engages in a clandestine affair and tries to keep people from knowing about it.

K5 The types of things he says.

Sutra:

"The other person is fond of speaking about calamities, auspicious events, and unusual changes. He may say that a Tathagata has appeared in the world at a certain place. He may

speak of catastrophic fires or wars, thus frightening people into squandering their family wealth without reason.

Commentary:

The other person is fond of speaking about calamities, auspicious events, and unusual changes. What does the person who is possessed by the demon like to speak about? He likes to talk about calamities, which are unlucky events. He may say a calamity is going to occur in a certain place, or that something auspicious is going to happen somewhere, or that an unusual event is going to take place. **He may say that a Tathagata has appeared in the world at a certain place.** He may say, "You know what? Such-and-such a Buddha has now appeared in the world at such-and-such a place."

He may speak of catastrophic fires or wars. He may say, "The three disasters – flood, fire, and wind – and the eight difficulties are upon us." Or, "The kalpa is coming to an end!" Or he might warn people, "Be careful, war is about to break out there." Or, "The Soviet Union is about to go to war with a certain country!" He speaks in this way, **thus frightening people into squandering their family wealth without reason.** He always says things that capture people's attention and cause them to be alarmed. When people hear what he says, they panic, "Oh no! There's going to be war. Will my life be in danger?" He might say, "The war is starting. If you give me some money immediately, I'll guarantee your safety. If you don't pay me, you will lose your life!" He is always saying such things to cheat people.

If you want to determine whether a person is genuine or phony, whether he is a bodhisattva or a demon, you can look for the following things: First, see whether he has any desire for sex; and second, see whether he is greedy for money. If he cheats people to satisfy his lust and greed for wealth, then he is not genuine. How might he be greedy for wealth? For example, he may say, "A great calamity is nearly upon us! The world is coming to an end. An atomic bomb is going to explode at such-and-such a place. A hydrogen bomb will be set off at another place." He says such things to frighten people into giving him their money. If you wake up to his tricks, then even if he emits light, makes the earth quake, or does something else spectacular, you shouldn't believe in him, because he is greedy. A person without greed is true; a greedy person is a phony. My method is a practical and effective truth-detector.

[January 1983]

If we had no greed or desires, then we would have no trouble. If you have greed and desire, then all sorts of things will happen. All the myriad things, beings, and species in the world are born from greed and desire. Thus it is said, "When not a single thought is produced, the entire substance manifests." If you don't have thoughts of greed and desire, then the Buddha-nature will appear. "When the six sense faculties suddenly move, one is covered by clouds." Once the eyes, ears, nose, tongue, body, and mind become attached to a state, it's like the sky clouding over so that the sun cannot shine. Fundamentally, what causes the six sense faculties to move? Greed and desire. Because you are unable to give up greed and desire, the six sense faculties turn into the six thieves and the six consciousnesses come into being. If you had no greed and desire, then the thieves of the six sense faculties would no longer be thieves, and the six consciousnesses would no longer be consciousnesses. Everything would return to the source, and all troubles would disappear. Everyone should pay attention to this. It all depends on whether or not you have greed and desire. If you do, then you have not separated yourself from the demons yet. If you do not, then you have joined with the Buddhas.

K6 Giving the name and pointing out the harm.

Sutra:

"This is a strange ghost that in its old age has become a demon. It disturbs and confuses the good person. But when it tires of doing so, it will leave the other person's body. Then both the disciples and the teacher will get in trouble with the law.

Commentary:

This is a strange, weird ghost that, after a long time, **in its old age has become a demon. It disturbs and confuses the good person. But when it tires of doing so, it will leave the other person's body.** Eventually, it gets bored of playing this game. It has had enough, and so it stops possessing the person. When that happens, **then both the disciples and the teacher will get in trouble with the law.** The authorities arrest them, accuse them of rabble-rousing, and either execute them or punish them in some other way.

[January 1983]

This is the time to study, and we must keep studying the states, one by one, until we finish. Then everyone will have a better understanding. Right now we've just started studying, and some will understand, while others won't. When each of you comes to the front, you are not here to interrogate anyone, but just to investigate what you have seen and understood with everyone else. The person who just came up here had a correct understanding. When the form skandha is obliterated, the view of self is emptied, so that one no longer has a sense of self, and all physical objects, all things with form and appearance, are also emptied. If you don't understand this, you can read over the sutra text a few more times, and then you'll naturally understand.

All religions operate in the realm of the five skandhas. Later on the text talks about how both the teacher and the disciples get in trouble with the law. The words "teacher and disciples" indicate that this is talking about religion. Being satisfied with their small achievements, they set up their own religion and claim that it is the real one. Without my having to mention any religions by name, everyone should know what I'm talking about. If you want to know which skandhas those religions fall under, what level they have reached, then you have to gain a thorough understanding of the fifty skandha-demon states.

Instead of just asking questions, you should look into them yourselves. We are all studying together, and it shouldn't be that one person answers everyone else's questions, because our wisdom is equal. In our investigation, if everyone agrees to a principle, then we will consider it correct. We are gathering everyone's opinions, and when we publish the fifty skandha-demon states in the future, each person's opinion should be included. This is a joint investigation, not one person answering others' questions. Anyone can speak out and express an opinion.

Why do we have only two people reading aloud? Because these two people have passable Chinese and English. They are giving a general explanation of the meaning, and if what they say is incomplete, people can speak up. People should not be simply asking questions. This is not like when we lectured on the *Brahma Net Sutra*. This meeting is investigatory in nature, and everyone is equal. There's no need to request the dharma or do anything. Everyone should just investigate and study together. No one is debating with anyone else, and anyone can express an opinion. Do you all think this is a good method?

[January 1983, another day]

Disciple: The sutra text says that the teacher and disciples will both fall into the hells?

Venerable Master: Right, that's referring to the cultivator!

Disciple: Is the cultivator one of the disciples?

Venerable Master: Not necessarily. The teacher is also that way; he's also a cultivator. An example of this was the People's Church. You can tell by whether or not a person has lust. If he has lust, then he is a demon. If he doesn't, then he's proper and he's a Buddha. That's where the difference lies. If he hasn't cut off lust, then he can't subdue his mind. He may be able to sit there and enter samadhi, but while in samadhi, he is still greedy and seeking. "He covertly indulges his greedy desires." That's how you can recognize him.

| K7 | Instructions to be aware and not become confused. |

Sutra:

"**You should be aware of this in advance and not get caught up in the cycle of transmigration. If you are confused and do not understand, you will fall into the Relentless Hells.**

Commentary:

You should be aware of this in advance and not get caught up in the cycle of transmigration. You should awaken to this early on and not enter the demon king's cycle of birth and death. **If you are confused and do not understand,** in the future **you will fall into the Relentless Hells.**

| J2 | Greedy for adventure. |
| K1 | Samadhi leads to craving and seeking. |

Sutra:

"**Further, Ananda, in the unhindered clarity and wonder that ensues after the feeling skandha is gone, this good person is untroubled by any deviant mental state and experiences perfect, bright concentration. Within samadhi, his mind craves to roam about, so he lets his subtle thoughts fly out as he greedily seeks for adventure.**

Commentary:

Further, Ananda, in the unhindered clarity and wonder that ensues after the feeling skandha is gone, this good person who cultivates samadhi **is untroubled by any deviant mental state and experiences perfect, bright concentration. Within samadhi, his mind** has another false thought and **craves to roam about,** that is, "to go out the top of his head and roam around in his spiritual body." That means his spirit goes out and runs around to various places. **So he lets his subtle thoughts fly out as he greedily seeks for adventure.** His spirit flies out and wants to go everywhere, to see the sights and have some fun.

| K2 | A demon dispatches a deviant force to possess a person. |

Sutra:

"**At that time a demon from the heavens seizes the opportunity it has been waiting for. Its spirit possesses another person and uses him as a mouthpiece to expound the sutras and explain the teachings.**

Commentary:

At that time a demon from the heavens seizes the opportunity it has been waiting for. The demon king in the heavens again becomes jealous and waits for an opening to get in. **Its spirit possesses another person.** It again sends a member of its retinue to possess another person **and uses him as a mouthpiece to expound the sutras and explain the teachings.** It comes to disturb the cultivator. Why does the cultivator get possessed by a demon? Simply because he is greedy for adventure; he longs to travel, to roam far and wide. As soon as he entertains the thought of roaming, that gives the demon king the chance to disturb him. The demon would not come if the cultivator did not have that thought.

| K3 | The person who is possessed causes trouble. |

Sutra:

"**This person, unaware that he is possessed by a demon, claims he has reached unsurpassed nirvana. When he comes to see that good person who seeks to roam, he arranges a seat and explain the teachings. His own body does not change its appearance, but those listening to the lecture suddenly see themselves sitting on jeweled lotuses and their entire bodies transformed into clusters of purple-golden light. Each person in the audience experiences that state and feels he has obtained something unprecedented.**

Commentary:

This person, unaware that he is possessed by a demon, claims he has reached the wondrous fruition of **unsurpassed nirvana. When he comes to see that good person who seeks to**

roam, that is, the cultivator who had a false thought about his spiritual body going out the top of his head and roaming everywhere, **he arranges a seat and explain the teachings. His own body does not change its appearance.** In the previous passage, the person's own body took on the appearance of a bhikshu, of Shakra, of a lay woman, of a bhikshuni, and various other forms. But in this case his body does not change. There are different kinds of demons, and you should not consider experiencing an unusual state to be something good. If one occurs and you don't recognize it, a demon can possess you. Here, the body of the person who is speaking the teachings doesn't change, **but those listening to the lecture suddenly see themselves sitting on jeweled lotuses and their entire bodies transformed into clusters of purple-golden light.** Suddenly, everyone feels as if he is sitting on a jeweled lotus and his whole body has turned into a cluster of purple-golden light. **Each person in the audience experiences that state and feels he has obtained something unprecedented.** They think this is rare and unusual, something they have never seen before. They believe it to be a good state, but actually it is a demonic state.

K4 The cultivator becomes deluded and confused.

Sutra:

"**The good person is beguiled and fooled into thinking the other is a bodhisattva. Lust and laxity corrupt his mind. He breaks the Buddha's moral precepts and covertly indulges his greedy desires.**

Commentary:

The good person is beguiled and fooled into thinking the other is a bodhisattva. Not only this person, but all those listening to these teachings are very stupid. Their minds are confused, and they think, "He's really a bodhisattva! He can make me sit on a jeweled lotus and turn the color of purple-golden light." You should ask yourself if you are really seated on a lotus blossom and radiant with purple-golden light. Actually it is all false. How can you, an ordinary person, have such a state? Isn't this a demon king that has come to fool you? Why would a bodhisattva make such a state appear? What is the bodhisattva trying to get from you?

Lust and laxity corrupt his mind. The minds of those listening to these teachings are moved as well, and they start having thoughts of lust. **He breaks the Buddha's moral precepts.** They don't keep the Buddha's precepts anymore. You should all remember: After you take the precepts, never be deceived by such states of confused belief. Even if a dharma-speaker displays mighty spiritual powers, you should look him over carefully and see if he is greedy. If he is out for money or if he has lust, then he's not genuine. He's a phony. If a person does not have any lust, greed, or ulterior motives, then he is genuine. If he violates the Buddha's moral precepts, then he's a fraud. **And** he **covertly indulges his greedy desires.** He engages in licentious conduct on the sly.

K5 The types of things he says.

Sutra:

"The other person is fond of saying that Buddhas are appearing in the world. He claims that in a certain place a certain person is actually a transformation body of a certain Buddha. Or he says that a certain person is such and such a bodhisattva who has come to teach humankind. People who witness this are filled with admiration. Their wrong views multiply, and their wisdom of modes is destroyed.

Commentary:

The other person is fond of saying that Buddhas are appearing in the world. The person possessed by the demon likes to roam about, and then based on his adventures, he talks about strange and mysterious things. The things he says are so mysterious that no one can conceive of them. He says, "All the Buddhas have now come into the world to save people." **He claims that in a certain place a certain person is actually a transformation body of a certain Buddha.** "He's really Buddha so-and-so, whose transformation body has come here to save living beings." **Or he says**

that a certain person is such and such a bodhisattva who has come to teach humankind.

For example, one of my disciples says that the disciples of a certain teacher say that their teacher is a bodhisattva. That's ridiculous. What kind of bodhisattva? A ghost bodhisattva. They're just cheating people. I'll tell you something: A real Buddha or bodhisattva would never admit that he was a Buddha or a bodhisattva. Nor would he let his disciples advertise for him, saying, "Our teacher is a bodhisattva." I never told you to talk like that. Why do some of you say that your teacher is a Buddha? You must never speak that way about me. Haven't I told you I'm a ghost? Just tell them your teacher is a ghost. I don't want to be called a bodhisattva or a Buddha. How pathetic those people are! Here the person says, "This is a bodhisattva who has come to teach the world! He has come to save us in this Dharma-ending Age."

People who witness this are filled with admiration. Since they have childish views and don't really understand the Buddhadharma, they think, "Wow! He's a bodhisattva! Fantastic! Let's hurry and go hear him speak the dharma and ask him to be our teacher!" For example, yesterday someone came to steal the dharma. I asked him who his teacher was, and he said it was so-and-so. That's the kind of situation this is referring to. They are filled with awe and admiration. "We'll take this bodhisattva as our teacher, and study bodhisattva practices with him. Since he's a bodhisattva, of course all the people he teaches can become bodhisattvas, too." As a result, **their wrong views multiply,** gradually growing thicker and thicker, **and their wisdom of modes is destroyed.** Their wisdom of all modes and all their various kinds of wisdom are eradicated. The seeds of their wisdom are destroyed. It's that dangerous!

[January 1983]

There's not a very great difference between what is true principle and what is not true principle. It's a very subtle difference, and so it's not easy for us to have dharma-selecting vision and to distinguish between proper dharma and deviant teachings, or good and evil. If a person is proper, then everything he does will be open and upright. If he is deviant, then he will always be taking risks hoping to gain advantages; he will do disgraceful things. Good people try to help others, while evil people harm others. Once we recognize these points, we will have a clear understanding.

K6 Giving the name and pointing out the harm.

Sutra:

"**This is a drought ghost that in its old age has become a demon. It disturbs and confuses the good person. But when it tires of doing so, it will leave the other person's body. Then both the disciples and the teacher will get in trouble with the law.**"

Commentary:

This is a drought ghost that in its old age has become a demon. Wherever a drought ghost goes, there will be no rainfall. The drought will last at least six months, and it may go on for one, two, three, or five years. As long as the ghost is in the area, there will be no rain. While young, it is a ghost. But as it ages, it becomes more crafty and villainous and turns into a demon. A derogatory proverb about old people says: "To be old and not to have died is to be a rascal." That is even more the case with ghosts. If a ghost grows old and doesn't die, it becomes a demon. **It disturbs and confuses the good person. But when it tires of doing so,** after it has played its tricks for a long time, the demon becomes bored with the whole affair. Having lost interest, **it will leave the other person's body. Then both the disciples and the teacher will get in trouble with the law.** They are arrested and put in prison. They may be executed or face life imprisonment. It is just as if they were in the hells.

K7 Instructions to be aware and not become confused.

Sutra:

"**You should be aware of this in advance and not get caught up in the cycle of transmigration. If you are confused and do not understand, you will fall into the Relentless Hells.**"

Commentary:

You should be aware of this in advance and not get caught up in the demon king's cycle of transmigration. Don't join the demon's retinue. **If you are confused and do not understand,** if you don't recognize the workings of the demon king, then **you will follow the demon king and fall into the Relentless Hells.**

J3 Greed for union.
K1 Samadhi leads to craving and seeking.

Sutra:

"**Further, in the unhindered clarity and wonder that ensues after the feeling skandha is gone, this good person is untroubled by any deviant mental state and experiences perfect, bright concentration. Within samadhi, his mind craves spiritual oneness, so he clarifies his concentrated thought as he greedily seeks for union.**

Commentary:

Further, in the unhindered clarity and wonder that ensues after the feeling skandha is gone, this good person is untroubled by any deviant mental state and experiences perfect, bright concentration. Within samadhi, his mind craves spiritual oneness. He wants to join in close connection with all sages. **So he clarifies his concentrated thought as he greedily seeks for union.** He forcefully uses subtle thoughts that have been settled and made clear. Because of his one secret thought of craving for union, he gives the demon king a chance to come and disturb him.

K2 A demon dispatches a deviant force to possess a person.

Sutra:

"**At that time a demon from the heavens seizes the opportunity it has been waiting for. Its spirit possesses another person and uses him as a mouthpiece to expound the sutras and explains the teachings.**

Commentary:

The demon sees its chance, so it dispatches a spirit that quickly possesses a person and speaks the teachings through him.

K3 The person who is possessed causes trouble.

Sutra:

"This person, unaware that he is actually possessed by a demon, claims he has reached unsurpassed nirvana. When he comes to see that good person who seeks union, he arranges a seat and explains the teachings. Neither his own body nor the bodies of those listening to the lecture go through any external transformations. But he makes the minds of the listeners become 'enlightened' before they even hear him speak, so they experience changes in every thought. They may have the knowledge of past lives or the knowledge of others' thoughts. They may see the hells or know all the good and evil events in the human realm. They may speak verses or spontaneously recite sutras. Each person is elated and feels he has obtained something unprecedented.

Commentary:

This possessed **person** is **unaware that he is actually possessed by a demon.** He **claims he has reached** the wondrous fruition of **unsurpassed nirvana. When he comes to see that good person,** the cultivator **who seeks union, he arranges a** dharma **seat,** ascends it, **and explains the teachings. Neither his own body nor the bodies of those listening to the lecture go through any external transformations.** His own appearance does not change, nor do the appearances of his listeners change. Nothing happens on the outside. It is not as in a previous passage, where the listeners saw themselves sitting on precious lotus flowers or saw their own bodies radiating purple-golden light. Nor is it as when they saw the person explaining the teachings change into a bhikshu, a bhikshuni, Shakra, a woman, and so forth. There are no such transformations.

But instead **he makes the minds of the listeners become "enlightened" before they even hear him speak.** After their "enlightenment," they feel as if they are drunk or having a dream in which they strike it rich. This "enlightenment" is not true enlightenment. It is an illusory state, like watching a movie or taking an hallucinogenic drug. They see everything in an altered state **so** that in their minds **they experience changes in every thought.**

They may have the knowledge of past lives, but again the knowledge of past lives they attain is not real. What they see is totally illusory. Or they may have the knowledge of others' thoughts. They may see all of the states in the hells. **Or** they may **know all the good and evil events in the human realm. They may** casually be able to **speak verses** on their own, **or** they may **spontaneously recite sutras. Each person is elated and feels he has obtained something unprecedented.** They all say, "He truly is a bodhisattva! He's really a Buddha! He has made me enlightened! He has given me the power of knowing past lives." However, the experience lasts only while they are listening to the lecture. That is why it is not genuine.

[May 1989]

Layperson: Venerable Master, dharma masters, and good advisors. I'd like to share something which is closely related to everyone's cultivation.

When the feeling skandha comes to an end, the cultivator tends to be in a state of anxiety in which he craves clever and skillful expedients. He wants to merge with the cosmic principle, unite with potentials, and convert living beings. When he has this kind of anxiety, several things may happen. For example, some people who have never read sutras before will become possessed by demons, and then they will be able to explain many sutras. There are many "cultivators" in Taiwan who have read very little of the sutras and who may have violated the substance of the precepts they received. Yet they want to obtain clever and skillful expedients; when they see other people explaining sutras and gaining a large following, they hope to quickly attain wisdom themselves so that they can also explain sutras to many people. Having such a thought they become possessed by demons as they sit in meditation.

Many people who seem to be very good at explaining sutras are actually possessed by demons. Of course, if a person strictly follows the precepts, diligently recites mantras and sutras, and cultivates very hard, then he may not be possessed. However, there are some people who are very casual about holding precepts and who do not recite sutras or bow to the Buddhas; yet when they go onstage and close their eyes, after two or three days not only they themselves, but also those in the audience who gave rise to false thinking will be able to lecture very well on the sutras without having studied them before.

I don't think this will happen at the Venerable Master's Way-places. If you go to other Way-places where the dharma-protecting spirits don't do a good job and you give rise to false thinking and greedy attachments, then you may have these states, especially if you like to meditate. People who don't meditate usually don't have these states. There is an elderly woman in Taiwan who was basically illiterate, but after three or five days, she could write beautiful Chinese calligraphy. I've seen many cases like this, where people suddenly "become Buddhas" in a few days' time. That woman had not been able to explain sutras before, but after three days, she was very good at explaining them. Such strange things really happen.

That is why everyone wants to learn deviant devices and no one wants to learn the proper dharma. If you explain the Buddhadharma to them, they won't listen. Those of us here are probably more aware of such phenomena. These states probably won't happen to people at this Way-place, but you have to be careful when you go out.

Venerable Master: These are all cases of people being possessed by fox spirits. This is what is meant by "its spirit possesses a person."

K4 The cultivator becomes deluded and confused.

Sutra:

"The good person is beguiled and fooled into thinking the other is a bodhisattva. His thoughts become entangled in love. He breaks the Buddha's moral precepts and covertly indulges his greedy desires.

Commentary:

The good person is beguiled and fooled into thinking the other is a bodhisattva. The cultivator is extremely stupid and thinks the possessed person is a bodhisattva. **His thoughts become entangled in love.** He falls in love with the demon. **He breaks the Buddha's moral precepts,** not abiding by them, **and covertly indulges his greedy desires.** He has licentious relations on the sly.

K5 The types of things he says.

Sutra:

"He is fond of saying that there are greater Buddhas and lesser Buddhas, earlier Buddhas and later Buddhas; that among them are true Buddhas and false Buddhas, male Buddhas and female Buddhas; and that the same is true of bodhisattvas. When people witness this, their initial resolve is washed away, and they easily get carried away with their wrong understanding.

Commentary:

He is fond of saying that there are greater Buddhas and lesser Buddhas. What does this demon like to say? It says, "You people study the Buddhadharma, but do you know what Buddhas are all about? There are great Buddhas and small Buddhas, old Buddhas and young Buddhas." He further elaborates that there are **earlier Buddhas and later Buddhas; that among them are true Buddhas and false Buddhas.** The demon king claims that he is a true Buddha, while other Buddhas are false Buddhas. He also says that there are **male Buddhas and female Buddhas.** He insists, "Intercourse between men and women creates Buddhas. It is the origin of Buddhas; it is the bodhi mind." Of course this confuses people. They think, "Oh, so that's how one becomes a Buddha!" and then they indulge in wild debauchery. They would rather die than not engage in lust.

And he says **that the same is true of bodhisattvas**, maintaining that there are great and small bodhisattvas, and male and female ones, too. Actually, anyone who becomes a Buddha or a bodhisattva is male. There are no female Buddhas or bodhisattvas. Guanyin Bodhisattva may manifest in the form of a woman in order to teach and rescue women. **When people witness this** and hear him saying such things, they think, "He's right. I always see Guanyin Bodhisattva depicted as a female. That's proof right there." Such people do not understand the Buddhadharma. Guanyin Bodhisattva is neither male nor female. The bodhisattva responds to each living being and appears in an appropriate form to teach and transform that being. It is very difficult to distinguish manifestations of bodhisattvas from manifestations of demons, because demons also have spiritual powers and the ability to transform themselves. How can you tell if someone is a demon? Observe to see whether he has lust or greed. **Their initial resolve is washed away.** They change their minds and forsake their original resolve to cultivate, **and they easily get carried away with their wrong understanding.**

K6　Giving the name and pointing out the harm.

Sutra:

"**This is a mei-ghost that in its old age has become a demon. It disturbs and confuses the good person. But when it tires of doing so, it will leave the other person's body. Then both the disciples and the teacher will get in trouble with the law.**"

Commentary:

This is a mei-ghost, a ghost that falls into the category of *li*, *mei*, and *wang liang* ghosts, **that in its old age has become a demon. It disturbs and confuses the good person** who is cultivating samadhi. **But when it tires of doing so** eventually, **it**

will leave the other person's body. **Then both the disciples and the teacher will get in trouble with the law.** They will be arrested and imprisoned.

K7　Instructions to be aware and not become confused.

Sutra:

"**You should be aware of this in advance and not get caught up in the cycle of transmigration. If you are confused and do not understand, you will fall into the Relentless Hells.**

Commentary:

You should be aware of this in advance and not get caught up in the cycle of transmigration. You should wake up at the very start and avoid entering the demon king's cycle of rebirth. **If you** lack wisdom and **are confused, and** you **do not understand** what is going on, **you will fall into the Relentless Hells.**

J4　Greed to analyze things.
K1　Samadhi leads to craving and seeking.

Sutra:

"**Further, in the unhindered clarity and wonder that ensues after the feeling skandha is gone, this good person is untroubled by any deviant mental state and experiences perfect, bright concentration. Within samadhi, his mind craves to know the origins of things, so he exhaustively investigates the nature of physical things and their changes from beginning to end. He intensifies the keenness of his thoughts as he greedily seeks to analyze things.**

Commentary:

Further, in the unhindered clarity and wonder that ensues after the feeling skandha is gone, this good person who is cultivating samadhi **is untroubled by any deviant mental state and experiences perfect, bright concentration. Within samadhi, his mind craves to know the origins of things.** He decides that he wants to study the principles of the physical world. **So he**

exhaustively investigates the nature of physical things and their changes and transformations **from beginning to end,** to find out what they are all about. **He intensifies the keenness of his thoughts,** honing his mental concentration **as he greedily seeks to analyze,** differentiate, and understand **things** in the physical world.

K2   A demon dispatches a deviant force to possess a person.

Sutra:

"**At that time a demon from the heavens seizes the opportunity it has been waiting for. Its spirit possesses another person and uses him as a mouthpiece to expound the sutras and explain the teachings.**

Commentary:

At that time a demon from the heavens sees him and says, "Aha! You've had a greedy thought. Great! Now I can send one of my retinue to snare you." And so it **seizes the opportunity it has been waiting for.** Once again, the demon king sends one of its followers and **its spirit possesses another person and uses him as a mouthpiece to expound the sutras and explain the teachings** of the demon king.

[January 1983]

Disciple: I've noticed that every state of the thinking skandha begins with the phrase "in the unhindered clarity and wonder that ensues after the feeling skandha is gone, [he is] untroubled by any deviant mental state." What does the phrase "untroubled by any deviant mental state" mean? Does it mean the person is without deviant knowledge and views? Or does it mean that he does not have improper thoughts? When the cultivator reaches this level, what is his state like?

Venerable Master: "In the unhindered clarity and wonder that ensues after the feeling skandha is gone." There has to be unhindered clarity for it to be wonderful, and it must be wonderful for there to be unhindered clarity. When he attains this state in the feeling skandha, he feels very much at ease. "[He is] untroubled by any deviant mental state." That means he doesn't encounter any such state. If he has some skill in the feeling skandha, he basically shouldn't encounter any deviant mental state. And yet, for no apparent reason, he does encounter one. This deviant mental state is a thief from outside – a deviant demon, ghost, or freak that comes from outside. Originally, he shouldn't have encountered such beings, but in the end he had thoughts of love, seeking, greed, selfishness, or self-benefit. Having reverted to these old faults, he encountered those beings. If he didn't have these old faults, he would be able to continue making progress.

If you understand all the states that come up without being swayed by them, then you won't be troubled by deviant mental states. As soon as you're turned by a state, however, it will be able to trouble you. Basically, he isn't supposed to be troubled by deviant mental states, and yet he gets turned – is this a contradiction? No, it's because his thought of desire has opened the door to thieves. He covertly indulges his greedy desires. He sneaks around engaging in immoral conduct and does not abide by the rules and precepts. He says, "What do precepts matter?" and claims to be enlightened. I don't dare to transgress the rules, because I'm not enlightened.

K3 The person who is possessed causes trouble.

Sutra:

"This person, unaware that he is possessed by a demon, claims he has reached unsurpassed nirvana. When he comes to see that good person who seeks to know the origins of things, he arranges a seat and explains the teachings. His body has an awesome spiritual quality which subdues the seeker. He makes the minds of those gathered beside his seat spontaneously compliant, even before they hear him speak. He says to all those people that the Buddha's nirvana, bodhi, and dharma body are there before them in the form of his own physical body. He says, 'The successive begetting of fathers and sons from generation to generation is itself the dharma body, which is permanent and

never-ending. What you see right now are those very Buddhalands. There are no other pure dwellings or golden features.'

Commentary:

This is really a case of "everyone being a Buddha!" That's just the approach this demon uses. **This person is unaware that he is possessed by a demon.** He doesn't have any idea that he has been caught by a demon, because he gets muddled and loses awareness when he becomes possessed. The demon takes total control and becomes his spokesman. He **claims he has reached** the **unsurpassed** wondrous fruition of **nirvana. When he comes to see that good person who seeks to know the origins of things,** who seeks thorough understanding of the physical world, **he arranges a seat and explains the teachings. His,** the demon king's, **body has an awesome spiritual quality which subdues the seeker,** the good person who seeks the source. **He makes the minds** of this person and **of those gathered beside his seat spontaneously compliant, even before they hear him speak.** Their minds are already subdued and respectful.

He says to all those people that the Buddha's nirvana, bodhi, and dharma body are there before them in the form of his own physical body. He says, "What are bodhi and nirvana? They are right here in my flesh body. **The successive begetting of fathers and sons from generation to generation is itself the dharma body, which is permanent and never-ending.** Fathers beget sons, and the sons grow up to become fathers who in turn beget sons. This succession of generations is the permanent, indestructible dharma body. **What you see right now are those very Buddhalands.** These now are the Buddhas' lands. **There are no other pure dwellings or golden features.** There aren't any other pure lands to dwell in or any other golden appearances. Those are all phony." That's how he talks. He has a ghostly quality and a demonic quality. Don't I often use the expression "demonic energy?" This is what demonic energy is. Because he has a demonic energy from the demon possessing him, people are taken in by what he says.

K4　The people become deluded and confused.

Sutra:

"Those people believe and accept his words, forgetting their initial resolve. They offer up their lives, feeling they have obtained something unprecedented. They are all beguiled and confused into thinking he is a bodhisattva. As they pursue his ideas, they break the Buddha's moral precepts and covertly indulge their greedy desires.

Commentary:

Those people believe and accept his words. When they hear him speaking such principles, they say, "That makes sense: Fathers beget sons, and the sons in turn beget their sons, generation after generation. That's the permanent and indestructible dharma body. That's actually the way it is." They all believe it **forgetting their initial resolve.** They lose their former proper outlook and proper thought. Their faith in the demon king is far stronger than their faith in the proper dharma. When demon kings and heterodox sects tell them what to do, they don't dare disobey. When a true teacher tells them to do something, they waver between doubt and belief. The demon king confuses them with its demonic power so that they believe whatever it says.

If you told a demon king to lecture on this sutra, he would not do it. Why not? As soon as he did, his true identity would be exposed. That's why I said that if you asked certain people in America who falsely claim to be experts in the Buddhadharma to explain this sutra, they wouldn't dare do it. They are afraid of being exposed.

They offer up their bodies and **lives** to the demon king, **feeling they have obtained something unprecedented. They are all beguiled and confused into thinking he is a bodhisattva.** They are truly pitiable. They think the demon is a bodhisattva. **As they pursue his ideas,** studying with the demon and learning his magic, **they** no longer maintain, but instead break, **the Buddha's moral**

precepts and covertly indulge their greedy desires. They secretly indulge in lust.

K5　The types of things he says.

Sutra:

"**He is fond of saying that the eyes, ears, nose, and tongue are the Pure Land, and that the male and female organs are the true place of bodhi and nirvana. Ignorant people believe these filthy words.**

Commentary:

How terrible this demon king is! **He is fond of saying that the eyes, ears, nose, and tongue,** body, and mind **are the Pure Land.** "You don't have to look anywhere else for the dharma door of the Pure Land," he tells them. "It's just the six sense faculties." **And** he also says **that the male and female organs are** the seeds of bodhi – **the true place of bodhi and nirvana.** Can you imagine speaking like that? **Ignorant people believe these filthy words.** People without any knowledge or wisdom say, "Oh? I've never seen or heard anything like this before. So that's what bodhi and nirvana are!" With total disregard for their own lives, they race along the road to death for all they are worth. They believe in such impure talk.

K6　Giving the name, and pointing out the harm.

Sutra:

"**This is a poisonous ghost or an evil paralysis ghost that in its old age has become a demon. It disturbs and confuses the good person. But when it tires of doing so, it will leave the other person's body. Then both the disciples and the teacher will get in trouble with the law.**

Commentary:

This is a poisonous ghost or an evil paralysis ghost, also known as a kumbhanda ghost, **that in its old age has become a demon. It disturbs and confuses the good person** who cultivates samadhi. **But when it tires of doing so, it will leave the other**

person's body. Then both the disciples and the teacher will get in trouble with the law.** The authorities intervene and impose restrictions upon the disciples and the teacher. They are arrested and imprisoned.

K7 Instructions to be aware and not become confused.

Sutra:

"You should be aware of this in advance and not get caught up in the cycle of transmigration. If you are confused and do not understand, you will fall into the Relentless Hells.

Commentary:

You should be aware of this well **in advance and not get caught up in the cycle of transmigration.** Don't fall into the demon king's snare. **If you are confused and do not understand, you** certainly **will fall into the Relentless Hells.**

J5 Greed for spiritual responses.
K1 Samadhi leads to craving and seeking.

Sutra:

"Further, in the unhindered clarity and wonder that ensues after the feeling skandha is gone, this good person is untroubled by any deviant mental state and experiences perfect, bright concentration. Within samadhi, his mind craves revelations from afar, so he pours all his energy into this intense investigation as he greedily seeks for imperceptible spiritual responses.

Commentary:

Further, in the unhindered clarity and wonder that ensues after the feeling skandha is gone, this good person who cultivates samadhi **is untroubled by any deviant mental state and experiences perfect bright concentration.** At that time he is no longer vulnerable to possession by demons or externalists. **Within samadhi, his mind** suddenly **craves revelations from afar.** "Revelations from afar" refers to knowledge of what is happening, no matter how far away. For instance, he might be in San Francisco and want to know what is happening in New York. If he can know about it, he has experienced what is called a revelation from afar. **So he pours all his energy into this intense investigation as he greedily seeks for imperceptible spiritual responses.** He intensifies his investigation of this matter of faraway revelations, seeking for psychic responses. For example, as soon as he sits in meditation in San Francisco, he may be able to see clearly what his relatives and friends are doing in New York, and hear clearly what they are saying. Later, he finds out that what he saw and heard is exactly what was really happening at the time. That's the kind of spiritual response he would like to attain.

K2 A demon dispatches a deviant force to possess a person.

Sutra:

"At that time a demon from the heavens seizes the opportunity it has been waiting for. Its spirit possesses another person and uses him as a mouthpiece to expound the sutras and the teachings.

Commentary:

At that time a demon from the heavens notices that your samadhi is about to be perfected, and it becomes jealous. It **seizes the opportunity it has been waiting for** and sends its demon descendant there to wait for an opening. As soon as it sees a chance, **its spirit possesses another person and uses him as a mouthpiece to expound the sutras and the teachings.**

K3 The person who is possessed causes trouble.

Sutra:

"This person, completely unaware that he is possessed by a demon, claims he has reached unsurpassed nirvana. When he comes to see that good person who seeks revelations, he arranges a seat and explains the teachings. He briefly appears to his listeners in a body that looks a hundred or a thousand years old. They experience a defiling love for him and cannot bear to part with him. They personally act as his servants, tirelessly making the four kinds of offerings to him. Each member of the assembly believes that this person is his former teacher, his original good and wise advisor. **They give rise to love for his teachings and stick to him as if glued, feeling they have obtained something unprecedented.**

Commentary:

This is really dangerous. **This person, completely unaware that he is possessed by a demon, claims he has reached unsurpassed nirvana.** He claims he has been certified when he has not, and that he has attained what he has not. He hasn't attained unsurpassed nirvana, but claims he has. **When he comes to see that good person who** greedily **seeks revelations** from afar and imperceptible spiritual responses, **he arranges a seat and explains the teachings.**

He, the person possessed by the demon, **briefly appears to his listeners in a body that looks a hundred or a thousand years old.** You should know that this vision is temporary. When the people in the assembly see him with the white hair of an old man and the skin of a child, they think he must be an old cultivator – an old bhikshu. **They experience a defiling love and cannot bear to part with him.** This defiling love refers to a devotion that stains and pollutes them. Once there is love, there is defilement. With defilement, you lose purity.

All the listeners want to follow this demon day and night. Why? They are deluded by its charisma. **They personally act as his** slaves and **servants, tirelessly making the four kinds of offerings to him.** The four kinds of offerings are:

1. food and drink,
2. clothing,
3. bedding and sitting mats, and
4. medicine.

They never grow weary of making such offerings to him.

Again, one wonders why. A genuine cultivator, a true disciple of the Buddha, will not have people draw near him and serve him in this way. It is only because the demon has a kind of charisma that everyone draws near him and likes to stay with him.

Each member of the assembly believes that this person is his former teacher. They get so confused that each believes the possessed person was **his original good and wise advisor.** They think, "Oh! He was my teacher in the past!" **They give rise to love for his teachings and stick to him as if glued, feeling they have obtained something unprecedented.** "It's never been like this before," they think.

[January 1983]

She does whatever he tells her to do. It's not as simple as making the four kinds of offerings of food, clothing, bedding, and medicines. She has to offer her body, mind, and life to him and engage in lust with him. The difference lies in the practice of lust. If a person has lust, then what he does is deviant. If he has no lust, then he is proper.

You should never listen to a person who says, "When you are enlightened, you can do whatever you want, including indulge in lust." Those are the words of a big demon king. Before you are enlightened, you may transgress the rules because you do not know any better. But if you say that you are enlightened, that you understand, and yet you deliberately transgress the rules and precepts, then what enlightenment have you obtained? It's as if you are driving in reverse.

People nowadays don't investigate true principles. All they know about is getting enlightened. They hear someone say that after he is enlightened, he doesn't have to follow the rules, so they repeat his words and say: "Oh! He doesn't have to follow any rules. Since he's enlightened, he can smoke, drink, play around with women, and do anything at all."

The most important thing is lust: if he has lust and he indulges in impure conduct all the time, then he's a demon. If he is not greedy for money and he is free of lust, then he is genuine.

In this case, he announces to those he meets, "In a former life you were my wife," or "You were the empress," or "You were my such and such when I was the emperor," and so forth; he makes these statements in order to arouse lust in people. By doing this in public, he hopes to cheat people and exploit the situation.

Again, one wonders why. A genuine cultivator, a true disciple of the Buddha, will not have people draw near him and serve him in this way. It is only because the demon has a kind of charisma that everyone draws near him and likes to stay with him.

K4 The cultivator becomes deluded and confused.

Sutra:

"The good person is beguiled and fooled into thinking the other is a bodhisattva. Attracted to the other's thinking, he breaks the Buddha's moral precepts and covertly indulges his greedy desires.

Commentary:

The good person is beguiled and fooled to the utmost **into thinking** that because **the other** person can transform himself, he **is a** Buddha or a **bodhisattva**. Fox spirits can display transformations and so can goblins, demons, ghosts, and weird creatures. But it never occurs to him that the ability to transform does not necessarily mean someone is a bodhisattva or a Buddha. What good roots does he have to enable him to encounter real bodhisattvas or Buddhas? **Attracted to the other's thinking**, he draws near the person who is possessed by the demon. **He breaks the Buddha's moral precepts**. This is the important point. How do we know he is a demon? We can tell from the fact that he breaks the precepts **and covertly indulges his greedy desires** by engaging in lust.

K5 The types of things he says.

Sutra:

"He is fond of saying, 'In a past life, in a certain incarnation, I rescued a certain person who was then my wife (or my mistress, or my brother). Now I have come to rescue you again. We will stay together and go to another world to make offerings to a certain Buddha.' Or he may say, 'There is a Heaven of Great Brilliance where a Buddha now dwells. It is the resting place of all Tathagatas.' Ignorant people believe his ravings and lose their original resolve.

Commentary:

Whenever he sees someone, **he is fond of saying** the same things that Liu Jintong, whom I mentioned before, used to say. She would tell her victim that he had been her son in one past life and her husband in another past life. Now this person says, "**In a past life, in a certain incarnation,**" perhaps in his hundred-and-first life or his hundred-and-second life, "**I rescued a certain person who was then my wife,**" **or** he says, "who was then **my mistress,**" or, "who was then **my brother,**" and so forth. "**Now I have come to rescue you again. We will** always **stay together and** never part. We will **go to another world to make offerings to a certain Buddha.**"

Or he may say, "There is a Heaven of Great Brilliance that we are going to." Actually the heaven he refers to is the place where the demon king resides. He says, "It is the place **where a** true **Buddha now dwells**, and all the Buddhas you presently believe in are phony. **It is the resting place of all Tathagatas.** When they are tired from teaching and rescuing beings in the world, they go to the Heaven of Great Brilliance to rest." When those **ignorant people** hear him they **believe his ravings, and** as a result they **lose their original resolve,** which had been based on proper faith.

K6 Giving the name and pointing out the harm.

Sutra:

"This is a pestilence ghost that in its old age has become a demon. It disturbs and confuses the good person. But when it tires of doing so, it will leave the other person's body. Then both the disciples and the teacher will get in trouble with the law.

Commentary:

This is a pestilence ghost that, after some three thousand or five thousand years, **in its old age has become a demon. It disturbs and confuses the good person,** attempting to destroy his samadhi power. **But** after a while, **when** it has played all its tricks and the game isn't new anymore, **it tires of doing so. It** becomes bored and **will leave the other person's body. Then both the disciples and the teacher will get in trouble with the law.** Once the demon goes, the person will lose all his awesomeness and charisma. Then people will start to doubt him. Eventually he will be taken to court and put in jail.

K7 Instructions to be aware and not become confused.

Sutra:

"You should be aware of this in advance and not get caught up in the cycle of transmigration. If you are confused and do not understand, you will fall into the Relentless Hells.

Commentary:

You should be aware of this in advance. You should awaken to this principle beforehand **and not get caught up in the cycle of transmigration.** Don't fall into the demons' snare. Don't enter the demonic cycle of birth and death. **If you are confused and do not understand** this principle, **you will fall into the Relentless Hells** for sure.

J6	Greed for peace and quiet.
K1	Samadhi leads to craving and seeking.

Sutra:

"**Further, in the unhindered clarity and wonder that ensues after the feeling skandha is gone, this good person is untroubled by any deviant mental state and experiences perfect, bright concentration. Within samadhi, his mind craves deep absorption, so he restrains himself with energetic diligence and likes to dwell in secluded places as he greedily seeks for peace and quiet.**

Commentary:

Further, in the unhindered clarity and wonder that ensues after the feeling skandha is gone, this good person who is cultivating samadhi **is untroubled by any deviant mental state and experiences perfect, bright concentration. Within samadhi, his mind** develops a craving. He **craves deep absorption** in that principle. **So he restrains himself with energetic diligence and likes to dwell in secluded places as he greedily seeks for peace and quiet.** He maintains firm self-control and is very strict with himself. He puts great effort into cultivation. He likes to reside in places that are *yin*, lacking in sunlight. He prefers places where there aren't any people, perhaps a cave somewhere deep in the mountains or in some isolated valley. He picks a secluded spot, for he likes still and quiet places. Because he is too greedy for peace and quiet, demons will come. In cultivation, people should not be greedy. Don't be greedy for good things, and don't be greedy for bad things. The ordinary mind is the Way. Just act ordinary, and don't be greedy. No matter what you may be greedy for, it's not right.

K2	A demon dispatches a deviant force to possess a person.

Sutra:

"**At that time a demon from the heavens seizes the opportunity it has been waiting for. Its spirit possesses another** person and uses him as a mouthpiece to expound the sutras and the teachings.

Commentary:

This is the same situation as before. **At that time a demon king from the heavens seizes the opportunity it has been waiting for.** When the chance comes, **its spirit possesses another person and uses him as a mouthpiece to expound the sutras and teachings.** It sends a member of its demonic retinue to possess another person who then comes and speaks the sutras and the teachings for him.

K3 The demon's words and deeds that mislead others.

Sutra:

"This person, unaware that he is possessed by a demon, claims he has reached unsurpassed nirvana. When he comes to see that good person who seeks seclusion, he arranges a seat and explains the teachings. He causes all of his listeners to think they know their karma from the past. Or he may say to someone there, 'You haven't died yet, but you have already become an animal.' Then he instructs another person to step on the first person's 'tail' and suddenly the first person cannot stand up. At that point, all in the assembly pour out their hearts in respect and admiration for him. If someone has a thought, the demon detects it immediately. He establishes intense ascetic practices that exceed the Buddha's moral precepts. He slanders bhikshus, scolds his assembly of disciples, and exposes people's private affairs without fear of ridicule or rejection. He is fond of foretelling calamities and auspicious events, and when they come to pass, he is not wrong in the slightest.

Commentary:

This person is **unaware that he is possessed by a demon.** He **claims,** as demon kings do, that **he has reached unsurpassed nirvana.** What proof is there that someone is a demon? For the most part, demons praise themselves.

They say, "Do you know me? I've already obtained nirvana." Or it may be, "I've realized the first fruition of arhatship," or, "I've reached the fourth fruition of arhatship," or, "I'm a bodhisattva now. Do you recognize me?"

As soon as someone talks like that you don't have to ask to know he is a demon. A Buddha would never say, "I'm a Buddha. Hurry up and bow to me. If you don't bow now, you'll miss your chance. Since I'm a Buddha, you're really stupid if you don't bow to me." Anyone who claims to be a Buddha, a bodhisattva, or an arhat is nothing but a demon. You can know immediately, without question, that it is a demon talking. A Buddha would never say he was a Buddha. A bodhisattva who has come into the world would never say he was a bodhisattva. Even if other people said he was a bodhisattva, he would not admit it. Even if he were a Buddha, and someone said, "Yes, I know you are a Buddha," he would not acknowledge it. One who is truly enlightened would not admit to that either. If someone says, "I'm enlightened," don't be taken in by him – he doesn't even measure up to a dog. Don't listen to his bluster and self-aggrandizing.

Listen to sutras so that you can have a demon-spotting mirror. Then when demons, ghosts, and weird beings show themselves, you will recognize them. But if you don't understand the Buddhadharma, you will not know what they are saying, and you will be cheated by them.

When he, the person who has been possessed by the demon, **comes to see that good person who seeks seclusion, he arranges a seat and explains the teachings.**

[January 1983]

This "person" is referring to the cultivator, not to another person. He has been possessed by a demon, but he doesn't realize it. He thinks that he has really become enlightened and realized the fruition. He thinks, "What great spiritual skill I have now!" He is not aware of his own mistake. "When people come to see that good person…" This phrase is referring to good men and women from outside, who come in quest of the teaching. They want to hear him explain the teachings because they know that he has spiritual powers. When they come, he arranges a seat and gives a lecture to teach and transform them.

Now we are bringing up each person's opinion for everyone to look into, and we don't have to say which opinion is right and which one is wrong. We are studying true principles; true principles are real gold. Whatever does not agree with true principle is wrong. Why do I say that the *Shurangama Sutra* is real? Because it explains the principles so clearly and honestly that it exposes the demons from the heavens and those of external ways for what they are. It exposes those who pretend to be good and wise advisors, so they have no recourse but to claim that the *Shurangama Sutra* is false. They try to pass off fish eyes as pearls; they stir up confusion and then exploit the situation.

[January 1983, another day]

In this case, people from outside come and invite him. He doesn't go to them first. "When people come to see that good person" means people from outside approach the cultivator who seeks seclusion. They invite him to go to where they are and explain the sutras and he goes. Do you understand? It is absolutely impermissible to alter the sutra text. This is the only meaning and there is no other explanation. Any other explanation would not make sense; it would be a forced and artificial interpretation.

He causes all of his listeners to think they know their karma from the past. Each person feels he knows, as if in a dream, what he was in his previous lives. One says, "Oh, in my last life I was a watchdog." Another person says, "In my previous life I was a cat." Someone else says, "In my past life I was a chicken." Another person says, "In my past life I was a cow." None of them were human beings.

Or he, the demon, **may say to someone there, "You haven't died yet but you have already become an animal."** What does he say? He says, "You were a dog in your past life, and even though you haven't died yet, you've become a dog again. Don't you believe me?" **Then he instructs another person to step on the first person's "tail."** He says to someone else, "He doesn't believe what I'm telling him. Go behind him and stand on his tail and then see if he can get up." Then that person stamps his foot on the ground and says he is standing on the first person's tail, **and suddenly the first person cannot stand up.** Wouldn't you say those were great spiritual powers? After the demon said the person had a tail and told someone to step on it, the person could not get up. The person has no choice but to believe. "He says I'm an animal, and now I really do have a tail. Otherwise, how could he step on it and prevent me from standing up?"

At that, all in the assembly pour out their hearts in respect and admiration for him. "It's magic," they say. "He knows the person is going to be an animal even before the person has died. He must be a Buddha or a living bodhisattva." Actually, they've been duped by a ghost and don't even realize it. They see a ghost or a demon king, and mistake it for a bodhisattva. Living beings are really upside-down.

If someone has a doubt, the demon detects it immediately. Someone in the assembly may be skeptical and think, "How can that be? It isn't reasonable." As soon as he starts to doubt, the demon knows it and says, "So you don't believe me?" These people take one look, "Oh! He's really a bodhisattva! I didn't say what was on my mind, and he knew about it. He exposed my doubt. That's incredible." After that he doesn't dare to disbelieve.

He establishes intense ascetic practices that exceed the Buddha's moral precepts. He says, "The Buddha's vinaya is not enough. I'm establishing a new vinaya for you. I want you to be new Buddhas, and I am creating a new Buddhism. The previous one is obsolete and inapplicable. This is the scientific era, the nuclear age, and everything must be modernized and improved. The old way of thinking is no longer useful. The old Buddhism cannot be applied either." That is how he changes Buddhism. He says that people can be elders or bhikshus or anything they want.

[January 1983]

There are old-fashioned religions and trendy religions. No one believes in religions they consider old-fashioned, but everyone chases madly after trendy things. Of all the dharma spoken by the Buddha, the most important part is precepts. Nowadays, people consider the Buddha really old fashioned, and they want to find something more up-to-date. Their search takes them right into the demon king's lair. None of the external sects are free from greed and desire. They are insatiable, and they desire to benefit themselves at the expense of others.

I cannot say that we at the City of Ten Thousand Buddhas are definitely in accord with the proper dharma. Nevertheless, I ask each of you who has followed me for so many years: Have I ever asked you to hand your wealth and property over to the temple? Why have I never done this? Because I'm very old-fashioned. I want to uphold and honor the precepts. The precepts tell us to give to others, not to demand that others give to us while we don't give anything to them.

At the City of Ten Thousand Buddhas, our revenue comes very naturally. We don't scheme for contributions. We receive enough income as it is. If we were to try to cheat people of their money, how would we be any different from demons? People who tell others to donate their personal and family wealth and their own lives and their families' lives to the Way-place are totally misguided. I'm not like them. I do not want anyone's wealth, nor do I desire any beautiful women. I want neither fame nor a good reputation. In fact, I have quite a notorious reputation, not a good one. The very mention of my name gives some people a headache, especially those goblins, demons, ghosts, and freaks.

He slanders bhikshus, saying, "Bhikshu? What's a bhikshu?" He makes fun of the name. He says, "You say he's a bhikshu? I say he's a loach!"[2]

---

2. A loach is a kind of carp. In Chinese, "bhikshu" and "loach" end with the same sound.

He also **scolds his assembly of disciples.** He scolds his disciples however he pleases. He may tell them, "You're a dog," or "You are a cat," or "You're a rat," or "You're a pig." The disciples hear his scolding and accept whatever he says, thinking he is a bodhisattva. "You say I'm a pig, so I'm a pig." "You say I'm a dog, so I'm a dog." "You say I'm a cat, so I'm a cat." They don't dare talk back. This demon king has such tremendous power that he manages to delude people into believing everything he says.

And he **exposes people's private affairs.** For instance, a man and a woman may have done something indecent, and he will say to the woman, "You did such and such with a certain man in a certain place."

The woman thinks to herself, "How did he know?"

Or he may expose them in public, saying, "These two are despicable. They did something improper, something unspeakable, in such-and-such a place. Ask her about it – she wouldn't dare deny it." It turns out that they have in fact done it, and they don't dare to deny it. He does this to show people that he has spiritual powers and that he knows everything that is going on. He exposes their private matters **without fear of ridicule or rejection.** He divulges people's secrets and is not afraid that they will scorn him.

He is always **fond of foretelling calamities and auspicious events.** He likes to say things such as, "You'd better be careful. Tomorrow is going to be an unlucky day for you. Someone might try to poison you, so watch what you eat or you may die of poisoning." He foretells both unlucky and lucky events, **and when they come to pass, he is not wrong in the slightest.** When the events happen, they turn out to be exactly as he predicted. So how could people not believe in him? Such demon kings are far more efficacious than bodhisattvas.

K4　Giving the name and pointing out the harm.
K5　Instructions to be aware and not become confused.

Sutra:

"This is a ghost with great powers that in its old age has become a demon. It disturbs and confuses the good person. But when it tires of doing so, it will leave the other person's body. Then both the disciples and the teacher will get in trouble with the law. You should be aware of this in advance and not get caught up in the cycle of transmigration. If you are confused and do not understand, you will fall into the Relentless Hells.

Commentary:

This is a ghost with great powers that in its old age has become a demon. Ghosts become demons when they get old, just as people who don't practice virtuous deeds become rascals in their old age. As I have told you, the Chinese have a saying, "To be old and not to have died is to be a rascal." When people are old and experienced, they can make trouble. In the same way, old ghosts become demons. **It disturbs and confuses the good person.** Jealous of the cultivation of other people, the ghost destroys their samadhi power. **But when it** eventually **tires of doing so, it will leave the other person's body** and no longer possess him.

Then both the disciples and the teacher will get in trouble with the law. That's equivalent to their falling into the hells. There's a saying:

> Someone deluded transmits his delusion,
> So after the transmission, neither one understands.
> The teacher falls into the hells,
> And the disciple burrows in after him.

The same principle applies here. Because he hasn't met a teacher who truly understands, the disciple is also muddled. When he sees his teacher going to the hells, he follows his teacher there. The teacher turns around and says, "What did you come here for?"

The disciple replies, "I saw you coming here, so of course I came along."

The teacher says, "Oh no! This isn't a good place. You shouldn't have come."

"But you came first. How could I not have followed you? I study with you, after all. I should go wherever you go," says the disciple.

The teacher thinks, "Ah, I've landed in the hells myself, and brought my disciple with me as well. I've really done wrong to you. I'm very sorry!" **You should be aware of this in advance and not get caught up in the cycle of transmigration. If you are confused and do not understand, you will fall into the Relentless Hells.**

J7 Greed to know past lives.
K1 Samadhi leads to craving and seeking.

Sutra:

"Further, in the unhindered clarity and wonder that ensues after the feeling skandha is gone, this good person is untroubled by any deviant mental state and experiences perfect, bright concentration. Within samadhi, his mind craves more knowledge and understanding, so he diligently toils at examining and probing as he greedily seeks to know past lives.

Commentary:

Further, in the unhindered clarity and wonder that ensues after the feeling skandha is gone, this good person is untroubled by any deviant mental state and experiences perfect, bright concentration. Within samadhi, his mind craves more knowledge and understanding. While in samadhi, he wants to know more things, to have the knowledge of past lives. He works with intense vigor and does not fear suffering. **So he diligently toils at examining and probing as he greedily seeks to know past lives.**

K2	A demon dispatches a deviant force to possess a person.

Sutra:

"At that time a demon from the heavens seizes the opportunity it has been waiting for. Its spirit possesses another person and uses him as a mouthpiece to expound the sutras and teachings. This person, unaware that he is possessed by a demon, claims he has reached unsurpassed nirvana. When he comes to see that good person who seeks knowledge, he arranges a seat and explains the teachings.

Commentary:

At that time a demon from the heavens seizes the opportunity it has been waiting for. Its spirit possesses another person and uses him as a mouthpiece to expound the sutras and teachings. This person, unaware that he is possessed by a demon, not realizing that he's been taken over by a demon, **claims he has reached unsurpassed nirvana. When he comes to see that good person who seeks knowledge, he arranges a seat and explains the teachings.**

K3	The demon's words and deeds that mislead others.

Sutra:

"There in the assembly, inexplicably, that person may obtain an enormous precious pearl. The demon may sometimes change into an animal that holds the pearl or other jewels, bamboo tablets, tallies, talismans, letters, and other unusual things in its mouth. The demon first gives the objects to the person and afterwards possesses him. Or he may fool his audience by burying the objects underground and then saying that a 'moonlight pearl' is illuminating the place. Thereupon the audience feels they have obtained something unique. He may eat only medicinal herbs and not partake of prepared food. Or he may eat only one sesame seed and one grain of wheat a day and still look robust. That is because he is sustained by the power of the demon. **He slanders bhikshus and scolds his assembly of disciples without fear of ridicule or rejection.**

Commentary:

There in the assembly, inexplicably, for no reason whatsoever, in the place where the lecture is being given, **that person may obtain an enormous precious pearl.** It may be a diamond or something like a "wish-fulfilling pearl." **The demon may sometimes change into an animal.** The person who is giving the lecture changes into an animal himself, explaining that bodhisattvas can transform into anything. The animal **that** he changes into **holds the pearl or other jewels, bamboo tablets,** or **tallies.** Tallies were used for official purposes in ancient times. Words were written on a piece of bamboo, which was then split, so that part of the words appeared on each piece. When it was time to use the tallies, they would be put together. If the tallies matched, it would be a certified match. If the two parts did not match, that would mean it was inauthentic. **Talismans** are used to subdue and catch demons, ghosts, goblins, and weird creatures. **And** the animal might carry **letters and other unusual things in its mouth.** All of these are strange, rare, and valuable objects. **The demon first gives the objects to the person and afterwards possesses him.**

Or he may fool his audience by burying the objects underground and then saying that a 'moonlight pearl' is illuminating the place. He buries the pearl in the ground and then tricks his listeners, telling them, "There is a pearl which resembles the bright moon, emitting light there." **Thereupon the audience feels they have obtained something unique.** "Wow! This has to be for real. This can't be a demon," they say. He is clearly a demon, yet they insist that he isn't. Alas for those who listen to his explanations!

He may eat only medicinal herbs and not partake of prepared food. The demon often eats only herbs, not regular food. He doesn't eat good food. He may eat ginseng or other tonics and nourishing supplements. When I was in Hong Kong I met a person who said he didn't eat ordinary food. He acted as a medium for people who sought long life, sons, blessings, or other things. Whenever he stayed in people's homes, he would announce he didn't eat ordinary food. What did he eat then? Walnuts. Walnuts are very nourishing – full of oil. If you eat them, your brain will be very good. You only have to eat a little to be full; if you usually eat one bowl of rice, you only have to eat half a bowl of walnuts to be full. He also ate pine nuts. At any rate, he ate the most nutritious items. **Or he may eat only one sesame seed and one grain of wheat a day and still look robust.** Even so, he stays really fat, fatter than a pig. **That is because he is sustained by the power of the demon.**

He slanders bhikshus and scolds his assembly of disciples without fear of ridicule or rejection. He does nothing but slander those who have left the home-life. "Left-home people? What home did they leave? They don't cultivate at all. Left-home people aren't greedy for money? The more the better is their attitude." Or he says, "Why do you believe in him? He's just a person, after all. You're really an idiot." When people have faith in the bhikshus, he calls them idiots. He scolds his own disciples, calling them animals and all sorts of things. He's totally unafraid of any rebuttals.

[May 1989]

Disciple: "When he comes to see that good person who seeks knowledge, he arranges a seat and explains the teachings."

Venerable Master: This means the demon. It goes to see the person who seeks knowledge of past lives.

Disciple: "There in the assembly, inexplicably, that person may obtain an enormous precious pearl. The demon may sometimes change into an animal." Is this another demon?

Venerable Master: No, it's the same one.

Disciple: Does the person possessed by the demon transform into an animal?

Venerable Master: Yes. To everyone, he appears to be an animal. He takes on a bizarre appearance. "First, the demon gives them to the person, and afterwards possesses him." "The person" is the one who seeks knowledge of past lives.

Disciple: The person who seeks knowledge of past lives is already possessed by a demon and has changed into an animal. And he's also holding the pearl and other gems in his mouth.

Venerable Master: He gives them to the people who are listening to his lecture. It isn't just one person. Perhaps he selects one among them. This is all hypothetical. It doesn't necessarily have to happen that way. Don't think that it has to be that way just because the Buddha said it. This is an example, and you should be able to understand other situations by inference. Don't be so rigid. Be flexible in your understanding, so that the next time such a situation occurs, you'll know, "Oh, this is the same as that example." Here he turns into an animal, but in another case he might turn into a Buddha.

Disciple: What about when it "Afterwards possesses him"? Whom does the demon possess?

Venerable Master: The demon possesses everyone.

Disciple: Are there other demons that come to possess everyone?

Venerable Master: No, the same demon can have innumerable transformation bodies. It can possess that person as well as other people.

Disciple: So it jumps around from one to the other?

Venerable Master: It doesn't jump. It isn't just one; it can transform into many.

Disciple: Oh, so it can possess you, and it can also possess someone else. I never knew demons were so powerful!

Venerable Master: Demons are about as powerful as Buddhas. It's just that the one is deviant and the other is proper. What demons do is deviant, and what Buddhas do is proper. That's the difference. There's a person from Taiwan who has had such experiences. We can ask him to speak now. [To the layman] Tell everyone the whole story about how the demon transmitted the mind-dharma to you.

Layman: Venerable Master, dharma masters, and good advisors. I will talk about my experiences in non-Buddhist religions, what I saw and understood. Perhaps my experiences are not quite the same as the states caused by the demons from the heavens described by the Buddha. These demons can transform in endless ways, and what I saw is only one of their states. As I share my experience, keep in mind that it is not the whole picture. The demons from the heavens manifest in many ways. They may or may not go through a medium. If you practice with an improper mind in an external sect, the demon can appear to you in the form of a person when you are meditating; it doesn't need a medium.

This sutra text says, "There in the assembly, inexplicably, that person may obtain an enormous precious pearl." Because it says "There in the assembly," I think that there are three parties: the medium, the speaker, and the listeners. The Venerable Master interprets "the person" as referring to the possessed person. That is one interpretation. However, from what I understand and from the other explanations that I've read, I think "the person" refers to someone who hasn't been possessed yet. Why? Because the Buddha spoke the *Shurangama Sutra* in order to warn those who are not yet possessed, but whose minds have already gone astray. If they are not alert, they will be possessed by demons. The Buddha wants to warn them. When the skandhas of form, feeling, and thinking come to an end, you should be especially cautious, for you may experience many of these states, and you need to know how to deal with them.

Two years ago, I went to the home of a layman who shaved his head like a monk's. He said that while meditating, a demon from the heavens possessed him and said, "Let me give you a 'wordless book from heaven,' or such and such a sutra." People went there because they were looking for a quick way to get enlightened. At that Way-place, they used all kinds of methods, and I either saw or heard them talk about every one of the first thirty skandha-demon states. For example, I saw the tallies, gems, and treasure troves. I also witnessed them eating meals of one sesame seed and one grain of wheat, or eating gluttonously. For example, in the case of "obtaining an enormous pearl" when you are meditating, someone will say, "May I give you this pearl?" If your mind is moved and you wish to have it, then through the medium, you stretch your hands out to take it. Once you accept it, you're in for trouble.

I'll talk about my personal experience. When I went to a certain place two years ago, the layman told me, "I can give you a wordless book from heaven. If you practice according to it for three years, you can obtain great spiritual powers." That day my mind was rather swayed, and I thought, "If you want to give me a 'wordless book from heaven,' fine."

He said, "To accept it, raise both hands, and I'll give it to you."

After I received it, I went home, and the next day I kept reciting things that I did not understand. It sounded like Japanese, and then Thai, and then I was singing army songs dating from the Japanese Meiji reign, songs which I had never sung before. Although my voice is usually pretty bad, when I was singing those army songs, I could sing very high and very low, and it sounded better than the singers on television. I think the "wordless book from heaven" is something like the tallies mentioned in the sutra.

There are two possibilities in the place where the teachings are being explained. The first is that you have not been possessed by the demon, and you cannot see what is happening. If you have not ended the form skandha, then you cannot see, either. In the other case, when you are meditating, the possessed person can see, and so can you.

In one case, you and the possessed person are both in samadhi, and you can see whatever he gives you. You can also see the external state, but it's just an illusion that he conjures up. In the other case, you cannot see, but your mind moves. The person says, "Can I give you this thing?" If you say, "Yes," then things change. However, if you say, "I don't want it," then the demon from the heaven cannot possess you, because it has to follow its own rules, too. As far as I know, all the external sects in Taiwan fall under the first thirty skandha-demon states, before the thinking and consciousness skandhas have been ended.

Our present interpretation may differ somewhat from the real incidents I just spoke of. In such situations, the demons from the heavens may appear in these ways to harm you and prevent you from attaining the Way. Since everyone is at a different level of cultivation, they appear in different ways each time. I just wanted to offer this for everyone to consider.

Sutra:

"He is fond of talking about treasure troves in other locations, or of remote and hidden places where sages and worthies of the ten directions dwell. Those who follow him often see strange and unusual people.

Commentary:

He is fond of talking about treasure troves in other locations. What does he like to say? He says, "Hey, in a certain place there are gold, silver, and all kinds of jewels. Do you want some?" He spreads such rumors to delude the assembly. **Or** he is fond of talking **of remote and hidden places where sages and worthies of the ten directions dwell.** He tells people, "There are Buddhas and Bodhisattvas cultivating there without your knowing it." **Those who follow him often see strange and unusual people.** They may give off light or have other strange characteristics.

K4 Giving the name and pointing out the harm.

Sutra:

"This is a ghost or spirit of the mountain forests, earth, cities, rivers, and mountains that in its old age has become a demon. The person it possesses may advocate promiscuity and violate the Buddha's precepts. He may covertly indulge in the five desires with his followers. Or he may appear to be vigorous, eating only wild plants. His behavior is erratic, and he disturbs

and confuses the good person. But when the demon tires, it will leave the other person's body. Then both the disciples and the teacher will get in trouble with the law.

Commentary:

What kind of creature is this? **This is a ghost or spirit of the mountain forests, earth, cities, rivers, and mountains that in its old age,** after a long time, **has become a demon. The person it possesses may advocate promiscuity and violate the Buddha's precepts.** His lust-filled thoughts cause him to break the precepts. **He may covertly indulge in the five desires with his followers,** the people who are with him. The five desires are wealth, sex, fame, food, and sleep. **Or he may appear to be vigorous, eating only wild plants. His behavior is erratic.** He does not sit in meditation or cultivate. He only engages in unbeneficial ascetic practices, **and he disturbs and confuses the good person,** causing him to stop cultivating. **But** after a while, **when the demon tires** and grows bored, **it will leave the other person's body. Then both the disciples and the teacher will get in trouble with the law.**

K5 Instructions to be aware and not become confused.

Sutra:

"**You should be aware of this in advance and not get caught up in the cycle of transmigration. If you are confused and do not understand, you will fall into the Relentless Hells.**

Commentary:

You should be aware of this in advance and not get caught up in the cycle of transmigration. Awaken to this early on, and don't fall into the demon's trap. Don't enter the demonic cycle of birth and death. **If you are confused and do not understand, you will fall into the Relentless Hells.**

J8	Greed for spiritual powers.
K1	Samadhi leads to craving and seeking.

Sutra:

"Further, in the unhindered clarity and wonder that ensues after the feeling skandha is gone, this good person is untroubled by any deviant mental state and experiences perfect, bright concentration. Within samadhi, his mind craves spiritual powers and all manner of transformations, so he investigates the source of transformations as he greedily seeks for spiritual powers.

Commentary:

Further, in the unhindered clarity and wonder that ensues after the feeling skandha is gone, this good person who is cultivating the Way and practicing samadhi **is untroubled by any deviant mental state and experiences perfect, bright concentration. Within samadhi, his mind craves spiritual powers.** He has another false thought. He decides he wants to have great spiritual powers **and all manner of transformations,** so that he can display the eighteen transformations in midair. He wants to be able to emit water from the upper part of his body and fire from the lower part; he wants to emit fire from the upper part of his body and water from the lower part. He longs to be like the arhats who can manifest these eighteen transformations while floating in the air, **so he investigates the** fundamental **source,** the principle **of** these **transformations, as he greedily seeks for spiritual powers.**

[January 1983]

A person is still vulnerable to possession by demons even after he has broken through the form and feeling skandhas. Breaking through the skandhas of form, feeling, thinking, formations, and consciousness is a very ordinary matter. It doesn't mean he truly has samadhi power and won't get possessed anymore. He is at a very high level; but even at that high level, he can still be possessed. Why? Because he still harbors love and greed in his mind. He may be greedy for knowledge, for spiritual powers, or for responses. His greed opens the door. He cannot become free from demonic possession just by thinking about it. In fact, he will only be more liable to become possessed.

K2 A demon dispatches a deviant force to possess a person.

Sutra:

"At that time a demon from the heavens seizes the opportunity it has been waiting for. Its spirit possesses another person and uses him as a mouthpiece to expound the sutras and teachings.

Commentary:

The demon that has been lying in wait sees its chance and sends a spirit to possess a person, through whom it speaks the sutras and explains the teachings.

K3 The demon's words and deeds that mislead others.

Sutra:

"This person, truly unaware that he is possessed by a demon, also claims he has reached unsurpassed nirvana. When he comes to see that good person who seeks spiritual powers, he arranges a seat and explains the teachings. The possessed person may hold fire in his hands and, grasping a portion of it, put a flame on the head of each listener in the fourfold assembly. The flames on top of their heads are several feet high, yet they are not hot and no one is burned. Or he may walk on water as if on dry land; or he may sit motionless in the air; or he may enter into a bottle or stay in a bag; or he may pass through window panes and walls without obstruction. Only when attacked by weapons does he feel ill at ease. He declares himself to be a Buddha and, wearing the clothing of a lay person, receives bows from bhikshus. He slanders dhyana meditation and the moral regulations. He scolds his disciples and exposes people's private affairs without fear of ridicule or rejection.

Commentary:

This person is **truly unaware that he is possessed by a demon.** He **also claims** that **he** himself **has reached** the wondrous fruition of **unsurpassed nirvana. When he comes to see that good person who seeks spiritual powers, he arranges a seat and explains the teachings.**

The possessed person may hold fire in one of **his hands and, grasping a portion of it** with his other hand, **put a flame on the head of each listener in the fourfold assembly.** One by one he puts a flame atop the heads of each of the people in the audience. **The flames on top of their heads are several feet high.** When he puts the flames there, they are small, and they grow bit by bit until they are several feet high. **Yet they are not hot and no one is burned.** They do not spread or set anything else on fire. **Or he,** the possessed person, **may walk on water as if on dry,** flat **land; or he may** walk or **sit motionless in the air.** There is nothing holding him up in the air, but he can sit in it.

Or he may enter into a bottle or stay in a bag; or he may pass through window panes and walls without obstruction. The doors and windows may be closed, but he can easily pass through them without opening them. He's not hindered in the least.

Only when attacked by weapons does he feel ill at ease. He is afraid of being cut by knives and pierced by spears. That is because he still has a physical form which obstructs him. Although he has five of the spiritual powers, he still fears being wounded by weapons. **He declares himself to be a Buddha and, wearing the clothing of a lay person,** not the attire of left-home people, **receives bows from bhikshus.** Dressed as a layperson, he receives bows from left-home people. **He slanders dhyana meditation and the moral regulations** as being useless and incorrect. And **he scolds his** own **disciples and exposes people's private affairs.** He discloses people's secrets **without fear of ridicule or rejection** by others.

Sutra:

"He often talks about spiritual powers and self-mastery. He may cause people to see visions of Buddhalands, but they are unreal and arise merely from the ghost's power to delude people. He praises the indulgence of lust and does not condemn lewd conduct. He uses indecent means to transmit his teachings.

Commentary:

He often talks about various sorts of **spiritual powers and self-mastery. He may cause people to see visions of Buddhalands** throughout the ten directions, **but they are unreal and arise merely from the ghost's power to delude people.** He himself does not have any real skill in cultivation. What **he praises** most is **the indulgence of lust.** He says, "It's truly the most wonderful thing there is. It's the source of bodhi and nirvana." **And he does not condemn lewd conduct.** He says, "There's nothing wrong with it. Don't bother holding precepts." **He uses indecent means to transmit his teachings.** He uses all this impure behavior as a means to transmit his teachings.

K4 Giving the name and pointing out the harm.

Sutra:

"This is a powerful nature spirit: a mountain sprite, a sea sprite, a wind sprite, a river sprite, an earth sprite, or a grass-and-tree sprite that has evolved over long ages. It may be a dragon-goblin; or a rishi who has been reborn as a goblin; or again a rishi who, having reached the end of his appointed time, should have died, but whose body does not decay and is possessed by a goblin. In its old age it has become a demon. It disturbs and confuses the good person. But when it tires of doing so, it will leave the other person's body. Then both the disciples and the teacher will get in trouble with the law.

Commentary:

This is a powerful nature spirit: a mountain sprite, a sea sprite, a wind sprite, a river sprite, an earth sprite; or a grass-

and-tree sprite that has evolved over long ages. **It may be a dragon-goblin; or** it may be **a rishi who,** having cultivated for perhaps a thousand, two thousand, three thousand, or five thousand years, **has been reborn as a** demon-**goblin** at the end of his life.

Or again, it may be **a rishi who, having reached the end of his appointed time, should have died, but whose body** after his death **does not decay** or change, **and is possessed by a goblin.**

In its old age it has become a demon. It disturbs and confuses the good person's power of samadhi. **But eventually, when it tires of doing so, it will leave the other person's body.** So long as the demon is there, the person possesses awesome spiritual power. But once the demon leaves, **then both the disciples and the teacher will get in trouble with the law** and their activities will be curtailed.

K5   Instructions to be aware and not become confused.

Sutra:

"**You should be aware of this in advance and not get caught up in the cycle of transmigration. If you are confused and do not understand, you will fall into the Relentless Hells.**

Commentary:

Ananda, **you should be aware of this in advance and not get caught up in the** demonic **cycle of transmigration.** Don't fall into the demons' snare. **If you are confused and do not understand, you will fall into the Relentless Hells.**

J9   Greed for profound emptiness.
K1   Samadhi leads to craving and seeking.

Sutra:

"**Further, in the unhindered clarity and wonder that ensues after the feeling skandha is gone, this good person is untroubled by any deviant mental state and experiences perfect, bright concentration. Within samadhi, his mind craves to enter** cessation, so he investigates the nature of transformations as he greedily seeks for profound emptiness.

Commentary:

He looks into how things in a state of existence can transform into nothingness, and how nothingness can transform into things which exist. He studies the way these transformations take place, hoping to experience a profound state of emptiness.

K2 A demon dispatches a deviant force to possess a person.

Sutra:

"**At that time a demon from the heavens seizes the opportunity it has been waiting for. Its spirit possesses another person and uses him as a mouthpiece to expound the sutras and teachings.**

Commentary:

At that time a demon from the heavens seizes the opportunity it has been waiting for. The demon watches and waits, and when it sees a chance, **its spirit possesses another person and uses him as a mouthpiece to expound the sutras and teachings.** The demon speaks through that person's mouth.

K3 The demon's words and deeds that mislead others.

Sutra:

"**This person, unaware that he is possessed by a demon, claims he has reached unsurpassed nirvana. When he comes to see that good person who seeks emptiness, he arranges a seat and explains the teachings. In the midst of the great assembly, his physical form suddenly disappears, and no one in the assembly can see him. Then out of nowhere, he abruptly reappears. He can appear and disappear at will, or he can make his body transparent like crystal. From his hands and feet he releases the fragrance of sandalwood, or his excrement and urine may be sweet as thick rock candy. He slanders the** precepts and is contemptuous of those who have left the home life.

Commentary:

This person is **unaware** and does not realize **that he is possessed by a demon** from the heavens. He **claims he has** already **reached** the wonderful fruition of **unsurpassed nirvana. When he comes to see that good person who seeks** the deep **emptiness** of cessation, **he arranges a seat and explains the teachings. In the midst of the great assembly, his physical form suddenly disappears, and no one in the assembly can see him.** The demon's spiritual powers cause the possessed person's body to suddenly vanish. He was there giving the lecture, but suddenly no one can see him. This is the "emptiness of people and phenomena." People and phenomena are both gone. **Then,** after a few minutes, from **out of nowhere, he abruptly reappears. He can appear and disappear at will.** If he wants to appear, he appears. If he wants to disappear, he disappears. He is in control and can do either with ease.

Or he can make his body appear **transparent like crystal,** so you can see right through it. **From his hands and feet,** at the flick of a wrist, **he releases the fragrance of sandalwood, or his excrement and urine may be sweet as thick rock candy. He slanders the precepts.** He says, "Don't bother about holding precepts. That is a Theravada matter. Why should you hold them? There is no great meaning in it." **And** he **is contemptuous of those who have left the home-life.** He says, "Don't leave the home-life. If you want to cultivate, go ahead and cultivate. You don't have to leave home to do it. What difference is there between being a layperson and a left-home person anyway?" That's how he slanders left-home people.

Sutra:

"He often says that there is no cause and no effect, that once we die, we are gone forever, that there is no afterlife, and that there are no ordinary people and no sages. Although he has

obtained a state of empty stillness, he covertly indulges his greedy desires. Those who give in to his lust also adopt his views of emptiness and deny cause and effect.

Commentary:

He often says that there is no cause and effect. "Don't believe in the law of cause and effect," he says. "It's totally wrong. There is no such thing." He says **that once we die we are gone forever.** "Once you die, you are gone forever, just like a light that gets snuffed out." He says **that there is no afterlife, and that there are no ordinary people and no sages.** "There's no such thing as rebirth, nor are there common people or sages. Those are just figures of speech."

Although he has obtained a state of empty stillness, he covertly indulges his greedy desires. Although he's arrived at some sort of theory of emptiness, he indulges in lust on the sly. **Those who give in to his lust adopt his views of emptiness.** As victims of the demon's energy, the people who engage in lust with him also come to believe that everything is empty **and deny cause and effect.** They feel there is no need to believe in cause and effect.

K4 Giving the name and pointing out the harm.

Sutra:

"This is an essence that was created during an eclipse of the sun or moon. Having fallen on gold, jade, a rare fungus, a unicorn, a phoenix, a tortoise, or a crane, the essence endowed it with life, so that it did not die for thousands or tens of thousands of years and eventually became a spirit. It was then born into this land and in its old age has become a demon. It disturbs and confuses the good person. But when it tires of doing so, it will leave the other person's body. Then both the disciples and the teacher will get in trouble with the law.

Commentary:

What is this? **This is an essence that was created during an eclipse of the sun or moon.** When there is an interaction between the sun and moon, an eclipse of the sun and moon, an essence falls to the ground. **Having fallen on gold, jade, a** certain kind of **rare fungus, a unicorn, a phoenix, a tortoise, or a crane, the essence endowed it with life, so that it did not die for thousands or tens of thousands of years and eventually became a spirit. It was then born into this land and in its old age has become a demon. It disturbs and confuses the good person** who is cultivating samadhi.

But eventually, **when it tires of doing so, it will leave the other person's body.** It will cease to possess him. **Then both the teacher and** his **disciples will get in trouble with the law.** They will be restrained by the law.

[January 1983]

Venerable Master: You must use dharma-selecting vision and wonderful-contemplative wisdom to regard this kind of state. When you contemplate, don't get attached and think, "I'm contemplating." Wonderful-contemplative wisdom functions like a mirror; it's similar to the great perfect mirror wisdom. However, while the great perfect mirror wisdom reveals the actual appearance of all phenomena effortlessly, wonderful-contemplative wisdom requires the power of contemplation in order to be clearly aware. If you can maintain an objective point of view, then you won't be ensnared by such improper views. If you recognize the state, then you won't be turned by it.

Disciple: I have a question. Monkey (in the book *Journey to the West*) was born from a rock. How did that rock give birth to a monkey? Can such phenomena occur after a rock has been exposed to the essence of the sun and moon over several tens of thousands of years? Is Monkey's case the same as that described in the sutra? That is, there is an essential energy created during an eclipse of the sun and the moon, and it is absorbed by such things as gold, jade, a rare fungus, a unicorn, a phoenix, a tortoise, or a crane, transforming them into demons. From reading the book, it seems to me that Monkey had a few good roots. He knew that transmigration entailed a lot of suffering, and so after eight hundred years, he started on a quest for the Way. He mastered various spiritual arts and later became a dharma protector in Buddhism.

Monkey was an example of a good being, but here the text is talking about spirits, sprites, ghosts, and monsters who turn into demons in their old age. Under what conditions do they turn into demons when they get old? It seems that these demons are like bandits because they do evil. Is it the case that some turn into demons while others don't, because some are good and others aren't?

Venerable Master: Monkey was only a demon, and there are many other cases which are similar. Monkey probably ran into trouble as he was cultivating at the level of the thinking skandha, and so as a result, he turned into a monkey that could ascend to the heavens and burrow into the earth. He is exactly what the *Shurangama Sutra* calls "a representative of the demons." As for other demons, when they are tired of being demons, of course they will also take refuge in the Triple Jewel. With a single thought of reflecting within and awakening, they can become disciples of the Buddha. Before they awaken, they are still demons. The older demons get, the greater their spiritual powers become. The young ones aren't that strong and their spiritual powers aren't that great. The older ones have inconceivable strength and spiritual powers, which is why they are called demons. Demons are even more powerful than ghosts. The Chinese have the term "demonic ghost" because ghosts can turn into demons.

Have you heard about the "as-you-wish demon woman?" She had been a ghost in the Zhou dynasty, but because she didn't follow the rules, she was struck by lightning. However, the lightning didn't destroy her completely, and she pulled herself back together with a concentrated effort. Then she cultivated and became a demon who went around taking people's lives, because she wanted to increase her own power and the power of her retinue. Each time she caused a person's death, the other demons would congratulate her: "You're really powerful!" It's similar to how other officials act toward an official who has just been promoted. A demon's power increases with the number of people it kills, until even ghosts have to follow its orders.

Later, when the as-you-wish demon woman met me, she took refuge with the Triple Jewel. Thus she was a demon who took refuge with the Buddha. Everything in this world is wondrous and inconceivable. This sutra describes only a small portion. If we were to go into detail, each skandha has myriads of different kinds of demons. The sutra mentions one kind to give people a general idea, so that they know to avoid thoughts of greed and craving. If you have no desire, you need not fear any demon whatsoever. If you are devoid of greed or desire, no demon can trouble you. Demons will come in only when they see that you've opened yourself up to them. If you always keep the doors closed, they won't come in.

Demons get born in the heavens because they have cultivated many blessings. The sutras talk about demons from the heavens, but you shouldn't think they are only in the heavens. They can go to the heavens, but they are not always there. Demons in the human realm that are endowed with spiritual powers can also be considered demons from the heavens. If the demons in the heavens need them to go there to cheer them on in battle and to increase their power, they can go at any time. Although they are born in the heavens, they still have desires and huge tempers and are incredibly stubborn. It's just because of their belligerent character that they become demons. If they weren't so aggressive and hot-tempered, then they would join the Buddhas' retinue. Those with bad tempers and heavy ignorance join the demons' retinue.

As for what kind of retribution they will receive in the future, that's a very distant question that cannot be answered. If they encounter someone with great spiritual powers but are rather resistant to being taught and transformed, they may be pulverized into nothingness. Even if they aren't pulverized, if they do a lot of evil and fail to reform, if they still turn away from enlightenment to unite with the worldly dust and continue to be confused, then they will have to undergo retribution and great suffering. They may fall among the animals and become foxes or weasels. It is the spirits of demons that cause them to turn into such creatures. They may become snakes or rats, or various other strange animals. These are all transformations of beings endowed with malicious demonic energy. Fierce beasts such as tigers are so powerful because they are aided by a bit of demonic power.

K5   Instructions to be aware and not become confused.

Sutra:

"**You should be aware of this in advance and not get caught up in the cycle of transmigration. If you are confused and do not understand, you will fall into the Relentless Hells.**"

Commentary:

You should be aware of this well **in advance and not get caught up in the cycle of transmigration** of the demon king. **If you are confused and do not understand,** if you do not wake up, **you will fall into the Relentless Hells.**

J10 Greed for immortality.
K1   Samadhi leads to craving and seeking.

Sutra:

"**Further, in the unhindered clarity and wonder that ensues after the feeling skandha is gone, this good person is untroubled by any deviant mental state and experiences perfect, bright concentration. Within samadhi, his mind craves long life, so he toils at investigating its subtleties as he greedily seeks for immortality. He wishes to cast aside the birth and death of the body, and suddenly he hopes to end the birth and death of thoughts as well, so that he can abide forever in a subtle form.**"

Commentary:

Further, in the unhindered clarity and wonder that ensues after the feeling skandha is gone, now that the skandha of feeling has become empty, clear, and subtle, **this good person** who is cultivating samadhi **is untroubled by any deviant mental state and experiences perfect, bright concentration. Within** that perfect, subtle **samadhi,** a change suddenly occurs. What is it? **His mind craves long life.** All of a sudden he thinks, "It would be most wonderful to live forever and not have to die." **So he toils at investigating its subtleties.** He painstakingly searches into its most esoteric and subtle aspects **as he greedily seeks for immortality.** He wants to live forever and never grow old.

He wishes to cast aside and renounce **the birth and death of the body,** literally "share-and-section birth and death." This refers to each individual's birth and death. Each person has a share, and each person has a section. What is meant by "share?" You have a body, and I have a body, too. You are a person, and I am also a person. You have your share, and I have my share. What about "section?" It is the life span, the interval from birth to death. "Section" can also refer to the physical stature – from head to toe.

And he **suddenly hopes to end the birth and death of thoughts as well.** Ordinary people undergo the physical birth and death of the body. A fourth stage arhat has ended that kind of birth and death, but still has to undergo the birth and death of thoughts[3]. This refers to the continual passage of thoughts – the ever-changing thought process in which one thought is produced and another perishes in an endless flow. When he no longer undergoes physical birth and death, he suddenly hopes to end the birth and death of thoughts as well, **so he can abide forever in a subtle form,** a very refined and attentuated form. To abide forever means to obtain eternal life.

K2 A demon dispatches a deviant spirit to possess a person.

Sutra:

"At that time a demon from the heavens seizes the opportunity it has been waiting for. Its spirit possesses another person and uses him as a mouthpiece to expound the sutras and teachings.

---

[3]. literally "change birth and death"

Commentary:

Right when he entertains a thought of greed for long life, **at that time a demon** king **from the heavens seizes the opportunity it has been** watching and **waiting for. Its spirit possesses another person.** The demon king sends one of its followers to possess a person **and uses him as a mouthpiece to expound the sutras and teachings** for the cultivator.

K3 The demon's words and deeds that mislead others.

Sutra:

"This person, unaware that he is possessed by a demon, claims he has reached unsurpassed nirvana. When he comes to see that good person who seeks long life, he arranges a seat and explains the teachings. He is fond of saying that he can go places and come back without hindrance, perhaps traveling ten thousand miles and returning in the twinkling of an eye. He can also bring things back from wherever he goes. Or he may tell someone to walk from one end of the room to the other, a distance of just a few paces. Then even if the person walked fast for years, he could not reach the wall. Therefore people believe in the possessed person and mistake him for a Buddha.

Commentary:

Since **this person**'s mind is totally controlled by the demon from the heavens, he himself is **unaware that he is possessed by a demon**. He **claims** that **he has reached** the wondrous fruition of **unsurpassed nirvana. When he comes to see that good person who seeks long life, he arranges a** dharma-**seat and explains the teachings.**

He is fond of saying that he can go places and come back without hindrance. What does this demon like to say? He says, "In this very moment I can go some place a thousand or even ten thousand miles away, and return in the same moment. I can go to Japan without taking a plane, buy merchandise and bring it back with me. If you don't believe it, I'll give you a demonstration." He is always showing off his spiritual powers. He wants people to see the inconceivable feats he can perform. He says, "I can go and come freely, in no time at all, **perhaps traveling ten thousand miles and returning in the twinkling of an eye.** I can go and return in the time it takes you to inhale and exhale."

Not only that, **he can also bring things back from wherever he goes.** He can buy things and bring them back. "You don't believe me?" he'll say. "See this item? It came from such and such a company in Japan – their exclusive model, only available for purchase on site." Then he shows them a radio or a tape recorder of Japanese make, which has not passed through customs or been imported, and which actually was manufactured by the company in Japan.

Or he may tell someone to walk from one end of the room to the other, a distance of just a few, maybe seven or eight, **paces. Then even if the person walked fast for years, he could not reach the wall.** He couldn't cover that small floor-space at a dead run even in a year's time. Seeing such displays, **therefore people believe in the possessed person and mistake him for a Buddha.** They think, "Oh! This is a Buddha coming to teach us the dharma."

Sutra:

"**He often says, 'All beings in the ten directions are my children. I gave birth to all Buddhas. I created the world. I am the original Buddha. I created this world naturally, not due to cultivation.'**

Commentary:

He often says, "You know, **all beings in the ten directions are my children. I gave birth to all Buddhas.** Do you know whose sons the Buddhas are? They are my sons." He shamelessly boasts that he gave birth to all Buddhas. "**I created the world. I am the original Buddha.** I was the first Buddha. There weren't any Buddhas before me. **I created this world naturally, not due to cultivation.** I created this world spontaneously. And I was already a Buddha when I came into the world. I didn't have to cultivate to become a Buddha."

K4 Giving the name and pointing out the harm.

Sutra:

"This may be a chamunda sent from the retinue of the demon in the Heaven of Sovereignty, or a youthful pishacha from the Heaven of the Four Kings that has not yet brought forth the resolve. It takes advantage of the person's luminous clarity and devours his essence and energy. Or perhaps without having to rely on a teacher, the cultivator personally sees a being that tells him, 'I am a vajra spirit who has come to give you long life.' Or the being transforms itself into a beautiful woman and engages him in frenzied lust, so that within a year his vitality is exhausted. He talks to himself; and to anyone listening he sounds like a goblin. The people around him do not realize what is happening. In most cases such a person will get in trouble with the law. But before he is punished, he will die from depletion. The demon disturbs and confuses the person to the point of death.

Commentary:

This may be a chamunda sent from the retinue of the demon in the Heaven of Sovereignty. Chamunda is a Sanskrit word that means "slave ghost," a ghost that does the work of a slave. It also means "jealous ghost" because it is always jealous of anything good that anyone else has. It tries to thwart people who want to study the Buddhadharma. If someone wants to be good, it drags him in a bad direction. It's a bad ghost. The demon in the Heaven of Sovereignty sends this kind of ghost to disturb the cultivator of samadhi. **Or** it may send **a youthful pishacha from the Heaven of the Four Kings.** Pishacha ghosts specialize in devouring essence. They eat the essence of various grains and plants and of humans as well. When men and women engage in sexual conduct, a kind of essence flows forth, and that's what they eat. Whenever people engage in sexual conduct, there are lots of ghosts waiting on the sidelines to eat the essence. It's very dangerous.

This is a pishacha ghost **that has not yet brought forth the resolve. It takes advantage of the person's luminous clarity and devours his essence.** Those who have not brought forth the resolve, such as the youthful pishacha and others, crave the cultivator's bright clarity and his soul. They consume his essence, but he remains unaware of it.

Or perhaps without having to rely on a teacher, the cultivator personally sees a being that tells him, "I am a vajra-wielding dharma-protecting **spirit who has come to give you long life.** Now I've come to give you longevity. You'll be able to live a long time." **Or** after saying that, **the being transforms itself into a beautiful woman and engages him in frenzied lust.** "Frenzied" means that they engage in this activity of lust over and over again, nonstop, **so that within a year his vitality is exhausted.** Under the strain, his vitality is depleted before a year is up. His essence, energy, and spirit all "dry up," because this is too excessive. The key word here is "frenzied." It's not describing any ordinary occurrence. It's not referring to the usual manner in which such activities are performed. It's certain that the beautiful woman says, "The more you indulge in lust, the longer your life will be. You will attain long life." In his greed for long life, he fails to realize his life is getting shorter by the minute. He's totally spent before a year is up.

At that time **he talks to himself**. Actually he's not talking to himself, he's conversing with the demon. **And** while he's doing so, **to anyone listening he sounds like a goblin**. He's conversing with the demon, but the people around him don't see it. I've encountered this kind of demon before.

I once met a man who was visited by a woman every night. She didn't come to him in the daytime, but every evening as soon as she came, everyone in the household could hear the clack-clack of a woman's high heels on the floor boards. Although they could hear the sound, they could not see her. Whenever the woman came, the man would strip, hop in bed, and have at it, not caring whether anyone was around or not. That was an instance of this type of ghost. Later on, a shaman in the area went to his home to exorcise the ghost. That night, when the demon came, she conversed with the shaman.

"Fine," she said. "You want to cure this man? All right, from today on he'll be fine. But from this point, I'm going to start coming to your household. We'll have a little duel of wits." After that, she actually went to the shaman's home, and his older brother engaged in this sort of improper activity from morning to night with the demon. I'll tell you, this demon is really powerful.

The people around him do not realize what is happening. They are not aware of this situation. **In most cases such a person will get in trouble with the law,** and his activities will be curtailed by the law. **But before he is punished,** before he is brought to trial, **he will die from depletion.** While still in prison, he dies from the total depletion of his essence, energy, and spirit. **The demon disturbs and confuses the person to the point of death.** The demon destroys the person's samadhi power to the extent that he perishes.

[January 1983]

When I was young, I liked to fight with demons. I fought with them until all the demon armies in the universe wanted to gang up on me. I nearly lost my life on many occasions. Because of this, later on, no matter how much I have wished to fight with demons again, I haven't dared to use any method against them. Many demons come to bully me, but I always practice forbearance and don't offer any opposition. I gather them in and influence them with kindness and compassion instead of subduing them with the function of subduing.

I remember that at the Virtue Society in Manchuria, the dean of the training school was called Xu Guilan. There were fifty or sixty students in the Virtue Society, and one of them became possessed by a demon. Xu Guilan, thinking that she had some authority as the dean of the training school, tried to get rid of the demon. She spat a mouthful of cold water at the possessed girl, but the demon didn't leave.

It said, "Okay, you want to get rid of me? Then I'll possess you instead, and see what you do about that!"

Thereupon, the possessed girl got better, and Xu Guilan herself was possessed by the demon. Earlier, Guo Hong said he had used this method of reciting a mantra and then spitting on the possessed person, and the person had run off. Probably the demon who possessed him didn't have enough power, and so it left. But the demon that possessed Xu Guilan wasn't afraid of being spat on with cold water, and it didn't go away. Then Xu Guilan started acting demonic. She could no longer live at the Virtue Society and had to move back home. The demon came to disturb her every day at her home, throwing her family into a turmoil.

What demon was this? It was a gibbon spirit, a very large one. When it came, it engaged in sexual intercourse with Xu Guilan. It would possess her body and torture her. Sometimes it would confuse her to the point that she would utter how much she loved it, and so on. Then they would have sex, and after it was over, Xu Guilan would be bleeding from her eyes, ears, nostrils, and mouth. The gibbon spirit sucked away all her energy and essence, leaving her paralyzed and near death.

The Virtue Society sent someone to see our monastery's abbot who was known throughout Manchuria as the Filial Son Wang. They had heard that he had great virtue and could subdue the demon, so they sought him out. However, the abbot would always ask me to take care of such matters. He never dealt with them himself, but always sent me to resolve whatever problems there were. This happened many times, such as when the family of Gao Defu in Danangou village was in trouble.

This time the abbot also asked me to go, and so I went. When they informed the gibbon spirit of my coming, guess what it said?

"Ah! You wasted your efforts asking him to come. It won't work. Even if you asked Ji Gong[4] to come, it wouldn't scare me."

It was not afraid of anything. When I went there, the gibbon spirit came, and we had a real fight! After two days of nonstop fighting, I finally subdued it. The woman recovered. I have been through many experiences such as this.

I'm not willing to interfere in other people's business anymore. For example, although I see that a certain person has an eagle spirit on her, and it is causing her head to shake involuntarily, I'm not going to do anything about it. I act as if I didn't see it. Why? Because I'm cultivating forbearance! Even if someone were to defecate on my head, I would bear it and not get angry. My motto now is that I will not contend with anyone. Guo Hong, you'd better be careful not to stir up trouble in the future. You must have a few good roots, or else that demon would easily have possessed you. This is no laughing matter.

K5 Instructions to be aware and not become confused.

Sutra:

"You should be aware of this in advance and not get caught up in the cycle of transmigration. If you are confused and do not understand, you will fall into the Relentless Hells."

Commentary:

Ananda, **you should be aware of this in advance,** understand the principle involved, **and not get caught up in the cycle of transmigration.** If you are aware of the demonic state, you won't fall into the demon's trap. You won't end up in the retinue of demons. But **if you are confused and do not understand,** there will be no politeness involved. It's certain **you will fall into the Relentless Hells.** You will not be shown the slightest favor.

---

[4]. the "Living Buddha"

I3 The Buddha exhorts those in the Dharma-ending Age.
J1 False boasting of accomplishment to sagely fruition.

Sutra:

"Ananda, you should know that in the Dharma-ending Age, these ten kinds of demons may leave the home-life to cultivate the Way within my dharma. They may possess other people, or they may manifest themselves in various forms. All of them will claim that they have already accomplished proper and pervasive knowledge and awareness.

Commentary:

Ananda, you should know that, especially **in the Dharma-ending Age, these ten kinds of demons,** the ones that appear in the ten demonic states associated with the thinking skandha, **may leave the home-life to cultivate the Way within my** Buddhadharma. **They may possess other people.** The demon kings may possess other people, **or they may manifest themselves in various forms.** They may display their spiritual powers as demon kings and manifest all kinds of forms. They may appear as Buddhas, bodhisattvas, arhats, or gods. Demon kings can manifest in any kind of body. **All of them will claim that they have already accomplished proper and pervasive knowledge and awareness.** "Proper and pervasive knowledge" refers to the Buddha, who has both proper knowledge and pervasive knowledge. "Proper knowledge" means knowing that "the mind produces the myriad phenomena." "Pervasive knowledge" means knowing that "the myriad phenomena are the mind itself." When someone has genuine proper and pervasive knowledge and views, he becomes a Buddha, one of proper and pervasive knowledge. However, demons pretend to be Buddhas and claim to have attained proper and pervasive knowledge.

When Shakyamuni Buddha was about to enter nirvana, he summoned the demon king and commanded him, "You should abide by the rules. Follow the rules from now on. Don't violate them."

The demon king replied, "So you want me to follow your rules? Fine. During the ending age of your dharma, I will wear your garments, eat your food, and defecate in your alms bowl." His meaning was that he would destroy the dharma from within.

When the Buddha heard that he was worried. He wept and said, "There's really nothing I can do about you. Your method is the most poisonous, the most destructive."

There is the saying: "The parasites on the lion's body eat the lion's flesh." This means that in the Dharma-ending Age, the demons are strong and the dharma is weak. There are a lot of demon kings. Therefore, cultivators must be very careful. What are demon kings like? In general, they are different from ordinary people. They have a demonic energy about them. There is something unusual about them, which reveals that they are demon kings.

[January 1983]

The Dharma-ending Age is a time when the dharma is weak and demons are strong. The *Song of Enlightenment* by Great Master Yong Jia says very clearly:

> Alas! In the evil time of the Dharma-ending Age,
> Living beings have few blessings;
>   it is difficult to train them.
> Far indeed from the sages of the past,
>   their deviant views are deep.
> Demons are strong, the dharma is weak;
>   many are the wrongs and injuries.
> Hearing of the door of the Tathagata's sudden teaching,
> They regret not destroying it as they would smash a tile.

"Alas" expresses a regretful sighing about the Dharma-ending Age. The evil time means this time is very evil and vile. All the monsters are appearing in the world.

The computer is one of the biggest monsters, and television is a small monster. The small monster helps the big one out and the big monster wants to devour all the people. It wants to take people's jobs away. This is a very evil age. Living beings have no blessings. They are tense and nervous from morning to night, and people suffer from diseases of the heart, liver, lungs, spleen, and kidneys. Such diseases strike people because they are infected with deviant energy. They have been poisoned too deeply.

You think it's nice to watch television, to talk on the phone, to listen to the radio, and to play with the computer, but you don't realize the harm that these things do to your heart, liver, spleen, lungs, and kidneys. They cause people to act inhuman and ghosts to act unlike ghosts. That's a sign that the world is starting to go bad. We have been born in a time when living beings have no blessings and are difficult to teach. You may advise them not to watch television or listen to the radio, but they insist on doing those things. Tell them not to listen to music, but they listen on the sly. It's not easy to teach the upside-down living beings in this terrible age.

"Far indeed from the sages of the past." They are very far from the Buddhas. "Their deviant views are deep." Everyone has deviant knowledge and deviant views; no one has proper knowledge and proper views. Their deviant views are too deep. "Demons are strong, the dharma is weak." In this age the demons prosper and the dharma is very feeble. "Many are the wrongs and injuries." You hurt me, and I hurt you. We hurt each other out of resentment. "Hearing of the door of the Tathagata's sudden teaching." If they hear of the Buddha's proper dharma-eye treasury, the dharma-door of the sudden teaching, "they regret not destroying it as they would smash a tile." They regret not being able to wreck it immediately, as they would smash a tile to bits. That's how much they hate the Buddhadharma. This is the way we are now.

Therefore, we Buddhists who live at the City of Ten Thousand Buddhas should not keep radios, televisions, or musical records in our homes; we should get rid of these. No matter how busy we are, we should attend the morning and evening ceremonies and the sutra recitations. We should not be absent from these activities. If you are a layperson and you cannot make it to the temple, you may do the morning and evening ceremonies, recite sutras, and investigate the

Buddhadharma at home. Don't spend your spare time watching television or listening to the radio, being no different from people of the outside world.

The City of Ten Thousand Buddhas is different from the outside world, and we should not let ourselves be influenced by the common crowd. All of you at the City of Ten Thousand Buddhas should devote your attention to the Buddhadharma and to studying and practicing the principles in the Buddhist sutras. If you memorize the *Shurangama Sutra*, that will make me extremely happy. Even at home, you should read and recite the *Shurangama Sutra*, the *Dharma Flower Sutra*, and the *Avatamsaka Sutra*. What's the point of coming to the City of Ten Thousand Buddhas if you don't understand the Buddhadharma at all? It's meaningless. If you don't understand anything and you have no idea what people are talking about during discussions, then your being here is too pitiful.

J2 They use lust in their teaching.

Sutra:

"They praise lust and break the Buddha's moral precepts. The evil demonic teachers and their demonic disciples that I just discussed transmit their teaching through licentious activity. Such deviant spirits take over cultivators' minds, and after as few as nine lives or as many as a hundred generations, they turn true practitioners entirely into followers of demons.

Commentary:

They praise lust. How can one tell if someone is a demon? Demons do not praise proper methods of practice. They praise lust and openly advocate sex. **And** they **break the Buddha's moral precepts.** They say, "The Buddha's precepts are useless. Don't keep them. The Buddha's precepts were for adherents of the initial vehicle to practice. We are great vehicle bodhisattvas, great vehicle Buddhas. Since we have already become Buddhas, we don't need to hold the precepts." **The evil demonic teachers** of dharma **and their demonic disciples,** the disciples of the demon kings, **that I just discussed transmit their teaching through licentious**

activity. They practice lust with each other and praise it, saying, "It is the finest and most wonderful dharma door. The principle of true emptiness and wonderful existence lies right within this." **Such deviant spirits,** that is, those who extol lust, **take over cultivators' minds.** Because the cultivators' minds are confused by the deviant demons who have possessed them, they crave sex and openly advocate lust. It's all because the demons have taken over their minds.

And after as few as nine lives or as many as a hundred generations, they turn true practitioners entirely into followers of demons. At the minimum, it takes nine lives. What does one "life" mean? Is it the period from a person's birth until his death? No. Rather, it refers to a period of a hundred years. Therefore nine lives is nine hundred years. At the most, it takes over a hundred generations. One generation represents thirty years, and so a hundred generations is three thousand years. It takes a minimum of nine lives to turn a true cultivator completely into a member of the demon's retinue.

At the other extreme, it might take as long as a hundred generations from the time the demon confuses him until he becomes part of the demon's retinue. Although he has been confused, he still has to pass through several more lives. Only after a long time does he officially join the demon's retinue. Before that time, his nature is not totally demonic. Do you know what demons are transformed from? Demons were originally people. A person who is not upright may become a demon, but it doesn't happen that fast. The demon king hounds him, follows him, and keeps confusing him. The process takes from as short a time as nine lives to as long as a hundred generations.

J3 They are beguiled by demons and fall into the hells.

Sutra:

"When their lives are over, they are bound to end up as one of the demonic hordes. They will lose their proper and pervasive knowledge and fall into the Relentless Hells.

Commentary:

When their lives are over, when the allotted time has passed, anywhere from nine lives to a hundred generations, and the practitioners die, **they are bound to end up as one of the demonic hordes.** They cannot become demon kings, since there is only one king. There are not that many demon kings. They can only become run-of-the-mill demons, common citizens of the demon populace. **They will lose their proper and pervasive knowledge.** They will lose proper knowledge and views and will have only wrong knowledge and views; and they will follow along in the deeds done by the demon king. **And** eventually they will **fall into the Relentless Hells.** After they use up their blessings as demons, their lives will end and they will fall into the hells.

J4 Exhortation to compassionately rescue them to repay kindness.

Sutra:

"You need not enter nirvana yet. Although you are completing your attainment to the level beyond learning, hold nonetheless to your vows to enter the Dharma-ending Age. Bring forth great compassion to rescue and take across living beings who have proper minds and deep faith. Do not let them become possessed by demons. Help them instead to attain proper knowledge and views. I have already rescued you from birth and death. By venerating the Buddha's words, you will be repaying the Buddha's kindness.

Commentary:

"Ananda, **you need not enter nirvana yet.** Don't enter nirvana yet. Stay here in the world and teach and transform living beings on my behalf. **Although you are completing your attainment to the level beyond learning, hold nonetheless to your vows to enter the Dharma-ending Age.** For all practical purposes, you have already attained the state beyond learning."[5] The Buddha says, "You should keep your compassionate vows. When the proper dharma is gone and the Dharma Image Age has passed, the Dharma-ending Age will come. At that time **bring forth great**

compassion to rescue and take across living beings who have proper minds and deep faith. Ananda, you should bring forth a mind of great kindness and compassion and save living beings whose minds are proper in the Dharma-ending Age."

Do not let them become possessed by demons. Rescue living beings and cause them to have deep faith in you, so that they will not be confused by the demon kings. Do not allow the demon kings to have their way with people. **Help them,** the living beings in the Dharma-ending Age, **instead to** be on guard and to **attain proper knowledge and views.** That means you and me, living beings right now, not anyone else. You should urge yourself on. Keep a proper attitude and outlook.

Shakyamuni Buddha says, "Ananda, **I have already rescued you from birth and death.** You have already ended birth and death. You are already a second-stage arhat, and you understand the way to reach the fourth stage of arhatship, so for all practical purposes we can say that your birth and death are now ended. **By venerating the Buddha's words, you will be repaying the Buddha's kindness.** Now listen to the Buddha's instruction; do what the Buddha tells you and don't forget it. By honoring and obeying the Buddha, you are repaying the Buddha's deep kindness."

What does it mean to repay the Buddha's kindness? If we listen to the Buddha's instructions, we are repaying the Buddha's kindness. If we want to repay the Buddha's kindness, we must obey the Buddha. If Ananda wants to repay the Buddha's kindness, Ananda should listen to the Buddha. If we want to repay the Buddha's kindness, we should also listen to the Buddha. We should listen to Shakyamuni Buddha and to the dharma masters when they explain the sutras and the principles. That's why at the very start I

---

5. At this point Ananda has realized the second fruition of arhatship, but has not yet actually attained the level beyond learning. However, the path of cultivation to reach that accomplishment is clear to him, so he can be considered as having attained that level.

said you all should listen to the Buddha. I'm not a Buddha; I should also listen to the Buddha. No matter what, we shouldn't ignore the Buddha's advice.

I4 Conclusion on the harm, and command to offer protection.
J1 Showing how the states come about from interaction.

Sutra:

"**Ananda, all ten of these states may occur in dhyana as one's mental effort interacts with the thinking skandha.**

Commentary:

Ananda, all ten of these states which have just been explained **may occur in** the still contemplation of **dhyana** when you have applied enough effort to reach that level. Where do those states come from? They can happen **as one's mental effort interacts with the thinking skandha**. They are changes that occur in the thinking skandha as a result of pressure applied in cultivation. When you are cultivating with maximum effort, such states will manifest. But when they manifest, don't "mistake a thief for your own son"; don't be confused by those states. When you meditate, your mental effort interacts with the thinking skandha. They engage in battle. It's like a war. If your samadhi power is victorious, then the thinking skandha will be conquered. But if the thinking skandha wins out and your skill in samadhi fizzles, you will be caught in a demonic state, and then these kinds of things will happen.

J2 Confusion will bring harm.

Sutra:

"**Dull and confused living beings do not evaluate themselves. Encountering such situations, in their confusion they fail to recognize them and say that they have become sages, thereby uttering a great lie. They will fall into the Relentless Hells.**

Commentary:

Dull and confused living beings do not evaluate themselves. Living beings are always getting attached to things. They are obstinate and inflexible, stupid and without wisdom. They do not take proper stock of themselves. **Encountering such situations, such demonic states, in their confusion they fail to recognize them.** The most important thing is that if you can recognize states, then you won't be turned by them. If you are clear about them, you will not be confused. If you don't understand, then you will be confused. Confusion is basically a lack of recognition. And what happens when people fail to recognize states?

They say that they have become sages. They say things like, "Do you know about me? I've become a Buddha already. And I'll tell you, it was really easy for me. It was cheaper than buying a couple pieces of tofu." That's really too easy, isn't it? Such people say that they are Buddhas, that they have realized the Way, that they are enlightened, that they have penetrated their meditation topic, and that they've got it all figured out.

For example, someone who came here today was of the same type as the "American Sixth Patriarch" who came a few days ago. He didn't bow to the Buddhas or stupas. The sutra describes the possessed person as not bowing in temples or to shrines. He didn't bow to the Buddha or listen to the dharma. He just ate lunch and left. The reason he left was that his demon dragged him away. He was so filled with demonic energy that he felt too uncomfortable to stay for even one minute more after eating his lunch. You should recognize what he was all about. His manner indicated that he thought he was already a Buddha, so he didn't need to bow to the Buddha.

Thereby uttering a great lie. They will fall into the Relentless Hells. He is bound to fall into the Relentless Hells in the future. Don't look only at the short term. It may take as little as nine lives, or it may take up to a hundred generations. He didn't listen to the Buddhadharma because of the demonic energy that had taken over him. Even if he wanted to listen, his entire body felt too uneasy, so he couldn't sit or stand still. I've told you about this before, and you should all pay attention. After this, whenever you go to a temple or Buddha hall, you must respect the temple rules.

Do what the other people are doing. Don't stand when everyone else is bowing to the Buddha. That looks very bad. Anyone who acts like that won't be able to study the Buddhadharma no matter where he goes. When you study the Buddhadharma, you must be receptive, humble, and sincere.

J3 Command to offer protection.

Sutra:

"**In the Dharma-ending Age, after my nirvana, all of you should pass on the Tathagata's teachings, so that all living beings can awaken to their meaning. Do not let the demons of the heavens have their way. Offer protection so that all can realize the Unsurpassed Way.**

Commentary:

In the Dharma-ending Age, after my nirvana, all of you should pass on the Tathagata's teachings. "All of you" refers to Ananda and all the great bodhisattvas, great arhats, and great bhikshus in the assembly, as well as to the great elders. Here the Buddha is exhorting them, "You must continue the transmission of the Tathagata's teachings down to the Dharma-ending Age, **so that all living beings can awaken to their meaning,** and so they can understand the principles of the *Shurangama Sutra*. Tell them about the fifty kinds of skandha demons, about the demons of the form, feeling, and thinking skandhas which I have explained for you. Be sure to propagate this teaching so everyone can hear it. **Do not let the demons of the heavens have their way.** If you let the demons do as they please, then you are in for trouble. **Offer protection** – maintain and support the Buddhadharma – **so that all can realize the** fruition of the **Unsurpassed Way.**

CHAPTER 5

The Formations Skandha

H4 The characteristics of the demons of the formations skandha.
I1 Overview of the beginning and end.
J1 In the beginning, one cultivates but has not yet broken through this region.
K1 Review of the ending of the previous thinking skandha.

Sutra:

"Ananda, when the good person who is cultivating samadhi has put an end to the thinking skandha, he is ordinarily free of dreaming and idle thinking, so he stays the same whether in wakefulness or in sleep. His mind is aware, clear, empty, and still, like a cloudless sky, devoid of any coarse sense-impressions. He contemplates everything in the world – the mountains, the rivers, and the earth – as reflections in a mirror, appearing without attachment and vanishing without any trace; they are simply received and reflected. He does away with all his old habits, and only the essential truth remains.

Commentary:

Ananda, when the good person. Which good person is being referred to here? The good person is the one who is developing the skill of directing the hearing inward to hear the inherent nature. He is cultivating the great Shurangama Samadhi. And who exactly is that person? He is simply whoever cultivates. "The good person" does not refer to any particular individual; it's not an exclusive title. If you cultivate, then it refers to you. If I cultivate, it refers to me. If he or she cultivates, it refers to him or her. Everyone has a share in it. That is, you have a share if you cultivate, but not if you don't. It's completely fair.

That good person is the one **who is cultivating samadhi**. Cultivation refers to diligently sitting in meditation, not to eating all day long. You should sit in meditation, listen to the sutras, and study the Buddhadharma. What should you cultivate? Samadhi power. How do you cultivate samadhi power? Sit in meditation. Samadhi arises from precepts, so the first step is to hold the precepts. Once you take the precepts, you must hold the precepts and never indulge in sexual misconduct. Men and women should observe propriety, as Lord Guan Yu[6] did. He was faithful to his wife all his life. He never drew near another woman. Do you see his ruddy face? It testifies to his magnanimous, proper energy. Now that you have taken the precepts, I want to tell you that you must remain faithful to your spouse. You may not get involved in extra-marital affairs and go looking for partners everywhere. Don't break the rules. You should accord with propriety and be open and upright in your conduct; only then will you attain samadhi. After taking the precepts, you will develop samadhi. From samadhi, wisdom will develop.

How do people get possessed by demons? If you have a little samadhi and your wisdom is insufficient, you may encounter demonic obstacles. If your skill in samadhi is deep enough, you will be able to conquer the demons.

[January 1983]

If you want to have proper samadhi, holding the precepts is certainly a prerequisite. It sets the foundation. Once we have a firm foundation, we can erect pillars on top of it. The pillars represent samadhi, and the foundation represents precepts. We must strictly uphold the precepts. This is very, very important. If you don't set a

---

6. A famous general in the Three Kingdoms period of China

good foundation, then the pillars will not stand, and your samadhi will be deviant.

What is meant by wisdom? Once the pillars are erected and the walls are put in, the house can be built. What's the use of a house? It can be a place for people to bow to the Buddhas and to hear lectures on the sutras. We can teach people to change their faults and renew themselves. That's the function of wisdom.

Precepts are the substance, samadhi is the appearance, and wisdom is the function. We should be very clear about this. If you lack precepts, then you won't have any samadhi. Without samadhi, you cannot develop wisdom. Likewise, if you don't set the foundation well, the pillars you erect will not be stable, the walls will cave in, and the house will collapse and be useless. Therefore, the three non-outflow studies of precepts, samadhi, and wisdom are all indispensable. We should pay close attention to this.

He **has put an end to the thinking skandha.** Among the five skandhas of form, feeling, thinking, formations, and consciousness, the thinking skandha is destroyed. In his mind's interaction with the thinking skandha, he has conquered it. Having broken through the thinking skandha, **he is ordinarily free of dreaming and idle thinking**. The state he has reached is not a state of not eating or not sleeping. In this state, one still sleeps and eats, but no longer dreams. Confucius once said, "Alas, I'm getting decrepit. It's been so long since I saw the duke of Zhou in a dream!"

This was the duke who protected the King Wu in the Zhou dynasty. Why didn't Confucius have any dreams? Probably it was because by that time in his life, Confucius had partially broken through the thinking skandha. However, since he was not aware of it, he wondered, "Hey! How come I don't dream anymore? Oh, I must be getting old." Confucius had some skill in cultivation, and it's likely that he had destroyed the thinking skandha without knowing it. He didn't understand, so he decided that he no longer had dreams because he was old. Once the thinking skandha is destroyed, dreams are gone.

So he stays the same whether in wakefulness or in sleep. If you have read classical Chinese literature, you may know a story called the *Warlord Defeats Duan at Yan* which relates how a warlord named Zheng married a girl named Jiang. She gave birth to Lord Zhuang and Gong Shuduan. Lord Zhuang was called "Born Upon Waking" because his mother was asleep when she started to give birth to him, and when she woke up, he was born.

To that cultivator, the state of wakefulness is the same as the state of sleep. In other words, when he's asleep, it's as if he were awake. He can be like that because he is not upside-down and thus has no dream-thinking. When you have broken through the thinking skandha, you can leave upside-down dream-thinking far behind and ultimately attain the state of nirvana. If you haven't broken through the thinking skandha, this upside-downness will not go away. You should pay attention to this point.

In our study of the Buddhadharma, the five skandhas discussed in the *Shurangama Sutra* are extremely important. Furthermore, you should know how to untie the six knots. If you do not understand these knots, then you will never be able to untie them and become free. If you can untie them, you will obtain freedom.

His mind is aware, clear, empty, and still. At this point he may be sleeping or awake, but for him, the two states are the same. What kind of state is this? The person actually sleeps very little. He's a light sleeper. He can replenish his energy just by closing his eyes for a while, unlike some people who sleep from dawn to dusk and from dusk to dawn. The reason they never seem to get enough sleep is because they have not broken through the thinking skandha. They tend to doze off a lot. When he breaks through the thinking skandha, he becomes alert and clear-minded. Waking and sleeping become the same for him. There is no difference. If you talk while he's sleeping, he will hear you. That's a subtle and wonderful state. Don't think you can scold him while he's asleep, for he knows what you are saying. He just doesn't let you know that he knows. What a wonderful state that is! Some beings in the heavens neither eat nor sleep, and are always alert and wide-awake.

"His mind is aware, clear, empty and still," **like a cloudless sky**. There's a Chinese saying, "No clouds for ten thousand miles – just ten thousand miles of sky." In the clear sky, the bright sun shines for thousands of miles around. In that state, the cultivator's mind is **devoid of any coarse sense-impressions**. All the shadows of coarse sense-data that characterized his former state are gone.

He contemplates everything in the world – the mountains, the rivers, and the earth – as reflections in a mirror, appearing without attachment and vanishing without any trace. His perception of the world and everything in it is like a bright mirror which reflects things and is empty when the things are gone. They leave no traces. No matter what state comes along, the cultivator does not become attached to it. When the situation passes, nothing remains. When it's gone, it's simply gone. It is said, "The mind of the past cannot be grasped, the mind of the present cannot be grasped, and the mind of the future cannot be grasped." The three minds cannot be obtained. That's why there is no attachment when they come, and no trace left when they go. **They are simply received and reflected.**

He does away with all his old habits. He empties himself of all old habits, stinking habits, evil habits, and bad habits. Take a look at the bad habits people have. Some people like to say really foul things – that's a stinky habit. Some people say mean things – that's an evil habit. Some people are generally arrogant and haughty. We have so many bad habits. But that cultivator has gotten rid of all those habits, **and only the essential truth remains**. The only thing left is the thought of essential truth, which is the eighth consciousness. At this point the first six consciousnesses and the seventh consciousness are all gone. Now only the eighth consciousness remains, and it must be transformed into the great perfect mirror wisdom of the Buddha. He has now reached this stage, but has not yet transformed it. That's what is meant by "only the essential truth remains."

K2	Introduction to the region of the formations skandha.

Sutra:

"**From this point on, as the origin of production and destruction is exposed, he will completely see all the twelve categories of living beings in the ten directions. Although he has not fathomed the source of their individual lives, he will see that they share a common basis of life, which appears as a mirage – shimmering and fluctuating – and is the ultimate, pivotal point of the illusory sense faculties and sense objects. This is the region of the formations skandha.**

Commentary:

From this point on, as the origin of production and destruction is exposed. This refers to the origin of birth and death, which lies in the subtle movements of the seventh and sixth consciousnesses. At this point, the thinking skandha has been destroyed, and the cultivator has reached the formations skandha. Therefore, as the origin is revealed, **he will completely see all the twelve categories of living beings in the ten directions.** He exhaustively understands each of the twelve categories, which include beings born from eggs up to beings not completely without thought.

Although he has not fathomed the source of their individual lives, he will see that they share a common basis of life, which appears as a mirage – shimmering and fluctuating. He does not completely understand how each individual came into being, but he does perceive the origin of all the twelve categories of beings. This origin appears to him like a mirage. Sometimes in the spring you may see what seems to be a body of water in the distance, but when you reach the spot there is no water. Zhuang Zi called this mirage a "wild horse," a poetic reference to the cloud of dust stirred up by a galloping horse. In the *Shurangama Sutra*, it's literally called "solar flames." It refers to the vapor that rises from the earth in the springtime, forming a mirage. It's said that wherever these mirages appear, the geomantic properties are pretty good. Thus, whether the

Buddhist sutras read "solar flames" or "wild horse," the reference is to mirages. "Shimmering" means that there's a bit of light, but it's not clear. "Fluctuating" means that the state of disturbance is not very great.

And is the ultimate, pivotal point of the illusory sense faculties and sense objects. The six sense faculties are the eyes, ears, nose, tongue, body and mind. These are all illusory, not real. In Chinese, "pivotal point" is expressed by characters for the pivot on which a Chinese door hangs and the place where the pivot is anchored so that the door can be opened and closed. Nowadays we use two metal hinges, but in ancient China the doors were hung on pivots that were anchored in holes. **This** situation **is** known as **the region of the formations skandha.**

J2 Ultimately it breaks up and reveals its false source.

Sutra:

"Once the basic nature of this shimmering fluctuation returns to its original clarity, his habits will cease, like waves subsiding to become clear, calm water. This is the end of the formations skandha. This person will then be able to transcend the turbidity of living beings. Contemplating the cause of the formations skandha, one sees that subtle and hidden false thoughts are its source.

Commentary:

Once the basic nature of this shimmering fluctuation returns to its original clarity, his habits will cease, like waves subsiding to become clear, calm water. The nature of this small amount of light is such that, after a long while, it will revert to its original stillness and clarity. Once it settles and becomes clear, the original, pure nature appears. When that happens, those kinds of habits will disappear like subsiding waves.

The thinking skandha is like a rapidly flowing torrent. The comparison was made earlier in the sutra. Now the analogy is to waves, as in a swift current or a torrent. When the waves subside, the water clears and settles. **This is the end of the formations skandha.** The thinking skandha is like a gushing torrent, whereas the formations skandha is like ripples on the water. When only the consciousness skandha remains, there are no more waves in the clear, settled water. This is called "the end of the formations skandha."

This person will then be able to transcend the state of **the turbidity of living beings. Contemplating the cause of the formations skandha, one sees that subtle and hidden false thoughts are its source.** When you reach this point you still have false thinking, but it is not so apparent. It is hidden and obscured, not easy to detect at all. These extremely subtle false thoughts are the source of the formations skandha.

I2   The ten speculations therein.
J1   Two theories on the absence of cause.
K1   Describes the source and shows the error.

Sutra:

"**Ananda, you should know that when the good person has obtained proper knowledge in his practice of shamatha, his mind is unmoving, clear, and proper, and it cannot be disturbed by the ten kinds of demons from the heavens. He is now able to intently and thoroughly investigate the origin of all categories of beings. As the origin of each category becomes apparent, he can contemplate the source of the subtle, fleeting, and pervasive fluctuation. But if he begins to speculate on that pervasive source, he could fall into error with two theories of the absence of cause.**

Commentary:

Ananda, you should know that when the good person has obtained proper knowledge in his practice of the still reflection of **shamatha** or concentration, **his mind is unmoving, clear, and proper.** Within samadhi, his mind becomes bright and concentrated, **and it cannot be disturbed by the ten kinds of demons from the heavens.** They can't disturb the cultivator. **He is now**

able to have the chance to **intently and thoroughly investigate** samadhi and fathom **the origin of all** twelve **categories of beings.**

As the origin of each category becomes apparent, as he exposes the source of each category, **he can contemplate the source of the subtle, fleeting, and pervasive fluctuation.** He contemplates this elusive state which is difficult to detect. The pervasive fluctuation is a subtle movement that occurs within the seventh consciousness. **But if he** suddenly initiates a change and **begins to speculate about that pervasive source** – the perfect inherent nature – **he could fall into error with two theories of the absence of cause.**

K2   Detailed explanation of their appearance.
L1   He sees no cause for the origin of life.
M1   He describes the measure of his vision.

Sutra:

"**First perhaps this person sees no cause for the origin of life. Why? Since he has completely destroyed the mechanism of production, he can, by means of the eight hundred merits of the eye organ, see all beings in the swirling flow of karma during eighty thousand eons, dying in one place and being reborn in another as they undergo transmigration. But he cannot see beyond eighty thousand eons.**

Commentary:

The **first** of the two theories of the nonexistence of cause is that **this person sees no cause for the origin of life.** He sees that, at the source of it all, there is no cause which makes a person a person. **Why? He has completely destroyed the mechanism of production.** That is, he has cut off the thinking skandha. The formations skandha is like ripples on the water. After he has broken through the thinking skandha, he has "destroyed the mechanism of production." The mechanism that produces false thoughts has been destroyed, and he does no more false thinking. Why did the text say earlier that a person has no more dreams after he breaks through the thinking skandha? It's because he has destroyed the mechanism that creates false thinking.

He can, by means of the eight hundred merits of the eye organ, see all beings in the swirling flow of karma during eighty thousand eons. Although each sense organ has a potential of twelve hundred merits, the eye organ does not function in total capacity and has only eight hundred merits. Once he breaks through the thinking skandha, he can see the events that occur within eighty thousand eons. He sees beings **dying in one place and being reborn in another as they undergo transmigration.** The flow of karma created by living beings in this world can be likened to a current or to the sea. He can see beings swirling in that flow over a period of eighty thousand great eons, dying in one place and being reborn in another, time after time. **But he cannot see** any of the events that occur **beyond eighty thousand eons.**

M2 He comes up with a wrong speculation.

Sutra:

"**Therefore, he concludes that for the last eighty thousand eons living beings in the ten directions of this and other worlds have come into being without any cause.**

Commentary:

Therefore, since he cannot see the events that occurred more than eighty thousand great eons ago, **he concludes that for the last eighty thousand eons living beings in the ten directions of this and other worlds have come into being without any cause.** They just come into being by themselves, without any cause or conditions. They are born spontaneously.

M3 He mistakes the principle and falls for an externalist teaching.

Sutra:

"**Because of this speculation, he will lose proper and pervasive knowledge, fall into externalism, and become confused about the bodhi nature.**

Commentary:

Because of this speculation, this conjecture that goes off-track, **he will lose proper and pervasive knowledge, fall into externalism,** join an external sect, **and become confused about the bodhi nature,** the nature of the bodhi mind.

L2 He sees no cause for the end of life.
M1 He describes the measure of his vision.

Sutra:

"**Second, perhaps this person sees no cause for the end of life. And why? Since he perceives the origin of life, he believes that people are always born as people and birds are always born as birds; that crows have always been black and swans have always been white; that humans and gods have always stood upright and animals have always walked on four legs; that whiteness does not come from being washed and blackness does not come from being dyed; and that there have never been nor will there be any changes for eighty thousand eons.**

Commentary:

What is the **second** view? **Perhaps this person sees no cause for the end of life.** The first is that he sees no cause for the beginning of things, and here he sees no cause for the end. **And why? Since he perceives the origin of life,** the beginning of all living beings, **he believes that people are always born as people and birds are always born as birds.** Believing that he has been enlightened and has attained great wisdom, he thinks he knows. What does he think he knows? He says, "People are people in life after life, and birds are birds in life after life."

Crows have always been black. They are black to begin with; they don't have to be dyed that color. **And swans have always been white.** They are white from birth. **Humans and gods have always stood upright.** Humans and celestial beings all walk erect. **And animals have always walked on four legs.** Animals walk horizontally, with their four legs on the ground. This is all fixed. **Their whiteness does not come from being washed, and their**

blackness does not come from being dyed. For example, crows are black, but they weren't dyed black. Also, swans did not have to be washed to become white. **And there have never been nor will there be any changes for eighty thousand eons.**

[January 1983]

Disciple: Since the person is able to see events that happened within twenty thousand, forty thousand, and even eighty thousand great eons, why is he unable to see people being reborn in other paths as they undergo transmigration?

Venerable Master: That's an interesting question. You must realize that although the text says he can see for twenty thousand great eons, he is actually under the influence of a false state. One thought is equivalent to limitless eons, and limitless eons are just one thought. He feels it is twenty thousand eons, but it may not really be that long; he is still caught up in a false state. Controlled by false thinking, he experiences a totally unreal state in which he sees pigs being pigs and cows being cows for twenty thousand eons. Although he feels that it's that way, his perception is not correct. If it were really twenty thousand eons, then of course pigs would undergo transmigration and would not remain as pigs during all that time! The fact that he claims that they do shows that he is totally fake. Although he says that he can see for twenty thousand great eons, it's not necessarily such a long time. That's only his own feeling.

For instance, Mr. Wu from Taiwan said, "Oh, I feel that I was together with so-and-so in the Sixth Patriarch's dharma assembly during the Tang dynasty."

That's just the kind of state we are discussing. The very fact that he feels this to be the case indicates that it is not true; if it were true, there would have to be some evidence. And he shouldn't go around advertising himself. If what he said were true, how could he bear to leave so soon after being reunited with that person? Has he really put everything down? Why is he going back to Taiwan to attend to other business? He made that claim just to confuse people. Those people, unable to distinguish right from wrong, exclaim, "Incredible! He must be psychic – he knows that he was with this person back in the Tang dynasty." So what? If you know that but you don't cultivate, you'll still fall and become a ghost.

Therefore, you have to perceive things clearly; it takes genuine wisdom to know why a person speaks a certain way. Mr. Wu saw that so-and-so was quite influential at the City of Ten Thousand Buddhas and at Gold Mountain Monastery, and he thought it would be advantageous to claim that he was associated with that person. That person silently acknowledged the claim, which was equivalent to saying, "Right, he and I really did study the dharma together in the assembly of the Great Master, the Sixth Patriarch." Notice how that elevates his own status. It is just like when another person came to the City of Ten Thousand Buddhas and talked about how we all supported him. These cases are very similar, but they used different methods to deceive people.

Pay close attention to this. As I said before, the false paves the way for the true. First there is the false, which makes people all muddled and confused. Later, some people who seek the truth set off in quest of the proper dharma. When people reach a dead-end, they begin to pursue the proper dharma. Therefore,

> That which is contrary is the movement of the Way.
> That which is weak is the function of the Way.
> Purity is the source of the turbidity.
> Movement is the foundation of stillness.

The Way contains opposites; when we study the Buddhadharma, we must have genuine dharma-selecting vision so that we can distinguish true teachings, false teachings, black methods, white methods, proper dharma, and deviant devices. If you can recognize them, you'll be all right. If you're so muddled that you don't recognize what's true and what's false, if you jump to conclusions without analyzing things carefully, then you're in for trouble.

For that reason, we should constantly investigate the *Shurangama Sutra*. The couplet on the main entrance to our Wayplace says, "The Avatamsaka Dharma Assembly and the Shurangama Platform." Since we are in the Shurangama Platform, we are now investigating the fifty skandha demons and afterwards we will study the perfect penetrations of the twenty-five sages. Then we can investigate the four clear, unalterable instructions on purity. In this way, we will investigate the *Shurangama Sutra*, passage by passage, section by section, until we understand it clearly. Nowadays the followers of demons, goblins, ghosts, and freaks claim that the *Shurangama Sutra* is false. Hearing them, people lose their faith and say, "Oh, the *Shurangama Sutra* is false; no matter what you say, it's false."

We should believe in reason. If a person's words make sense, we should believe them. If they don't make sense, if they do not accord with the proper dharma and the precepts, then even if what they say is true, we should regard it as false. How can we distinguish the true from the false, the black from the white? Don't be so muddled that you take wrong knowledge and views as correct, and proper knowledge and views as incorrect. To do that would be to seriously invert right and wrong. You would lose your vision and become blind, because you wouldn't be able to tell black from white. People who hold to wrong knowledge and views undergo the retribution of having no eyes, because they have blinded others and led others astray. Pay close attention to this. The law of cause and effect is very serious; it is not off by a bit. From my experience, I know that we cannot do even the slightest wrong deed, for if we do, we will soon have to undergo the retribution.

M2 He comes up with a wrong speculation.

Sutra:

"He says, 'As I now examine to the end of this life, I find the same holds true. In fact, I have never seen bodhi, so how can there be such a thing as the attainment of bodhi? You should

now realize that there is no cause for the existence of any phenomena.'

Commentary:

This person is able to see the events that occur within eighty thousand great eons, so **he says, "As I now examine to the end of this life,** the life of this physical body, **I find the same holds true."** Just like the living beings that he perceives within eighty thousand great eons, his body also has no source from which it comes. He says, **"In fact, I have never seen bodhi.** I have yet to see what bodhi looks like, **so how can there be such a thing as the attainment of bodhi?** I've looked throughout the eighty thousand great eons and haven't even caught a glimpse of bodhi, so why should I believe that it is possible to attain bodhi? **You should now realize that there is no cause for the existence of any phenomena**; for no reason whatsoever, they come into being." Actually, he can only see within the range of eighty thousand great eons, and he has no idea of what occurs beyond that period of time.

When the Buddha was in the world, an old man came to the monastery wishing to leave the home-life. The Buddha was away on the road and not at the monastery. The arhats there all took a look at the old man, who was probably over eighty years old, with wrinkled skin, white hair, and an unsteady gait. Whenever a person requested to leave the home-life, the arhats would look into his past causes and future effects. Now they contemplated the old man's causes and found that in the past eighty thousand eons he had not planted a single good root; he had not done any good deeds.

The great arhats said, "Since you didn't plant good roots, you cannot leave the home-life."

You shouldn't think leaving home is so easy. To leave home, you have to plant good roots for bodhi in life after life. So the arhats told the old man, "Although you wish to leave the home-life now, since you don't have any good roots, we can't allow you to leave home. You'd better go."

When the old man heard that, he began to cry. He began to weep as he thought about his unlucky fate. At such an advanced age, he had wished to leave the homelife and had been rejected by the Buddha's disciples. As he walked along crying, he thought, "I might as well commit suicide. I could hang myself or throw myself into the river. I don't want to live anymore." However, his one thought of sincerity evoked a response. The Buddha came back and asked him, "What are you crying for?"

He said, "I wanted to leave the home-life, but the Buddha wasn't at the monastery and the Buddha's disciples wouldn't allow me to leave home. They said that I hadn't planted any good roots or done any good deeds in the last eighty thousand great eons. That's why I think I'd be better off dead. There's no point in living."

The Buddha said, "Don't cry anymore. I will help you. I will let you leave the home-life. Come with me to the monastery." Thus the old man returned to the monastery and left the home-life under the Buddha. All of the Buddha's disciples were perplexed.

"Strange! The Buddha accepts only those who have good roots. Why did the Buddha accept that old man, who didn't have any good roots?" the disciples wondered.

The Buddha told them, "You arhats can only see the events that occur within eighty thousand great eons. You don't know what goes on beyond this period. More than eighty thousand great eons ago, this old man was a woodcutter in the mountains. One day he saw a tiger and climbed up a tree to save himself. The tiger started gnawing at the tree, intending to devour the man. When it had just about chewed through the tree, the man got so nervous that he cried out, 'Namo Buddha!' The tiger immediately left. When it had gone far away, the man climbed down from the tree and went home, saved from being eaten by the tiger. His one recitation of 'Namo Buddha' planted the seed for a good root more than eighty thousand years ago. It is now time for that seed to sprout and bear fruit. That's why he is now able to leave the home-life." The Buddha's explanation resolved his disciples' doubts.

The cultivator of samadhi says there is no cause for the existence of anything because he is unaware of the events occurring beyond the period of eighty thousand great eons.

M3 He mistakes the principle and falls for an externalist teaching.

Sutra:

"**Because of this speculation, he will lose proper and pervasive knowledge, fall into externalism, and become confused about the bodhi nature.**

Commentary:

Because of this speculation, he will lose proper and pervasive knowledge and views, **fall into externalism, and become confused about the bodhi nature.** He will not understand the bodhi nature.

K3 Concludes that it is an externalist teaching.

Sutra:

"**This is the first external teaching, which postulates the absence of cause.**

Commentary:

It maintains that there is no origin or cause for anything.

J2 Four theories regarding pervasive permanence.
K1 Describes their source and shows the error.

Sutra:

"**Ananda, in his practice of samadhi, the good person's mind is unmoving, clear, and proper and can no longer be disturbed by demons. He can thoroughly investigate the origin of all categories of beings and contemplate the source of the subtle, fleeting, and constant fluctuation. But if he begins to speculate on its pervasive constancy, he could fall into error with four theories of pervasive permanence.**

Commentary:

Ananda, in his practice of samadhi, the good person's mind is unmoving, clear, and proper. His proper mind has the wisdom that develops from samadhi, **and** it **can no longer be disturbed by demons.** By now, the demon kings can no longer use their tricks to disturb his samadhi. But sometimes transformations happen in his own formations skandha, causing him to have wrong ideas. These are known as "demons of one's own mind."

He can thoroughly investigate the origin of all categories of beings and contemplate the source of the subtle, fleeting, and constant fluctuation. He examines the ephemeral and elusive origin of all beings and finds a subtle movement a constant vibration. **But if he begins to speculate on its pervasive constancy,** that subtle fluctuation, **he could fall into error with four theories of pervasive permanence.** This person could give rise to wrong speculations and be ensnared in the views of pervasive permanence. What are the four theories?

K2 Detailed explanation of their appearance.
L1 He speculates that the mind and states are permanent.

Sutra:

"**First, as this person thoroughly investigates the mind and its states, he may conclude that both are causeless. Through his cultivation, he knows that in twenty thousand eons, as beings in the ten directions undergo endless rounds of birth and death, they are never annihilated. Therefore, he speculates that the mind and its states are permanent.**

Commentary:

First, as this person thoroughly investigates the nature of the **mind and its states, he may** come up with a wrong view and **conclude that both are causeless.** There is no source from which they spring.

Through his cultivation, he knows that in twenty thousand eons, as beings in the ten directions undergo endless rounds of

birth and death, they are never annihilated. Through the cultivation of samadhi, he becomes aware of the production and destruction of all living beings within twenty thousand eons. He sees them going through the endless cycle, being born and dying, over and over. Yet they are never annihilated. **Therefore, he speculates that the mind and its states are permanent** and will never change.

L2 He speculates that the four elements are permanent.

Sutra:

"Second, as this person thoroughly investigates the source of the four elements, he may conclude that they are permanent in nature. Through his cultivation, he knows that in forty thousand eons, as living beings in the ten directions undergo births and deaths, their substances exist permanently and are never annihilated. Therefore, he speculates that this situation is permanent.

Commentary:

What is the **second** theory? **As this person thoroughly investigates the source of the four elements** – earth, water, fire, and air – **he may conclude that they are permanent in nature.** He claims the natures of earth, water, fire, and air are permanent and indestructible. Actually earth, water, fire, and air are created from the false thoughts of living beings and have no substance at all. Without any substance, how can they be permanent? That is a misconception. **Through his cultivation, he knows that in forty thousand eons, as living beings in the ten directions undergo births and deaths, their substances exist permanently and are never annihilated. Therefore, he speculates that this situation is permanent.** He says that the nature of their births and deaths is permanent and unchanging. It has never been interrupted. That is the second theory.

L3 He speculates that the eight consciousnesses are permanent.

Sutra:

"Third, as this person thoroughly investigates the sixth sense faculty, the manas, and the consciousness that grasps and receives, he concludes that the origin of mind, intellect, and consciousness is permanent. Through his cultivation, he knows that in eighty thousand eons, as all living beings in the ten directions revolve in transmigration, this origin is never destroyed and exists permanently. Investigating this undestroyed origin, he speculates that it is permanent.**

Commentary:

Third, as this person thoroughly investigates the sixth sense faculty – the sixth (mind) consciousness, **the manas** consciousness, which was previously called the defiled consciousness, **and the consciousness that grasps and receives, he concludes that the origin of mind, intellect and consciousness** – of the sixth and seventh consciousnesses – **is** fundamentally **permanent**.

Through his cultivation of the skill of directing the hearing inward to listen to the inherent nature, **he knows that in eighty thousand eons, as all living beings in the ten directions revolve in transmigration,** undergoing repeated births and deaths, **this origin is never destroyed and exists permanently** and without change. **Investigating this undestroyed origin, he speculates that it is permanent** and not subject to change.

L4 He speculates that the cessation of thoughts is permanent.

Sutra:

"Fourth, since this person has ended the source of thoughts, there is no more reason for them to arise. In the state of flowing, halting, and turning, the thinking mind – which was the cause of production and destruction – has now ceased forever, and so he naturally thinks that this is a state of non-production and non-destruction. As a result of such reasoning, he speculates that this state is permanent.

Commentary:

Fourth, since this person has ended the source of thoughts, there is no more reason for them to arise. Once he breaks through the thinking skandha, the cause for false thoughts to arise is gone.

He has samadhi power over the thoughts in his mind. With an unmoving, clear, and proper mind, he has no opportunity to entertain false thoughts. **In the state of flowing, halting, and turning of the formations skandha, the thinking mind – which was the cause of production and destruction – has now ceased forever.** He no longer has false thoughts, **and so he naturally thinks that this is a state of non-production and non-destruction. As a result of such reasoning, he speculates that this state is permanent** and unchanging.

K3 Concludes that it is an externalist teaching.

Sutra:

"**Because of these speculations of permanence, he will lose proper and pervasive knowledge, fall into externalism, and become confused about the bodhi nature. This is the second external teaching, which postulates pervasive permanence.**

Commentary:

Because of these speculations, these four theories **of pervasive permanence, he will lose** the wisdom of **proper and pervasive knowledge, fall into externalism, and become confused about the bodhi nature**. Once he starts following external teachings, he will not be able to understand the bodhi nature. **This is the second external teaching, which postulates pervasive permanence.**

J3 Four upside-down theories.
K1 Describes the source and shows the error.

Sutra:

"**Further, in his practice of samadhi, the good person's mind is firm, unmoving, and proper and can no longer be disturbed by demons. He can thoroughly investigate the origin of all categories of beings and contemplate the source of the subtle, fleeting, and constant fluctuation. But if he begins to speculate about self and others, he could fall into error with theories of partial impermanence and partial permanence based on four distorted views.**

Commentary:

Further, in his practice of samadhi, the good person's mind is firm, unmoving, and proper and can no longer be disturbed by demons. When this good person cultivates and attains solid samadhi, his mind becomes proper, so (external) demons have no chance to obstruct him. However, demons may arise within his own mind. **He can thoroughly investigate the origin of all twelve categories of beings and contemplate the source of the subtle, fleeting, and constant fluctuation** that appears in the formations skandha at this stage in his cultivation.

But if he begins to speculate about self and others, he could fall into error with theories of partial impermanence and partial permanence based on four distorted views. Indulging in false thoughts about self and others, he creates demons in his own mind and comes up with four distorted views. He says that things are both permanent and impermanent, both produced and destroyed, both moving and still, both defiled and pure, and both alive and dead. He defends both sides of the issue and refuses to make a decision. He says, "This way is right, and that way is also right." He says things are impermanent, but he also says things are permanent. That's upside-down. His lack of resolution confuses people.

K2 Detailed explanation of their appearance.
L1 Speculation regarding self and others.

Sutra:

"**First, as this person contemplates the wonderfully bright mind pervading the ten directions, he concludes that this state of profound stillness is the ultimate spiritual self. Then he speculates, 'My spiritual self, which is settled, bright and unmoving, pervades the ten directions. All living beings are within my mind, and there they are born and die by themselves. Therefore, my mind is permanent, while those who undergo birth and death there are truly impermanent.'**

Commentary:

What does he say in his first theory? **First, as this person** who cultivates the Way **contemplates the wonderfully bright mind fully pervading the ten directions, he concludes that this state of profound stillness** and purity **is the ultimate spiritual self. Then he speculates, "My spiritual self, which is settled, bright and unmoving, pervades the ten directions.** My mind is in a state of unmoving suchness, replete with samadhi power and wisdom that are perfectly bright and unmoving."

He says, "Since my mind pervades the ten directions, **all living beings are** contained **within my mind, and there they are born and die by themselves,** over and over. **Therefore, my mind is permanent** and not subject to birth and death, **while those who undergo birth and death there are truly impermanent.** The living beings in my mind are continually undergoing birth and death. Therefore, they must be impermanent in nature. My mind pervades the ten directions, permanent and unchanging. But the beings within it, undergoing birth and death, are impermanent."

L2　Speculation regarding worlds.

Sutra:

"Second, instead of contemplating his own mind, this person contemplates in the ten directions worlds as many as the Ganges' sands. He regards as ultimately impermanent those worlds that are in eons of decay, and as ultimately permanent those that are not in eons of decay.

Commentary:

Second, instead of contemplating his own mind, this person contemplates in the ten directions worlds as many as the Ganges' sands. He does not look within his mind, as above when he saw his own mind pervading the ten directions. Rather, he looks outside at the worlds in the ten directions, as numerous as the Ganges' sands.

He regards as ultimately impermanent those worlds that are in eons of decay, and as ultimately permanent those that are not in eons of decay. He sees a certain world that has reached the eon of decay in the cycle of becoming, dwelling, decay and emptiness, and he claims that it is ultimately impermanent in nature. Seeing another world that is not in the eon of decay, he says that it is ultimately permanent. So there are both impermanence and permanence.

L3 Speculation regarding his body and mind.

Sutra:

"Third, this person closely examines his own mind and finds it to be subtle and mysterious, like fine motes of dust swirling in the ten directions, unchanging in nature. And yet it can cause his body to be born and then to die. He regards that indestructible nature as his permanent intrinsic nature, and that which undergoes birth and death and flows forth from him as impermanent.

Commentary:

In the **third** distorted theory, **this person closely examines his own mind and finds it to be subtle and mysterious.** He scrutinizes his own mind in its most subtle and mysterious aspects. These aspects, which are so elusive that they can hardly be perceived, characterize the formations skandha. These states are like tiny ripples on water, or **like fine motes of dust swirling in the ten directions.** The continuous flowing movement is **unchanging in nature. And yet it can cause his body to be born and then to die.** It causes his body to undergo repeated births and deaths.

He regards that indestructible nature of the flowing movement **as his permanent intrinsic nature.** He says, "This is the permanence of my own nature." **And that which undergoes birth and death and flows forth from him as impermanent.** He says, "All the beings that are born and die, over and over, flowing forth from this permanent nature of mine, are themselves impermanent in nature."

| L4 | Speculation regarding neither self nor others. |

Sutra:

"**Fourth, knowing that the skandha of thinking has ended and seeing the flowing of the skandha of formations, this person speculates that the continuous flow of the skandha of formations is permanent, and that the skandhas of form, feeling, and thinking which have already ended are impermanent.**

Commentary:

Fourth, knowing that the skandha of thinking has ended and seeing the subtle **flowing,** like ripples, **of the skandha of formations** as he cultivates, **this person speculates that the continuous flow of the skandha of formations is permanent.** Seeing no change in it, he concludes, "Oh, it must be permanent in nature." **And that the skandhas of form, feeling, and thinking which have already ended are impermanent.** Since they are gone, he thinks they must be impermanent.

| K3 | Concludes that it is an externalist teaching. |

Sutra:

"**Because of these speculations of impermanence and permanence, he will fall into externalism and become confused about the bodhi nature. This is the third external teaching, which postulates partial permanence.**

Commentary:

Because of these four wrong theories based on his **speculations of impermanence and permanence, he will** lose proper and pervasive knowledge, **fall into externalism, and become confused about the bodhi nature.** He says, "This part is permanent and that part is impermanent." Because he has these inverted theories and doesn't even understand their implications himself, he adopts the ideas of external teachings and becomes confused about the actual nature of bodhi. **This is the third external teaching, which postulates partial permanence.** This third inverted theory advocated by external sects maintains that things are partially permanent and partially impermanent.

J4 Four theories regarding finiteness.
K1 Describes the source and shows the error.

Sutra:

"**Further, in his practice of samadhi, the good person's mind is firm, unmoving, and proper and can no longer be disturbed by demons. He can thoroughly investigate the origin of all categories of beings and contemplate the source of the subtle, fleeting, and constant fluctuation. But if he begins to speculate about the making of certain distinctions, he could fall into error with four theories of finiteness.**

Commentary:

Further, in his practice of samadhi, the good person's mind is firm, unmoving, and proper and can no longer be disturbed by demons. This refers to any good person who cultivates the samadhi of directing the hearing inward to listen to his own nature, thus attaining perfect penetration of the ear organ. When he has broken through the three skandhas of form, feeling and thinking, he has solid samadhi and his mind is proper. Thus, the demons of the heavens and those of external sects cannot affect him in any way.

When the two skandhas of form and feeling still existed, the demons from the heavens were able to disturb his mind directly. When he reached the thinking skandha, the demons could no longer do so; they had to possess another person in order to disrupt his samadhi. Now, at the stage of the formations skandha, the demons cannot disturb his samadhi even if they possess another person. That's what is meant by a "firm, unmoving, and proper" mind. The demons can not get at him.

He can thoroughly investigate the origin of all twelve **categories of beings and contemplate the source of the subtle, fleeting, and constant fluctuation.** He contemplates this most concealed, ephemeral nature of living beings, within the subtle movement of the formations skandha. **But if he begins to**

speculate about the making of certain distinctions. He ponders and reflects, and makes four kinds of distinctions, which will be discussed below. **He could** then **fall into error with four theories of finiteness.** Once he gets to thinking, he comes up with four theories of finiteness which belong to external teachings.

K2 Detailed explanation of their appearance.
L1 Speculation regarding the three periods of time.

Sutra:

"First, this person speculates that the origin of life flows and functions ceaselessly. He judges that the past and the future are finite and that the continuity of the mind is infinite.

Commentary:

The first of the four distinctions regards the three periods of time – the past, the present, and the future. It's said, "You may search for the mind in the three periods of time, but the mind is not there." The mind of the past cannot be obtained, the mind of the present cannot be obtained, and the mind of the future cannot be obtained. Why not? Let's consider the past. What is the past? The past has already gone by, so the mind of the past cannot be obtained. As for the present, it never stops. Right now, you say this is the present, but it has already become the past. If you then say this is the present, it too has passed. The present never stays fixed, so where is your present mind? What about the future mind? The future has not come yet. Since it hasn't arrived, it doesn't exist, either. Therefore,

> You may search for the mind in the three periods of time,
> > but it is not there.
> Where there is no mind,
> > false conditions do not exist.

Since even the mind is gone, where could there be any false thoughts? If you can understand this principle, you will find that there actually aren't any! In the treasury of the Tathagata, there is nothing at all.

This cultivator, however, has developed an attachment. What is he attached to? The ideas of finite and infinite. He says things are either finite or infinite, setting up so-called "theories" of what is finite and infinite. **First, this person speculates that the origin of life flows and functions ceaselessly.** In the state of the formations skandha, he conjectures that the origin of the twelve categories of living beings flows and functions without interruption. This ceaseless flowing and functioning is a manifestation of the formations skandha.

At that time, **he judges that the past and the future are finite.** He says that the past and the future are both bounded, but that's nonsense. How could the past and the future be finite? Based on his false speculations and attachments, he says that they are finite, but in fact, they are infinite. In the course of cultivation, his mind has become muddled, and he has no wisdom. Having broken through the thinking skandha, he gets confused and strays off the proper path in the formations skandha. That's why he makes conjectures of the finite and the infinite. **And** he reckons **that the continuity of the mind is infinite.** He says, "This present mind continues without interruption in the present. It has no limit or boundary, and is infinite."

L2   Speculation regarding what he hears and sees.

Sutra:

"**Second, as this person contemplates an interval of eighty thousand eons, he can see living beings; but earlier than eighty thousand eons is a time of stillness in which he cannot hear or see anything. He regards as infinite that time in which nothing is heard or seen, and as finite that interval in which living beings are seen to exist.**

Commentary:

What is the second distinction? It is the distinction of what he can see and hear and what he cannot see and hear. He takes what he can see and hear as one side, and what he cannot see and hear as the other side, so he falls into duality again. Neither side is the Middle Way.

Second, as this person contemplates an interval of eighty thousand eons, he can see living beings. When he sits in meditation, his samadhi allows him to contemplate an interval as long as eighty thousand great eons, and he can perceive all the twelve categories of beings within that time. **But earlier than eighty thousand eons is a time of stillness in which he cannot hear or see anything.** He can see with extreme clarity the events within the interval of eighty thousand eons. He can see beings undergoing endless rounds of birth and death. But he cannot see or hear what is happening outside of that interval.

He regards as infinite and unbounded **that time in which nothing is heard or seen, and as finite** and bounded **that interval in which living beings are seen to exist.** He falls into duality again, becoming attached to existence and nonexistence. Attaching to nonexistence means clinging to emptiness. Attaching to existence means clinging to forms. Neither accords with the Middle Way. Therefore the Buddha criticizes such a person for following an external sect.

L3 Speculation regarding self and others.

Sutra:

"**Third, this person speculates that his own pervasive knowledge is infinite and that all other people appear within his awareness. And yet, since he himself has never perceived the nature of their awareness, he says they have not obtained an infinite mind, but have only a finite one.**

Commentary:

Third, this person speculates that his own pervasive knowledge is infinite. The third distinction is the distinction between self and others. "Others" refers to living beings, and "self" refers to the cultivator himself. He makes yet another false speculation and becomes attached to it. He says, "I feel that I possess the wisdom of pervasive knowledge." What is meant by pervasive knowledge? Pervasive knowledge means there is nothing that is not known; therefore, it has the quality of being infinite.

And he says **that all other people,** all living beings, **appear within his awareness.** They are all contained within his wisdom.

And yet, since he himself has never perceived the nature of their awareness, he says they have not obtained an infinite mind, but have only a finite one. Living beings have not obtained a boundless mind, but he himself has. Because he does not know the nature of their knowledge, he says that they have not obtained a boundless mind and do not have boundless wisdom, but have only a bounded wisdom. That is the distinction of self and others.

L4 Speculation regarding production and destruction.

Sutra:

"Fourth, this person thoroughly investigates the formations skandha to the point that it becomes empty. Based on what he sees, in his mind he speculates that each and every living being, in its given body, is half living and half dead. From this he concludes that everything in the world is half finite and half infinite.

Commentary:

Fourth, this person thoroughly investigates the formations skandha to the point that it becomes empty. What is the fourth distinction? It is that of the living and the dead. He examines the formations skandha to the utmost extent, until it becomes empty. **Based on what he sees** and understands from his investigations, **in his mind he speculates that each and every living being, in its given body, is half living and half dead.** This is another false speculation and false attachment. He sees any given living being's body as half living and half dead. Since living beings are like that he draws conclusions about the whole world. **From this he concludes that everything in the world is half finite and half infinite.** Life is on the side of the finite, and death is on the side of the infinite. That's his conjecture. The more he runs, the farther away he gets.

K3 Concludes that it is an externalist teaching.

Sutra:

"**Because of these speculations about the finite and the infinite, he will fall into externalism and become confused about the bodhi nature. This is the fourth external teaching, which postulates finiteness.**

Commentary:

Because of these four **speculations about the finite and the infinite.** What does he conjecture? If it's not finite, then it's infinite. If it's not infinite, then it's finite. He keeps going back and forth like this, and generally does not stay on the Middle Way. He either goes too far or does not go far enough. Either he runs far away, or he doesn't even take a single step. Therefore, **he will** lose proper and pervasive knowledge and **fall into externalism.** External teachings either go too far, or else they don't go far enough. Neither going too far nor coming up short is the Middle Way. We should cultivate the Middle Way. The Buddha spoke of the ultimate truth of the Middle Way as neither falling into emptiness nor falling into existence. If you lean to the side of emptiness or the side of existence, then you fall into duality. It's called an external teaching because there are two sides. **And** he will **become confused about the** true **bodhi nature.** He does not recognize bodhi. **This is the fourth external teaching, which postulates finiteness.**

J5 Four kinds of sophistry.
K1 Describes the source and shows the error.

Sutra:

"**Further, in his practice of samadhi, the good person's mind is firm, unmoving, and proper and can no longer be disturbed by demons. He can thoroughly investigate the origin of all categories of beings and contemplate the source of the subtle,** fleeting, and constant fluctuation. But if he begins to speculate on what he knows and sees, he could fall into error with four distorted, false theories, which are total speculation based on the sophistry of immortality.

Commentary:

Further, in his practice of samadhi, the good person's mind is firm, unmoving, and proper and can no longer be disturbed by demons. This refers to all good people who are cultivating and abiding in samadhi; this samadhi is cultivated by many people, not just one. Since the cultivator has a steady mind in which samadhi and wisdom are equally balanced, there is no opening for the demons to get at him. But although external demons cannot bother him, internal demons arise. Internal demons are the demons created from transformations in his own mind.

He can thoroughly investigate the origin of all categories of beings and contemplate the source of the subtle, fleeting, and constant fluctuation. He looks into the origin of the twelve categories of living beings, examining the primal purity of their nature. The constant fluctuation is a very subtle, attenuated motion that occurs in the formations skandha.

But if he begins to speculate on what he knows and sees. Before he has such thoughts, there is no problem. But as soon as those thoughts arise, there is trouble. As it's said, "Opening the mouth is a mistake. Entertain a thought is wrong." As soon as you have a false thought problems arrive.

He could fall into error with four distorted, false theories, which are total speculation based on the sophistry of immortality. Total speculation refers to the "nature that is totally speculation and attachment," which I have discussed before. It is a kind of false attachment. He becomes attached to something that is not true.

[January 1983]

Looking into the question of "Who is reciting the Buddha's name?" is called "investigation." As I have said many times before, investigation means concentrating on one thing.

With concentration, it is efficacious.
With distraction, nothing is obtained.

Concentration can be compared to drilling a hole with an awl or to using a diamond drill to drill steel. The drill penetrating to the other side represents enlightenment. "Who is reciting the Buddha's name?" refers to reciting in one's mind.

"Investigating" means searching, which is different from "speculating." Searching means concentrating and looking in one place, searching for "Who?" It means looking into a principle. Speculating, on the other hand, is not a single thought. Rather, it involves thinking about this and about that, and making comparisons. Speculation means having a lot of false thoughts, while investigation consists of one false thought. One who is speculating thinks about several things and cannot make up his mind. He thinks about the heavens and wonders what kind of clothes God wears, what kind of hat he wears, how big his eyes are, how long his ears are, and how wide his nose is. He speculates on God's measurements, trying to measure God's size in inches and feet. But ultimately, is God really the way he speculates him to be? He's never seen God, so his measurements may not be right.

He also thinks about the earth, speculating on the earth's gravitational pull. How big is the earth's center? How large is the earth's surface area? How many specks of dust are there on the earth? He estimates that the earth is composed of a hundred million times eighty-four thousand specks of dust amassed together. He's guessing and calculating on his own, but probably even a computer wouldn't be able to compute this figure. He tries to use himself as a computer to compute it but he can't come up with the head or tail of an answer, so he thinks it's rather freaky.

Therefore, "investigating" does not fall under the formations skandha; it is not under form, feeling, thinking, formations, or consciousness. "Reciting" means you recite in your mind, concentrating single-mindedly. For example, when you recite "Namo Amitabha Buddha," there is only the phrase "Namo Amitabha

Buddha," and you have no other false thoughts. This is called fighting poison with poison. If you have lots of false thoughts, then the poison is too great and you will surely die.

K2 Detailed explanation of their appearance.
L1 Eight sophistries.

Sutra:

"First, this person contemplates the source of transformations. Seeing the movement and flow, he says there is change. Seeing the continuity, he says there is constancy. Where he can perceive something, he says there is production. Where he cannot perceive anything, he says there is destruction. He says that the unbroken continuity of causes is increasing and that the pauses within the continuity are decreasing. He says that the arising of all things is existence and that the perishing of all things is nonexistence. The light of reason shows that his application of mind has led to inconsistent views. If someone comes to seek the dharma, asking about its meaning, he replies, 'I am both alive and dead, both existent and nonexistent, both increasing and decreasing.' He always speaks in a confusing way, causing that person to forget what he was going to say.

Commentary:

First, this person, who is about to go down the path of confusion, **contemplates the source of transformations** in his formations skandha. **Seeing the movement and flow, he says there is change.** He observes the flowing of the formations skandha and says it is undergoing changes. **Seeing the continuity, he says there is constancy.** Perceiving the formations skandha continuing on without cease, he calls it constancy. "Constant" means unchanging. Change implies impermanence, while lack of change implies permanence.

Where he can perceive something, he says there is production. When he contemplates the formations skandha, some areas are visible to him. He sees the subtle movements and describes them as "production." **Where he cannot perceive**

anything, he says there is destruction. He cannot detect the tiny movements of the formations skandha, so he says this is "destruction." In other words, he can perceive the events within eighty thousand great eons, so he says they have come into being. He cannot see the events beyond eighty thousand eons, so he says they have ceased to be. This is similar to the previous cases.

He says that the unbroken continuity of causes is increasing. When the causes continue without interruption, he says there's an increase. That's another aspect of the formations skandha that he perceives. **And that the pauses within the continuity are decreasing.** Within the continuity there are pauses, and he says they are a decrease. For example, when the twenty-five sages described their perfect penetrations, one of them talked about the pause between inhaling and exhaling. That is also a "pause." He calls the pauses within the continuity "decreasing." But you shouldn't follow his theories, because he is making up his own terminology based on his perceptions, and they are fundamentally untrue. Don't look for rational principles in his theories. He just made them up, and they are totally irrational. That's why these are considered the views of external sects. There is no truth in them.

He says that the arising of all things is existence. He watches things arise within the formations skandha, and he calls that existence. **And that the perishing of all things is nonexistence.** He calls the place where everything passes away and nothing exists "nonexistent." These are the four distorted theories. **The light of reason shows that his application of mind has led to inconsistent views.** If you examine his theories in light of reason, you see that they are all wrong. He used his mind in the wrong way. At this time, **if someone comes to seek the dharma, asking about its meaning,** requesting instruction on the principles of Buddhism, **he replies** to the person, **"I am both alive and dead, both existent and nonexistent, both increasing and decreasing."**

He always speaks in a confusing way. He invariably defends both sides of the issue. If he isn't talking about existence, then he's talking about nonexistence. If he's not discussing emptiness, then he's discussing form. Because he speaks from both sides, he cannot find the Middle Way, **causing that person** who is seeking the dharma **to forget what he was going to say.** Faced with the first person's nonsensical explanations, the questioner forgets all his questions and cannot recall what he came to seek instruction in. What kind of instruction would you call that? People come wanting to understand, but the cultivator confuses them until they lose all sense of what is right. They lose not only their train of thought, but also their original wisdom and clarity of mind. This person is confused, and he makes others confused, too.

L2 The sophistry of only "no."

Sutra:

"**Second, this person attentively contemplates his mind and finds that everything is nonexistent. He has a realization based on nonexistence. When anyone comes to ask him questions, he replies with only one word. He only says 'No.' Aside from saying 'no,' he does not speak.**

Commentary:

The person only knows about nothingness, so he talks in a crazy way. He denies the existence of everything. No matter what you ask him, he says "no." That's the only word he says. **Second, this person attentively contemplates** and examines **his mind and finds that everything is nonexistent.** Among the twelve categories of living beings, he feels that in the mind of the formations skandha, everything is gone. At the point where he sees nothing, **he has a realization based on nonexistence.** He thinks that he has attained wisdom based on "nonexistence." Actually, he doesn't understand. He has gone too far overboard, and his views are completely irrational. He develops an attachment to the idea of "nonexistence" and thinks he's enlightened. What did he enlighten to? The word "no."

So **when anyone comes to ask him questions, he replies with only one word.** People think he must be a seasoned cultivator, because he keeps his eyes shut and nurtures his spirit, not saying a word all day long. He eats nothing except a few bananas. Thinking that he is a sage, they request the dharma from him. When they do, he really knows how to put on an act by giving one-word replies. This tactic is called "One-word Chan." People call it that because they don't understand what he's talking about. No matter what you ask him, **he only says "No."**

"How should I cultivate?" you ask.

"No."

"Should I recite the Buddha's name?"

"No."

"Do you think it would be a good idea to observe the moral rules and receive the precepts?"

"No."

His continual response of "no" bewilders you and you forget what you were going to say. You wonder, "What does he mean by 'no'? No what?" You can't figure it out, but then it finally hits you, "Oh! There really is nothing. It's truly nothing." **Aside from saying "no," he does not speak.** You may ask him one question, ten questions, a hundred, a thousand, or ten thousand questions, but he will always answer "no." Then you think, "The Chan principles he's talking about must be too lofty; that's why we can't understand them."

L3   The sophistry of only "yes."

Sutra:

"Third, this person attentively contemplates his mind and finds that everything is existent. He has a realization based on existence. When anyone comes to ask him questions, he replies with only one word. He only says 'Yes.' Aside from saying 'yes,' he does not speak.

Commentary:

In the **third** kind of false sophistry, **this person attentively contemplates his mind and finds that everything is existent.** He looks into his mind and sees that the twelve categories of living beings all undergo birth and death in this place of existence. **He has a realization based on existence.** Actually, he has not realized any fruition. The sutra only says that in order to describe his mistake. He contemplates living beings and says, "Ah! They all exist." Perceiving this principle, he thinks he has become enlightened and has realized the fruition.

When anyone comes to ask him questions, he replies with only one word. No matter what principle he is asked about, **he only says "Yes."**

"Would it be a good idea for me to leave the home-life and become a monk?" you ask him.

"Yes."

"Would it be good for me to take the five precepts?"

"Yes."

"What would be the best thing for me to do?"

"Yes."

Aside from saying "yes," he does not speak. He doesn't say anything but "yes," so you think, "Oh! This is really One-word Chan. He must be a lofty Sanghan. The teaching he speaks is so wonderful that I don't even understand it." It's wonderful precisely because you don't understand it. For example, if you understand what I'm now lecturing in this sutra, then it's not wonderful.

"The dharma master keeps talking and talking, but I don't understand what's he saying," you may say.

In that case, it's wonderful for you. Simply because you don't understand, it is wonderful. Once you understand it, it's not wonderful anymore. Why not? Because you understand it! Whatever you don't understand is wonderful. Therefore, if you want the wonderful, don't study the Buddhadharma. If you don't study, then you won't know it and it will be wonderful.

Regardless of what you say, he says "yes." Why is that? He believes he has become enlightened on account of the word "yes," and so he's transmitting that teaching to you.

L4 The sophistry of existence and non-existence.

Sutra:

"Fourth, this person perceives both existence and nonexistence. Experiencing this branching, his mind becomes confused. When anyone comes to ask questions, he tells them, 'Existence is also nonexistence. But within nonexistence there is no existence.' It is all sophistry and does not stand up under scrutiny.

Commentary:

His fourth fallacious theory concerns existence and nonexistence. What is this theory? He says things both exist and do not exist. But he says things that don't exist cannot also exist and things that exist cannot also not exist. He does not know whether it's existent or nonexistent. He talks wildly, like a drunkard.

Fourth, this person perceives both existence and nonexistence within the formations skandha. He perceives the formations skandha to be like waves flowing ceaselessly, so he says that it exists. He says the pauses within the ceaseless flow are nonexistence. **Experiencing this branching, his mind becomes confused.** His state has produced a branching off, just like on a tree, so he declares that things both exist and do not exist. His mind is confused because he doesn't have any true wisdom or samadhi. His wisdom and his samadhi are not balanced. At this point he becomes attached and cannot find his way out of the mess. He's confronted with a wrong road and doesn't know which road is right.

When anyone comes to ask questions and request instruction in the dharma, **he tells them, "Existence is also nonexistence.** Things that exist also do not exist. **But within nonexistence there is no existence.** But things that do not exist cannot come into existence." What already exists is also nonexistent. However, what is nonexistent does not exist. Ultimately, what kind of theory is that? **It is all sophistry.** That kind of reasoning is fallacious. He doesn't know what he's saying. That's why I said that he talks like a drunkard.

And what he says **does not stand up under scrutiny.** There's no way to hold a reasonable discussion with him. What can you do then? You can only use my method, which is to slap him across the mouth and see if he still talks about existence and nonexistence. If you slap him, he might react by asking, "Why did you hit me?"

"But you don't exist, remember? So my slapping you also doesn't exist!" There's another tactic – you can take a knife and say, "Hey! I'm gonna kill you," and see whether or not he exists. You cannot reason with him. What he says cannot stand up under scrutiny, and you shouldn't ask him about it.

K3 Concludes that it is an externalist teaching.

Sutra:

"**Because of these speculations, which are empty sophistries, he will fall into externalism and become confused about the bodhi nature. This is the fifth external teaching, which postulates four distorted, false theories that are total speculation based on the sophistry of immortality.**

Commentary:

Because of these four theories or **speculations, which are empty sophistries.** His theories are impossible imaginings. The things he says simply cannot be. There is no truth in his doctrines. For that reason, **he will fall into externalism.** Why is it called an external teaching? Because the principles in it are improper. His knowledge and views are wrong, so the principles he expounds are not ultimate. They don't get to the bottom of things. **And** he will **become confused about the bodhi nature.** He doesn't know the true path to enlightenment. The genuine path of bodhi is not clear to him. **This is the fifth external teaching, which postulates four**

distorted, false theories that are total speculation based on the sophistry of immortality.

In the first theory, he says that he is both alive and dead, both existent and non-existent, both increasing and decreasing. In the second case, he answers all questions with the word "no." He says "No, no, no" all day long, never saying any other word. No matter what anyone says to him, he just says "no." If you ask a thousand or ten thousand questions, you'll get that many replies of "no."

In the third case, he says "yes" to everything.

"Can I be a thief?" you ask.

"Yes."

"Can I take the precepts?"

"Yes."

"Is it all right to eat excrement?"

"Yes."

"Is it all right to drink urine?"

"Yes."

"Can you die?"

"Yes."

"Can you go on living in this world?"

"Yes."

No matter what you say, he says "yes," a thousand or ten thousand times. There is nothing that is not a "yes." His "yes" signifies existence – everything exists.

In the fourth case, which is the one under discussion right now, he says that existence implies non-existence, but that non-existence does not imply existence. Ultimately, what kind of principle is that? It's the kind of principle that he expounds – these four distorted theories based on the sophistry of immortality. His theories are incoherent and unclear.

They are total speculation, with no reality to them. In the past I explained
1) the nature that is totally speculation and attachment,
2) the nature that arises dependent on something else, and
3) the perfectly accomplished real nature.

I don't know if everyone is clear about the principle.

What is the "nature that is totally speculation and attachment?" Suppose you see a rope lying on the ground on a night when there isn't much moonlight. You may think, "Oh, is it a snake?" That's the "nature that is totally speculation and attachment." Actually, it's a rope, but you make the false judgment that it is a snake. Suppose you see the silhouette of a tree or a plant on a moonless night, and you think, "Oh, could that be a ghost?" and you get scared.

Maybe at night you see a dog, and you think, "Oh, is that a wolf or a tiger?" That's the "nature that is totally speculation and attachment" at work. When you get a better look, you realize that it's just a dog, not a wolf or a tiger. That's the "the nature that arises dependent on something else." Based on the dog, your "nature that is totally speculation and attachment" comes into being. It is really a dog. What is a dog? It is an animal. Because you have the "nature that is totally speculation and attachment," you mistake it for a wolf, a tiger, or some sort of strange creature. The same thing happens when you see a plant.

You thought that rope was a snake, but when you get a better look, you see that it's only a rope. The rope is called the "nature that arises dependent on something else." What is the "nature that arises dependent on something else?" Well, what is the rope made from? It's made from hemp. The hemp is called the "perfectly accomplished real nature." Hemp can be made into a rope, and that is the "nature that arises dependent on something else." Based on the "perfectly accomplished real nature," the "nature that arises dependent on something else" comes into being. Then when you do not see and recognize it clearly, the "nature that is totally speculation and attachment" comes into being. Here the follower of this external teaching is the same. What he says isn't the way things really are. He comes up with these false theories that are totally based on speculation and attachment.

J6 The sixteen ways in which form can exist after death.
K1 Describes the source and shows the error.

Sutra:

"**Further, in his practice of samadhi, the good person's mind is firm, unmoving, and proper and can no longer be disturbed by demons. He can thoroughly investigate the origin of all categories of beings and contemplate the source of the subtle, fleeting, and constant fluctuation. But if he begins to speculate on the endless flow, he could fall into error with the confused idea that forms exist after death.**

Commentary:

Further, in his practice of samadhi, the good person's mind is firm, unmoving, and proper and can no longer be disturbed by demons. This refers to any good person who cultivates and attains solid samadhi. Because he has firm samadhi and a proper mind, the demon kings cannot have their way with him. Their tricks are all played out. But although the demons' tricks cannot touch him, demons can arise right within his own mind. These demons of the mind are the most difficult to subdue.

He can thoroughly investigate the origin of all twelve **categories of beings** – that is, the fundamental source of all living beings – **and contemplate the source of the subtle, fleeting, and constant fluctuation.** He observes the elusive, light, and fleeting original nature of the twelve categories of living beings. This original nature is just the formations skandha, which is characterized by subtle fluctuation. **But if he begins to speculate on the endless flow,** the subtle fluctuation which is like the continual motion of waves on the water, **he could fall into error with the confused idea that forms exist after death.** Speculating that there is existence after death, his mind becomes confused.

| K2 | Detailed explanation of their appearance. |

Sutra:

"He may strongly identify with his body and say that form is himself; or he may see himself as perfectly encompassing all worlds and say that he contains form; or he may perceive all external conditions as contingent upon himself and say that form belongs to him; or he may decide that he relies on the continuity of the formations skandha and say that he is within form.

Commentary:

He may strongly identify with his body and say that form is himself. The person who entertains this kind of wrong attachment may want to make his body tough and durable. He claims that form, which is comprised of the four elements, is simply himself. **Or he may see himself as perfectly encompassing all worlds and say that he contains form.** He may see that his own nature is perfectly fused and unobstructed, and that all worlds in the ten directions are contained in it. Therefore, he says that he contains form. What kind of form? He says, "I have an immense form." **Or he may perceive all external conditions as contingent upon himself and say that form belongs to him.** He may say that external conditions follow him everywhere, and that the four elements of form all belong to him. **Or he may decide that he relies on the continuity of the formations skandha and say that he is within form.**

Sutra:

"In all of these speculations, he says that forms exist after death. Expanding the idea, he comes up with sixteen cases of the existence of forms.

Commentary:

In all of these speculations, he says that forms exist after death. In the above discussion about form and external conditions, there were four theories. He said:

1. The four elements of form belong to him;

2. The four elements of form are himself;
3. Form is within himself, so that he is big and form is small; and
4. Apart from him, there is no form.

In general, his talk is nonsense. There is no logic in it. In these four theories, he speculates that there is existence after death.

Expanding the idea, he comes up with sixteen cases of the existence of forms. He takes the above four theories and applies them to the four skandhas of form, feeling, thinking, and formations, thus obtaining sixteen cases of the existence of forms. Another way to formulate the sixteen cases is to combine the four skandhas of form, feeling, thinking, and formations and the four elements of earth, water, fire, and air. It's useless to ask him how he came up with these views, because there is basically no logic in them. They don't make any sense. I cannot figure them out myself, because they are unclear to begin with.

Sutra:

"Then he may speculate that afflictions are always afflictions, and bodhi is always bodhi, and the two exist side by side without contradicting each other.

Commentary:

Four times four makes sixteen ways in which forms can exist. He sees that the four theories can be applied to each of the four skandhas of form, feeling, thinking and formations, or to the four elements of earth, water, fire and air. **Then he may speculate that afflictions are always afflictions, and bodhi is always bodhi.** He says that afflictions are afflictions forever, and bodhi is bodhi forever, and that the statement, "Afflictions are simply bodhi" is wrong. **And the two exist side by side without contradicting each other.** He claims that these two function side by side without disrupting each other, that they are mutually cooperative. But this idea is fundamentally wrong. It's basically impossible. Why does he talk like this then? Because he is confused about bodhi.

K3 Concludes that it is an externalist teaching.

Sutra:

"Because of these speculations about what exists after death, he will fall into externalism and become confused about the bodhi nature. This is the sixth external teaching, which postulates confused theories of the existence of forms after death in the realm of the five skandhas.

Commentary:

The four skandhas of form, feeling, thinking, and formations are multiplied by four to generate sixteen cases for the existence of forms. He says that forms exist after death, and so **because of these speculations about what exists after death, he will fall into externalism and become confused about the bodhi nature,** his inherent enlightened nature.

This is the sixth external teaching, which postulates confused theories of the existence of forms after death in the realm of the five skandhas. "The five skandhas" here actually refers only to the four skandhas of form, feeling, thinking, and formations, and not to consciousness. He says that after people die, they continue to have form and appearance. In his disoriented state of mind, he invents this kind of theory.

J7 Eight ideas about the non-existence of form.
K1 Describes the source and shows the error.

Sutra:

"Further, in his practice of samadhi, the good person's mind is firm, unmoving, and proper, and can no longer be disturbed by demons. He can thoroughly investigate the origin of all categories of beings and contemplate the source of the subtle, fleeting, and constant fluctuation. But if he begins to speculate on the skandhas of form, feeling, and thinking, which have already ended, he could fall into error with the confused idea that forms do not exist after death.

Commentary:

Further, in his practice of samadhi, the good person's mind is firm, unmoving, and proper. This refers to any person who cultivates samadhi power. He has solid samadhi and wisdom, **and can no longer be disturbed by demons.** Although his wisdom is not ultimate and true wisdom, the demon kings cannot do anything to him. However, he is not yet able to subdue the demons of his own mind. **He can thoroughly investigate the origin of all twelve categories of** living **beings and contemplate the source of the subtle, fleeting, and constant fluctuation.** He looks into the fundamental nature of all living beings, which is elusive, light and ephemeral and characterized by subtle movements.

But if he begins to speculate on the three skandhas of form, feeling, and thinking, which have already ended, he could fall into error with the confused idea that forms do not exist after death. He says that there is no existence after death. That's the kind of upside-down theory that he comes up with.

K2 Detailed explanation of their appearance.

Sutra:

"**Seeing that his form is gone, his physical shape seems to lack a cause. As he contemplates the absence of thought, there is nothing to which his mind can become attached. Knowing that his feelings are gone, he has no further involvements. Those skandhas have vanished. Although there is still some coming into being, there is no feeling or thought, and he concludes that he is like grass or wood.**

Commentary:

Seeing that his form skandha **is gone, his physical shape seems to lack a cause.** His body has no support. It's been given away. **As he contemplates the absence of thought, there is nothing to which his mind can become attached.** He has broken through the thinking skandha, and it is gone. There is no place left for his mind to get hung up. He has no more false thinking.

Knowing that his feelings are gone – that his feeling skandha is gone, **he has no further involvements** with external conditions. **Those** three **skandhas** of form, feeling, and thinking **have vanished. Although there is still some** very small trace **of coming into being,** that is, although the formations skandha still exists, **there is no feeling or thought, and he concludes that he is like grass or wood.** Since he's devoid of feeling and thinking, he considers himself to be the same as grass and wood.

Sutra:

"Since those qualities do not exist at present, how can there be any existence of forms after death? Because of his examinations and comparisons, he decides that after death there is no existence. Expanding the idea, he comes up with eight cases of the nonexistence of forms.

Commentary:

Since those qualities do not exist at present. "Qualities" refers not only to form, but to mind as well. He says that the material aspects of form and mind are gone now. This is referring to the four skandhas of form, feeling, thinking, and formations. Remember that he says his body is like grass or wood. That means he doesn't have any awareness. Although he is alive, there's nothing at all. **How can there be any existence of forms after death?** If he cannot find any sign of existence, anything with actual form and appearance, right now in his living state, how could there be anything with form after he dies?

Because of his examinations and comparisons, he decides that after death, there is no existence. He mulls over the idea, looking at it from all angles. "If there are no forms in life, how can there be any after death? There are no forms after death either." If there is no evidence of the skandhas of form, feeling, thinking, and formations while he is alive, then there shouldn't be any evidence of them after death either. Expanding the idea, he comes up with eight cases of the nonexistence of form. There are four cases of the nonexistence of the skandhas of form, feeling, thinking, and formations during life, and four cases of their nonexistence after death. They are all gone.

Sutra:

"From that, he may speculate that nirvana and cause and effect are all empty, that they are mere names and ultimately do not exist.

Commentary:

From that, because he reasons that the four skandhas do not exist, based on the eight cases of nonexistence **he may speculate that nirvana and cause and effect are all empty.** He says that there is no nirvana, and he denies cause and effect. If it were really that way, there would be no reason for people to cultivate or become Buddhas. Why? According to his theories, there isn't anything at all. He thinks **that they are mere names and ultimately do not exist.** They are nothing but names; they do not really exist. That's what he says.

K3 Concludes that it is an externalist teaching.

Sutra:

"Because of those speculations that forms do not exist after death, he will fall into externalism and become confused about the bodhi nature. This is the seventh external teaching, which postulates confused theories of the nonexistence of forms after death in the realm of the five skandhas.

Commentary:

He says that after death, there isn't anything at all. Everything is empty. **Because of those speculations that forms do not exist after death, he will fall into** a kind of **externalism and become confused about the bodhi nature. This is the seventh external teaching, which postulates confused theories of the nonexistence of forms after death in the realm of the five skandhas.** He says that there is no existence after death within the five skandhas. That's the sort of distorted theory that his mind comes up with.

J8 Eight kinds of negation.
K1 Describes the source and shows the error.

Sutra:

"**Further, in his practice of samadhi, the good person's mind is firm, unmoving, and proper and can no longer be disturbed by demons. He can thoroughly investigate the origin of all categories of beings and contemplate the source of the subtle, fleeting, and constant fluctuation. In this state where the skandha of formations remains, but the skandhas of feeling and thinking are gone, if he begins to speculate that there is both existence and nonexistence, thus contradicting himself, he could fall into error with confused theories that deny both existence and nonexistence after death.**

Commentary:

Further, in his practice of samadhi, the good person's mind is firm, unmoving, and proper and can no longer be disturbed by demons. Again, this refers to any good person who cultivates his samadhi power, making it strong and solid. Although external demons cannot get at him, the demons of his own mind are difficult to subdue. **He can thoroughly investigate the origin of all** twelve **categories of beings and contemplate the source of the subtle, fleeting, and constant fluctuation.** He observes the mind which is elusive and fleeting. At this point there are still subtle movements in the formations skandha.

In this state where the skandha of formations remains, but the skandhas of feeling and thinking are gone, if he begins to speculate that there is both existence and nonexistence, if he says that things both exist and do not exist, **thus contradicting himself.** His own "self" is obliterated. It no longer exists. If you were to say that things exist then he would also exist. If you say things don't exist, then he doesn't exist either. When he contradicts himself, he is also destroying himself. He denies his own theories.

He could fall into error with confused theories that deny both existence and nonexistence after death. He says that after he dies, there is neither existence nor nonexistence. Then what is there? Is "neither existence nor nonexistence" the Middle Way? No. He has no regard for the Middle Way, nor has he attained the Middle Way. This is where he has gone wrong and become confused.

K2 Detailed explanation of their appearance.

Sutra:

"**Regarding form, feeling, and thinking, he sees that existence is not really existence. Within the flow of the formations skandha, he sees that nonexistence is not really nonexistence.**

Commentary:

Regarding form, feeling, and thinking, the three skandhas that he has already broken through, **he sees that existence is not really existence.** He perceives a state of existence, and yet it is not really existence. **Within the flow of the formations skandha, he sees that nonexistence is not really nonexistence.** Within the subtle fluctuation of the skandha of formations, he sees that what does not exist also seems to exist. Therefore, there is neither existence nor nonexistence. He formulates this kind of theory.

Sutra:

"**Considering back and forth in this way, he thoroughly investigates the realms of these skandhas and derives an eightfold negation of forms. No matter which skandha is mentioned, he says that after death, it neither exists nor does not exist.**

Commentary:

Earlier he saw a situation in which the previously existing form, feeling, and thinking became nonexistent, and the flowing of the formations skandha, which could later cease to exist, was still existing then. **Considering back and forth in this way,** he investigates this way and that, trying to discover the underlying principle. **He thoroughly investigates the realms of these** four skandhas of form, feeling, thinking and formations, viewing them from all angles, **and derives an eightfold negation of forms.** There are eight cases, all of which deny the existence of forms. **No matter which skandha is mentioned,** he only has one answer – **he says that after death, it neither exists nor does not exist.** He says that after death, the skandhas of form, feeling, thinking, and formations are neither existing nor nonexistent.

Sutra:

"Further, because he speculates that all formations are changing in nature, an 'insight' flashes through his mind, leading him to deny both existence and nonexistence. He cannot determine what is unreal and what is real.

Commentary:

Further, because he speculates that all formations are changing in nature. He further investigates the nature of the formations skandha. Because the formations skandha has subtle movements, it is ever flowing and changing. Then **an "insight" flashes through his mind, leading him to deny both existence and nonexistence.** A mistaken insight occurs to him, and he decides that existence and nonexistence are both invalid. Is this the Middle Way? No, he doesn't understand the ultimate meaning of the Middle Way. That's why he has no regard for the Middle Way. He only considers existence and nonexistence. So **he cannot determine what is unreal and what is real.** Things are neither unreal nor real. You say something is real, but he denies it. You say it's unreal, but he denies that too. Since he maintains that it's neither real nor unreal, he is at a loss.

K3 Concludes that it is an externalist teaching.

Sutra:

"Because of these speculations that deny both existence and nonexistence after death, the future is murky to him and he cannot say anything about it. Therefore, he will fall into externalism and become confused about the bodhi nature. This

is the eighth external teaching, which postulates confused theories that deny both existence and nonexistence after death in the realm of the five skandhas.

Commentary:

Because of these various **speculations** which he made above **that deny both existence and nonexistence after death, the future is murky to him and he cannot say anything about it.** He says that after death there is both existence and nonexistence. He cannot perceive the future end of the formations skandha. Since he cannot know it, there is nothing he can discuss, nothing he can say. **Therefore, he will fall into externalism** by following an external teaching, **and** he will **become confused about the fundamental bodhi nature. This is the eighth external teaching, which postulates confused theories that deny both existence and nonexistence after death in the realm of the five skandhas.** He says that after one dies, there is existence and yet no existence in the realm of the five skandhas. Because his mind is utterly confused, he arrives at this kind of theory.

J9 Seven theories on the cessation of existence.
K1 Describes the source and shows the error.

Sutra:

"Further, in his practice of samadhi, the good person's mind is firm, unmoving, and proper and can no longer be disturbed by demons. He can thoroughly investigate the origin of all categories of beings and contemplate the source of the subtle, fleeting, and constant fluctuation. But if he begins to speculate that there is no existence after death, he could fall into error with seven theories of the cessation of existence.

Commentary:

Further, in his practice of samadhi, the good person's mind is firm, unmoving, and proper and can no longer be disturbed by demons. The good person who cultivates samadhi has developed solid samadhi power and a proper mind, so the demons have no way to bother him.

He can thoroughly investigate the origin of all twelve categories of living beings and contemplate the source of the subtle, fleeting, and constant fluctuation. He contemplates their hidden, light, and ephemeral nature. At this point, there are subtle fluctuations in the formations skandha. **But if, since he cannot perceive any state beyond the formations skandha, he begins to speculate that there is no existence after death, he could fall into error with seven theories of the cessation of existence.** This person could come to believe in seven kinds of cessation.

K2 Detailed explanation of their appearance.

Sutra:

"**He may speculate that the body will cease to exist; or that when desire has ended, there is cessation of existence; or that after suffering has ended, there is cessation of existence; or that when bliss reaches an ultimate point, there is cessation of existence; or that when renunciation reaches an ultimate point there is cessation of existence.**

Commentary:

He may speculate that the body will cease to exist. He contemplates that in all places where living beings have bodies, their bodies will eventually perish. These places are the four great continents – Jambudvipa in the south, Purvavideha in the east, Aparagodaniya in the west and Uttarakuru in the north – and also the six desire heavens.

Or he may surmise **that when desire has ended** – beyond the desire realm, in the heavens of the first dhyana (of the four dhyanas), known as the "ground of the happiness of leaving birth" – **there is cessation of existence.** In the first dhyana, you separate from the defilements of living beings and experience joy. **Or that after suffering has ended,** in the heavens of the second dhyana, known as the "ground of the joy of developing samadhi," **there is cessation of existence.** At this point, you feel joy because you have attained samadhi.

Or that when bliss reaches an ultimate point, there is cessation of existence. He may speculate that the state of ultimate bliss in the heavens of the third dhyana will also come to an end. The third dhyana is called the "ground of the wonderful bliss of leaving joy," because one transcends happiness and experiences a subtle bliss. He surmises that the third dhyana heavens will also cease to be. **Or** he judges **that when renunciation reaches an ultimate point** – in the heavens of the fourth dhyana, known as the "ground of the purity of renouncing thought" – **there is cessation of existence.** He surmises that the heavens of the four stations of emptiness, in which there is no hindrance of form, will also cease to be.

The time passes by very quickly. Without our realizing it, the summer is already over. In China, Confucius compared life to a ceaselessly flowing stream. Time that has gone by can never return. Someone also said, "An inch of time is worth an ounce of gold, but an ounce of gold can hardly buy back an inch of time." An inch of time is as valuable as an ounce of gold. If you lose gold, it's possible to recover it. Once time has gone by, however, there is no way to get it back. Therefore, time is even more valuable than gold. Thus, in Buddhism we say, "An inch of time is an inch of life." When time grows short, one's life is also shorter. We must certainly cherish our time and not casually let it go by in vain.

During this summer, we have begun our days at six o'clock in the morning, either meditating or studying the sutras. From early in the morning until nine o'clock at night every person has applied himself or herself diligently to cultivation. I believe that this period has been more precious than gold, more valuable than diamonds. Everyone has been together, being permeated and influenced by what we have heard and cultivated. This is a most precious and valuable time in our lives. It's a pity that the time has passed by in the twinkling of an eye. Although it is nearly over, the Buddhadharma that each of us has learned has planted a precious vajra seed in our mind, in the field of our eighth consciousness. In the future it will certainly bear the indestructible fruit of vajra, which is also the Buddha-fruit – we will become Buddhas.

When will we become Buddhas? It depends on how diligently we till and irrigate the fields. The seed has been planted in the ground, but just as in farming, we have to water it, pull the weeds, and till the soil, making it soft so that the seed can sprout. How do we pull the weeds out? Weeding means that at all times, we must guard against the arising of very subtle thoughts and get rid of all false thoughts.

Every day we must apply effort in our cultivation in this way, just as farmers tend and irrigate their fields. Give it some water and pull out the weeds, day by day, and the vajra seed you have planted in the ground will produce a bodhi sprout. After your bodhi sprout comes up and grows into a bodhi tree, it will bear the bodhi fruit. But you have to protect that bodhi sprout. If you neglect to water it and tend to it, then it will wither away. What is meant by watering? If you study the Buddhadharma every day, you are irrigating your bodhi sprout with the water of the dharma, and in time, your vajra fruit will ripen. If you don't continue to care for this vajra seed after the session is over, then it will not be easy for it to sprout. You must protect your vajra seed well. Don't go back to doing the things you used to like doing. Follow the rules and behave yourselves. Don't be as wild and reckless as you used to be. If you follow the rules, then you are in accord with the Buddhadharma. If you don't then you are not. We should certainly abide by the rules and regulations. Don't be so lax and unrestrained. This is my hope for each one of you.

During this summer session of lectures on the *Shurangama Sutra*, it has surely been the case that, "Once it enters your ears, it is forever a seed of the Way." As soon as the principles of this sutra pass through your ears, they remain forever in the field of your eight consciousness as seeds of bodhi.

Sutra:

"Considering back and forth in this way, he exhaustively investigates the limits of the seven states and sees that they have already ceased to be and will not exist again.

Commentary:

Considering back and forth in this way, he exhaustively investigates the limits of the seven states mentioned above **and sees that they have already ceased to be and will not exist again.** They don't seem to exist at present, and since they are already gone, they will not come into being again. These are the seven kinds of cessation of existence.

K3 Concludes that it is an externalist teaching.

Sutra:

"**Because of these speculations that existence ceases after death, he will fall into externalism and become confused about the bodhi nature. This is the ninth external teaching, which postulates confused theories of the cessation of existence after death in the realm of the five skandhas.**

Commentary:

Because of these speculations that existence ceases after death, in which he maintains that there is nothing what-so-ever after death, that everything is annihilated, **he will fall into externalism and become confused about the bodhi nature,** about the nature of proper enlightenment. **This is the ninth external teaching, which postulates confused theories of the cessation of existence after death in the realm of the five skandhas.** In his confused mind, he thinks that existence ceases after death in the realm of form, feeling, thinking, and formations.

J10 Five kinds of immediate nirvana.
K1 Describes the source and shows the error.

Sutra:

"**Further, in his practice of samadhi, the good person's mind is firm, unmoving, and proper and can no longer be disturbed by demons. He can thoroughly investigate the origin of all categories of beings and contemplate the source of the subtle, fleeting, and constant fluctuation. But if he begins to speculate** on existence after death, he could fall into error with five theories of nirvana.

Commentary:

Further, in his practice of samadhi, the good person's mind is firm, unmoving, and proper and can no longer be disturbed by demons. Since he has solid samadhi power and a pure and proper mind, the demon kings cannot affect him in any way.

He can thoroughly investigate the origin of all twelve categories of beings and contemplate the source of the subtle, fleeting, and constant fluctuation. He examines their mind, which is hidden, light, and clear and in which there is a subtle fluctuation. But if he begins to speculate on existence after death, he could fall into error with five theories of nirvana. Beyond the formations skandha, he perceives existence again. Based on the constant, ceaseless fluctuations in the formations skandha, he makes false conjectures of existence and comes to believe in five theories regarding nirvana.

K2 Detailed explanation of their appearance.

Sutra:

"He may consider the heavens of the desire realm a true refuge, because he contemplates their extensive brightness and longs for it; or he may take refuge in the first dhyana, because there his nature is free from worry; or he may take refuge in the second dhyana, because there his mind is free from suffering; or he may take refuge in the third dhyana, because he delights in its extreme joy; or he may take refuge in the fourth dhyana, reasoning that suffering and bliss are both ended there and that he will no longer undergo transmigration.

Commentary:

He may consider the heavens of the desire realm a true refuge. That's where he will go. He considers the heavens of the desire realm to be his refuge. Why? Because he contemplates their extensive brightness and longs for it. The heavens of the desire realm appear to be perfect and brilliant, so he gets attached to them and yearns to go there. He takes them as his haven, as the state of nirvana. He thinks the desire realm is a place of true happiness.

Or he may take refuge in the first dhyana, because there his nature is free from worry. He may think that the beings in the heavens of the first dhyana, the "ground of the joy of leaving birth," have left behind the worries and afflictions of living beings and experience a sense of joy. Thus he wishes to be born there. **Or he may take refuge in the second dhyana, because there his mind is free from suffering.** In his cultivation, he may reach the heavens of the second dhyana, where his mind no longer suffers, because he has developed samadhi. These heavens are known as the "ground of the joy of developing samadhi."

Or he may take refuge in the third dhyana, because he delights in its extreme bliss. He may believe that the bliss of the third dhyana is extremely fine. He thinks he will get whatever he wishes for there, so he considers those heavens to be a state of nirvana. **Or he may take refuge in the fourth dhyana, reasoning that suffering and bliss are both ended there and that he will no longer undergo transmigration.** He may say that in the fourth dhyana, the "ground of the purity of renouncing thought," suffering and bliss are both gone and so there is no further rebirth in the three realms. Since it is extremely pure, he considers it a state of nirvana and wants to take refuge there.

Sutra:

"**These heavens are subject to outflows, but in his confusion he thinks that they are unconditioned; and he takes these five states of tranquility to be refuges of supreme purity. Considering back and forth in this way, he decides that these five states are ultimate.**"

Commentary:

These heavens are subject to outflows, but in his confusion he "mistakes a thief for his own son" and **thinks that they are**

unconditioned; and he takes these five states of tranquility to be refuges of supreme purity. He feels that these five states are peaceful and secure, and that they are especially supreme and pure places of refuge. **Considering back and forth in this way,** going round and round, **he decides that these five states are ultimate.** He reckons they are all ultimate states where he can attain nirvana. He does not realize that these heavens are still subject to outflows.

K3 Concludes that it is an externalist teaching.

Sutra:

"**Because of these speculations about five kinds of immediate nirvana, he will fall into externalism and become confused about the bodhi nature. This is the tenth external teaching, which postulates confused theories of five kinds of immediate nirvana in the realm of the five skandhas.**

Commentary:

Because of these five **speculations** described above **about five kinds of immediate nirvana, he will fall into externalism and become confused about the bodhi nature.** He loses sight of the enlightened nature of bodhi. **This is the tenth external teaching, which postulates confused theories of five kinds of immediate nirvana in the realm of the five skandhas.** His theories are incorrect and upside-down.

I3 Conclusion on the harm, and command to offer protection.
J1 Showing how this happens due to interaction.

Sutra:

"**Ananda, all ten of these crazy explanations may occur in dhyana as one's mental effort interacts with the formations skandha. That is why these 'insights' appear.**

Commentary:

Ananda, all ten of these crazy, erroneous **explanations** discussed above **may occur in dhyana,** the "stilling of thought," **as one's mental effort interacts with the formations skandha.** What is the problem here? Before you have broken through the formations skandha, your cultivation of samadhi interacts and battles with the formations skandha. If your own proper knowledge and proper views are victorious, you can leap over this hurdle. If the formations skandha wins, then you become possessed by a demon. **That is why these crazy "insights" and crazy explanations appear.**

J2 Confusion will bring harm.

Sutra:

"Dull and confused living beings do not evaluate themselves. Encountering such situations, they mistake their confusion for understanding and say that they have become sages, thereby uttering a great lie. They will fall into the Relentless Hells.

Commentary:

Dull and confused living beings do not evaluate themselves. Living beings are stubborn, muddled, and unaware. They fail to reflect on who they are and what kind of disposition they have. **Encountering such situations,** when such states arise, they are confused, but because they don't have the guidance of a wise teacher who has clear vision, **they mistake their confusion for understanding and say that they have become sages.** They claim they have become enlightened and become Buddhas, **thereby uttering a great lie.** Because they tell such an outrageous lie, **they will** definitely **fall into the Relentless Hells.**

J3 Command to offer protection.

Sutra:

"After my nirvana, all of you should pass on the Tathagata's teachings, transmitting and revealing them to those in the Dharma-ending Age, so that living beings everywhere can awaken to these truths. Do not let demons arise in their minds and cause them to commit grave offenses. Offer protection so that wrong views will be eradicated.

Commentary:

After my nirvana in the future, Ananda and **all of you** in the great assembly **should pass on the Tathagata's teachings,** the words I have spoken, **transmitting and revealing them to those living beings in the Dharma-ending Age, so that living beings everywhere can awaken to these truths.** You should cause all living beings to understand these principles. **Do not let demons arise in their minds and cause them to commit grave offenses.** Don't let people create their own bad karma in this way. **Offer protection so that wrong views will be eradicated.** Maintain and support the Buddhadharma, and put an end to wrong views.

Sutra:

"**Teach them to awaken to true principles in body and mind, so that they do not stray off the unsurpassed path. Do not let them aspire to and be content with small attainments. You should become kings of great enlightenment and serve as guides of purity.**

Commentary:

Teach them to awaken to true principles in body and mind. Help living beings in the Dharma-ending Age to understand the real and ultimate doctrine in body and mind, **so that they do not stray off the unsurpassed path.** Don't let them chase after superficial teachings and fail to seek the fundamental dharma. When living beings meet a fork in the road, they will not know which branch to take. **Do not let them aspire to and be content with small attainments.** Don't allow those who aspire to the unsurpassed path of enlightenment to become complacent and satisfied with attaining a little. **You should become kings of great enlightenment and serve as guides of purity.** Be pure models and pure leaders. Do not be content with small attainments. Instead you should increase your efforts and advance.

Chapter 6

The Consciousness Skandha

H5	The characteristics of the demons of the consciousness skandha.
I1	Overview of the beginning and the end.
J1	In the beginning, one cultivates but has not yet broken through this region.
K1	Review of the ending of the previous formations skandha.

Sutra:

"**Ananda, when that good person, in cultivating samadhi, has put an end to the formations skandha, the subtle, fleeting fluctuations – the deep, imperceptible, pivotal source and the common foundation from which all life in the world springs – are suddenly obliterated. In the submerged network of the retributive karma of the pudgala, the karmic resonances are interrupted.**

Commentary:

Ananda, when that good person who is cultivating in the formations skandha, **in cultivating samadhi, has put an end to the formations skandha, the subtle, fleeting fluctuations – the deep, imperceptible, pivotal source and the common foundation from which all life in the world springs – are suddenly obliterated.** Those imperceptible, subtle movements, which characterize all the twelve categories of beings in the world and are the common source of their births, are suddenly wiped out. In

Chinese, the characters for "pivotal source" literally mean the large rope that forms the border of a net, or they can mean buttons and fastenings in clothing. They can also refer to the central point or axis.

Pudgala is a Sanskrit word translated as "that which goes on to repeated reincarnations," that which is born over and over again. It is also called "body while in a state of existence," and also "sentient being." Every sentient being is endowed with a "body while in a state of existence." When we die, we will have what is called "the body that exists while in between skandhas."

In the submerged network of the retributive karma of the pudgala, the bodies while in a state of existence, **the karmic resonances are interrupted.** In this interactive process of the mutual repayment of karma which runs very deep, cause and effect are suspended. "Karmic resonances" refers to cause and effect. Since the formations skandha has ceased, and birth and death have come to an end, cause and effect have been arrested. This is describing the end of the formations skandha and the beginning of the consciousness skandha.

K2   Introduction to the region of the consciousness skandha.

Sutra:

"There is about to be a great illumination in the sky of nirvana. It is like gazing east at the cock's final crow to see the light of dawn. The six sense faculties are empty and still; there is no further racing about. Inside and outside there is a profound brightness. He enters without entering. Fathoming the source of life of the twelve categories of beings throughout the ten directions, he can contemplate that source without being drawn into any of the categories. He has become identical with the realms of the ten directions. The light does not fade, and what was hidden before is now revealed. This is the region of the consciousness skandha.

Commentary:

There is about to be a great illumination in the sky of nirvana of the inherent nature. He's on the verge of a great awakening. He is about to get enlightened. By analogy, **it is like gazing east at the cock's final crow to see the light of dawn.** When the cock crows for the first and second time to announce the dawn, there is still no light in the east. The sky is still dark. But if you gaze eastward when the cock crows for the third and final time, you will see the first light of the day.

The six sense faculties are empty and still. The feeling skandha has ended, so the sense faculties no longer perceive. They are "empty." The thinking skandha has ended, so there is no more false thinking. Thus it is "still." At this point, there is no more feeling and no more false thoughts causing the mind to run about. **There is no further racing about.** That means the shifting and flowing of the formations skandha have also ceased. The fluctuations of the formations skandha had been like ceaseless ripples, but now they have subsided, and there is no more running about.

Inside and outside there is a profound brightness. At this point, when only the consciousness skandha remains to be broken through, there is a brilliant light both inside and out. **He enters without entering,** because the functions of the sense faculties and sense objects have been severed. The six sense faculties and six objects have united, and there are no longer any faculties or any objects. There is no further pairing between faculty and object. They are non-dual. The six faculties and six objects are no longer differentiated, so there is no flow for him to enter.

Fathoming the source of life of the twelve categories of beings throughout the ten directions, he can contemplate that source without being drawn into any of the categories. He penetrates deeply to the primal life-source of the twelve categories of beings. He can reflect upon this source without being attracted to any of the twelve categories of beings. They have no sway over him. He has no further involvement with the twelve categories of beings. **He has become identical with the realms of the ten**

directions. He is experiencing identity in substance with all realms everywhere. **The light does not fade.** This bright wisdom does not disappear, **and what was hidden before is now revealed.** The most secret and imperceptible states now become manifest. **This state is the region of the consciousness skandha.** It falls within the scope of the consciousness skandha.

J2　Ultimately it breaks up and reveals its false source.

Sutra:

"If he has become identical with the beckoning masses, he may obliterate the individuality of the six gates and succeed in uniting and opening them. Seeing and hearing become linked so that they function interchangeably and purely. The worlds of the ten directions and his own body and mind are as bright and transparent as vaidurya. This is the end of the consciousness skandha. This person can then transcend the turbidity of life spans. Contemplating the cause of the consciousness skandha, one sees that the negation of existence and the negation of nonexistence are both unreal, and that upside-down false thoughts are its source.

Commentary:

If he has become identical with the beckoning masses. Having severed connections of cause and effect with the twelve categories of living beings, he has become identical with them. However, he is not influenced by them. Since he has cut off all interaction with them, he is no longer reborn among them.

He may obliterate the individuality of the six gates. At this point, the entrances of the six sense faculties no longer function. They have been smelted. In what way do they no longer function? This does not mean that the eyes cannot see, the ears cannot hear, the nose cannot smell, or the tongue cannot taste. Rather, what happens is that the six faculties function interchangeably. If you break through the formations skandha, then you will experience this state. The eyes can still see, but they can also speak and eat. The ear, which could only hear before, can now see as well. You can also see with your nose and your mouth. Each sense faculty is capable of all six functions. That's what obliterating the individuality of the six gates means. The former signs of defilement are now gone.

And he may **succeed in uniting and opening them.** "Uniting" means the six sense faculties unite to become one. "Opening" means each faculty has the functions of all six. **Seeing and hearing become linked.** There is communication between them. They can help each other out just like neighbors who show mutual concern for each other. The six faculties are linked **so that they function interchangeably and purely.** Isn't that wonderful? This state is really sublime.

The worlds of the ten directions and his own body and mind are as bright and transparent as vaidurya. They are like that exquisite blue gem, which is so clear as to be transparent. **This is the end of the consciousness skandha.** When you reach this level you have put an end to the consciousness skandha, and so all five skandhas are gone. But before you reach this level, the consciousness skandha has not ended.

This person can then transcend the turbidity of life spans. Contemplating the cause of the consciousness skandha, one sees that the negation of existence and the negation of nonexistence are both unreal, and that upside-down false thoughts are its source. Questions of existence and nonexistence are elusive and intangible. Such upside-down false thoughts are the basis of the states that he attains.

I2   Ten attachments within this.
J1   Attachment to causes and that which is caused.
K1   When formations are gone, consciousness appears.

Sutra:

"Ananda, you should know that the good person has thoroughly seen the formations skandha as empty, and he must return consciousness to the source. He has ended production

and destruction, but he has not yet perfected the subtle wonder of ultimate serenity.

Commentary:

Ananda, you should know that the good person who cultivates samadhi **has thoroughly seen the formations skandha as empty.** Although he encountered so many demonic states, whether they were caused by demons from the heavens, demons of his own mind, or other kinds of demons, they did not sway his samadhi. Or it could have been that when he was cultivating samadhi, he didn't experience any demonic states at all. Or maybe when he encountered demonic states, he recognized them and did not become confused by them. Once he pierced through the confusion, the formations skandha was destroyed. Now he is at the beginning of the consciousness skandha. He has already fathomed the formations skandha and seen it as empty, **and he must return consciousness to the source.** Now he has to break through the consciousness skandha, and when he does, he will return to the source, to the treasury of the Tathagata. **He has already ended** the states of **production and destruction, but he has not yet perfected the subtle wonder of ultimate serenity.** He has yet to perfectly realize the nature of ultimate serenity.

K2 A wrong understanding leads to a mistake.

Sutra:

"He can cause the individual sense faculties of his body to unite and open. He also has a pervasive awareness of all the categories of beings in the ten directions. Since his awareness is pervasive, he can enter the perfect source. But if he regards what he is returning to as the cause of true permanence and interprets this as a supreme state, he will fall into the error of holding to that cause. Kapila the Sankhyan, with his theory of returning to the truth of the unmanifest, will become his companion. Confused about the bodhi of the Buddhas, he will lose his knowledge and understanding.

Commentary:

He can cause the individual sense faculties of his body to unite and open. Now in the consciousness skandha, he has a false mental attachment. He is at the point where he "has not yet perfected the subtle wonders of ultimate serenity," but he can make his six sense faculties function interchangeably. Each sense faculty has the abilities of all six. His eyes can talk and hear. His ears can eat and smell. The eyes, ears, nose, tongue, body, and mind can function interchangeably to perceive sights, sounds, smells, tastes, and objects of touch.

You may think that ears cannot eat but when one attains the interchangeable functioning of the six faculties, they can. "Where are their teeth?" you wonder. Ask your ears. They don't eat things the way we do, anyway. When they start to eat they may just naturally grow teeth, and their teeth, will not fall out. Perhaps they don't even use teeth. Or perhaps the teeth appear when they need them. This is the true ability of science. Each faculty has six functions.

"Unite" refers to how the six faculties join to become one faculty. "Open" refers to how one faculty opens up to have the functions of all six. Would you say these are spiritual powers? Is this science? No matter how much research scientists do, even if they can transplant human hearts, livers and other parts of the body, they cannot enable each sense faculty to have the functions of all six. That's something science cannot achieve. No matter how advanced science becomes, I don't think it will ever have that capability. If you develop science in your own nature, then you can have this kind of function.

He also has a pervasive awareness of all the categories of beings in the ten directions. Not only does he have the ability to unite and open his six sense faculties to function interchangeably, he also knows what is going on with all twelve categories of beings throughout the ten directions. He and other beings share a mutual awareness. **Since his awareness is pervasive,** he can know the dispositions of all beings in the ten directions, and **he can enter the perfect source,** the perfection of the original nature.

But if he regards what he is returning to as a cause of true permanence. Suppose he becomes wrongly attached to the place of his return. What is his attachment? He says that it is true permanence **and interprets this as a supreme state.** Since he believes it to be true permanence, he interprets this as a kind of supreme liberation and supreme view. If he didn't hold such a view, there would be no problem. But as soon as he holds this view, **he will fall into the error of holding to that cause.** He takes true permanence as the cause, but this is completely wrong. He thinks that place is characterized by true permanence. Actually he is still within consciousness, which is not true permanence. He becomes attached to a cause and what that cause pertains to. In fact this is not the cause, but he regards it as the cause. By attaching to it, he joins an external sect. He does business with them. He puts his investments there and forms a company. With what external sect does he get involved?

Kapila the Sankhyan, with his theory of returning to the truth of the unmanifest, will become his companion. Kapila founded the "religion of the yellow-haired." Earlier, we mentioned that the teacher of Matangi used a mantra of the Kapila religion, a mantra which came from the Brahma Heaven. The "truth of the unmanifest" postulates that there is nothing at all, that everything is transformed from the current state of the eighth consciousness. This religion teaches that all things are born from the "truth of the unmanifest." Once this cultivator becomes attached to this cause, he becomes friends with those of the "yellow-haired external sect." He incorporates with them, and it is not known when that corporation will ever end. Is it limited or unlimited?

Confused about the bodhi of the Buddhas, the way of enlightenment, **he will lose his knowledge and understanding.** He takes what is not a cause to be a cause. He shouldn't have set up this cause, but he did. Because he wrongly established that cause and what it pertains to, he no longer has true wisdom. He has lost it.

Where did it go? If you want to help him look for it you will lose yours, too.

K3 Giving the name and instructions to awaken.

Sutra:

"This is the first state, in which he concludes that there is a place to which to return, based on the idea that there is something to attain. He strays far from perfect penetration and turns his back on the City of Nirvana, thus sowing the seeds of externalism.

Commentary:

This is the first state, in which he concludes that there is a place to which to return, based on the idea that there is something to attain. His principle is wrong. In what way? **He strays far from perfect penetration.** What he does is completely opposed to "cultivating the perfect penetration of the ear organ by directing the hearing inward to listen to the inherent nature, thereby entering the flow and forgetting the source." Why? Because he has developed an attachment. **And** he **turns his back on the City of Nirvana.** What is this great City of Nirvana? It's where the four virtues of nirvana – permanence, bliss, true self, and purity – are found. **Thus** he is **sowing the seeds of externalism.** By postulating a nonexistent cause, he becomes attached to an external teaching. Since his premise is like the "truth of the unmanifest" of the Kapila religion, he makes friends with its adherents and joins their ranks.

J2 Attachment to an ability that is not actually an ability.
K1 When formations are gone, consciousness appears.

Sutra:

"Further, Ananda, the good person has thoroughly seen the formations skandha as empty. He has ended production and destruction, but he has not yet perfected the subtle wonder of ultimate serenity.

Commentary:

Further, Ananda, the good person who is cultivating samadhi **has thoroughly seen the formations skandha as empty.** He has thoroughly investigated and put an end to the formations skandha; it is empty for him. **He has already ended** the states of **production and destruction, but he has not yet perfected the subtle wonder of ultimate serenity.** He has not completely attained the bliss of ultimate serenity, because consciousness has not been ended yet. Consciousness and true suchness differ by only a little bit. Consciousness is subject to production and destruction, whereas true suchness is not. Right now, the eighth consciousness, which still has tiny traces of production and destruction, joins with true suchness, which is without production and destruction, and becomes what is called "the joined consciousness." Since the consciousness is in extremely close proximity to true suchness, they merge to form the joined consciousness. Since it is still a "joined" consciousness, the subtle wonder of ultimate serenity has not been perfected.

K2 A wrong understanding leads to a mistake.

Sutra:

"He may regard that to which he is returning as his own body and may see all beings in the twelve categories throughout space as flowing forth from his body. If he interprets this as a supreme state, he will fall into the error of maintaining that he has an ability which he does not really have. Maheshvara, who manifests his boundless body, will become his companion. Confused about the bodhi of the Buddhas, he will lose his knowledge and understanding.

Commentary:

He, the cultivator, **may regard that to which he is returning as his own body.** The place he is headed for is still within the production and destruction of the eighth consciousness. It is not actually his own body, but he thinks it is. **And** he has another false attachment, which is that **he may see all beings in the twelve**

categories – from egg-born beings to beings not entirely lacking thought – **throughout space as flowing forth from his body.**

"Do you know where living beings come from?" he asks. "They all come from my own body. I gave birth to them all."

It is like an earlier state in which the cultivator said, "All beings are my children – even the Buddhas, bodhisattvas, and arhats – I created them all. I can create Buddhas; I can create bodhisattvas; and I can create arhats." See what an egomaniac he is.

If he interprets this as a supreme state. He thinks it's supreme, but it really isn't. It's based on wrong knowledge and views and can hardly be called supreme. If it were truly supreme, it would accord with the Buddhadharma. So as you cultivate the Way and read the sutras, make sure you understand them clearly. **He will fall into the error of maintaining that he has an ability which he does not really have.** He says he is able to create all living beings, but in fact he has no such ability. That's just a speculation he makes with his false consciousness. He doesn't really have the ability, but he becomes attached to the idea that he does. Who has this kind of attachment?

It's the God **Maheshvara,** the lord of the Heaven of Great Sovereignty, which is the highest heaven in the form realm. Maheshvara is also called the Great Sovereign God. He has three flesh eyes which he was born with, and he also has the buddha eye in the middle of his forehead.

How many hands does he have? He has eight hands, four in front and four in back. The ones in front are good for picking things up, and the ones in back are handy for stealing things. Since one hand isn't enough, and two hands still aren't that powerful for picking up or stealing things, he has eight hands. He can pick up a lot of things, too. If he went into a department store, I'm sure the security officers who watch for shoplifters would have a hard time keeping an eye on him, because he has so many hands. He rides upon a magnificent white ox and carries a white whisk in one hand. He travels around with the greatest freedom. He says, "Take a look at me. I'm utterly at ease. You're nothing by comparison. I have total self-mastery." That is why he's called the Great Sovereign God.

The Great Sovereign God, **who manifests his boundless body, will become his companion.** This god is attached to the idea that he can manifest a boundless body, and he claims that all living beings are manifested by him. Now this person is cultivating the same dharma-door. He has the same attachment. He says that all living beings are manifested by him. Tell me, how can someone who has not accomplished Buddhahood create living beings? This is a false attachment; he thinks he has an ability that he doesn't really have. He makes friends with the Great Sovereign God and goes off to the Heaven of Great Sovereignty.

Confused about the bodhi of the Buddhas, he will lose his knowledge and understanding. He fails to recognize the genuine enlightenment. He doesn't have any genuine wisdom, and so he joins the demons of the heavens and the external sects.

K3 Giving its name and instructions to awaken.

Sutra:

"This is the second state, in which he draws conclusions about the workings of an ability based on the idea that he has such an ability. He strays far from perfect penetration and turns his back on the City of Nirvana, thus sowing the seeds for being born in the Heaven of Great Pride where the self is considered all-pervading and perfect.

Commentary:

This is the second state, in which he draws conclusions about the workings of an ability based on the idea that he has such an ability. Based on the idea that he is able to create living beings, he attains a fruition that seems all-pervasive and perfect. **He strays far from perfect penetration.** What he has done goes against the dharma-door of cultivating perfect penetration through the ear, of directing the hearing inward to listen to the inherent nature.

And he turns his back on the City of Nirvana. He also goes against the truth of the unproduced and undestroyed, **thus sowing the seeds for being born in the Heaven of Great Pride where the self is considered all-pervading and perfect.** He will eventually be reborn in the Heaven of Great Pride, which is the Heaven of Great Sovereignty.

Great pride means he looks down on everyone else. He is always up on his white ox, with his three eyes and eight arms, thinking he is quite marvelous. Riding freely about on his white ox, he feels smug and satisfied. Because he feels his lifestyle is so superb, he becomes arrogant. He claims, "I completely pervade everything, and I can accomplish everything."

J3 Attachment to a wrong idea of permanence.
K1 When formations are gone, consciousness appears.

Sutra:

"Further, the good person has thoroughly seen the formations skandha as empty. He has ended production and destruction, but he has not yet perfected the subtle wonder of ultimate serenity.

Commentary:

Further, the good person, who in his cultivation of samadhi has destroyed the formations skandha, **has thoroughly seen the formations skandha as empty. He has already ended** the mind of **production and destruction, but he has not yet perfected the subtle wonder of ultimate serenity.** He has not yet truly attained the bliss of ultimate serenity.

K2 A wrong understanding leads to a mistake.

Sutra:

"If he regards what he is returning to as a refuge, he will suspect that his body and mind come forth from there, and that

all things throughout space in the ten directions arise from there as well. He will explain that that place from which all things issue forth is the truly permanent body, which is not subject to production and destruction. While still within production and destruction, he prematurely reckons that he abides in permanence. Since he is deluded about non-production, he is also confused about production and destruction. He is sunk in confusion. If he interprets this as a supreme state, he will fall into the error of taking what is not permanent to be permanent. He will speculate that the Sovereign God (Ishvaradeva) is his companion. Confused about the bodhi of the Buddhas, he will lose his knowledge and understanding.

Commentary:

If he regards what he is returning to as a refuge, there will be doubts in his mind and **he will suspect that his body and mind come forth from there.** The previous false conjecture was that he himself produced all living beings. Now he thinks that he came forth from the place to which he is returning, **and that all things throughout space in the ten directions arise from there as well.**

He will explain that that place from which all things issue forth is the truly permanent body, which is not subject to production and destruction. "That place" refers to the refuge to which he is returning. He claims that it is not caught up in production and destruction. Why does he say that? Because he is mistaken in his basic assumption.

While still within the consciousness that is subject to **production and destruction, he prematurely reckons that he abides in permanence.** He speculates that it is eternal and unchanging. **Since he is deluded about non-production, he is also confused about production and destruction.** Since he doesn't understand the principle of non-production, he isn't clear about the principle of production and destruction, either. **He is sunk in confusion.** He becomes attached to the state and refuses to let go of it. He works on his cultivation right at that spot.

If he interprets this as a supreme state, he will fall into the error of taking what is not permanent to be permanent. If he considers it supreme, he is just adding attachments on top of attachments. He becomes attached to that permanence, but it is not true permanence. **He will speculate that the Sovereign God (Ishvaradeva) is his companion. Confused about the** nature of **bodhi of the Buddhas, he will lose his knowledge and understanding** and no longer have true wisdom.

K3 He gives it a name and warns us to be aware of it.

Sutra:

"This is the third state, in which he makes a false speculation based on the idea that there is a refuge. He strays far from perfect penetration and turns his back on the City of Nirvana, thus sowing the seeds of an distorted view of perfection.

Commentary:

This is the third state, in which he makes a false speculation based on the idea that there is a refuge. He establishes the idea that there is a refuge, and then makes false speculations about a false fruition. **He strays far from perfect penetration and turns his back on the City of Nirvana, thus sowing the seeds of an distorted view of perfection.** He turns away from the principle of perfect penetration and leaves it far behind, and he comes to hold a wrong view of perfection.

J4 Attachment to an awareness that is not actually awareness.
K1 When formations are gone, consciousness appears.

Sutra:

"Further, the good person has thoroughly seen the formations skandha as empty. He has ended production and destruction, but he has not yet perfected the subtle wonder of ultimate serenity.

Commentary:

Further, the good person has thoroughly investigated and seen the formations skandha as empty. **He has ended production and destruction.** He has destroyed the nature that is subject to production and destruction, **but he has not yet perfected the subtle wonder of** the bliss of **ultimate serenity.**

K2 A wrong understanding leads to a mistake.

Sutra:

"**Based on his idea that there is universal awareness, he formulates a theory that all the plants in the ten directions are sentient, not different from human beings. He claims that plants can become people, and that when people die they again become plants in the ten directions. If he considers this idea of unrestricted, universal awareness to be supreme, he will fall into the error of maintaining that what is not aware has awareness. Vasishtha and Sainika, who maintained the idea of comprehensive awareness, will become his companions. Confused about the bodhi of the Buddhas, he will lose his knowledge and understanding.**

Commentary:

Based on his idea that there is universal awareness, he formulates a theory. He deduces, from what he knows, that there is a universal awareness, and then formulates a view about it. What is his view? You'd never guess, and neither would I. He says **that all the plants in the ten directions are sentient.** In China, there is a saying,

"People are not plants; who can be without emotion?"

That statement implies that plants are insentient. But here the cultivator has decided that all plants are sentient, **not different from human beings.** They are the same as people in that they also have life. **He claims that plants can become people, and that** when people die they again become plants in the ten directions. After death, humans turn back into plants.

If he considers this idea of unrestricted, universal awareness to be supreme. He doesn't have the wisdom to selectively apply this theory of universal awareness. He tries to be special and mistakenly thinks his idea is a supreme one. **He will fall into the error of maintaining that what is not aware has awareness.** He claims to understand this principle, but actually he is ignorant. He does not understand, but insists that he does.

He is similar to two followers of external sects, **Vasishtha and Sainika.** "Vasishtha" is a Sanskrit name which means "avoid going near." How did he get such a name? He was a shepherd boy. One day the prince of Vaishali was outside playing. Happening upon the shepherd boy, the prince made him act as his bed and lay down and took a nap on top of the boy. This upset the shepherd boy, who went home and told his mother, "The prince of Vaishali used me as a bed and took a nap on top of me." Knowing that the prince would one day become the king and have a lot of power, the mother instructed her son, "From now on, don't hang around him. Avoid going near him. Keep your distance." That's how he got the name "avoid going near."

"Sainika" is also a Sanskrit name which means "endowed with an army." Judging from his name, he was probably someone who enjoyed serving in the military and had the air of a military man. These two people, **who maintained the idea of comprehensive awareness, will become his companions.** They believed they knew everything, and now they become this cultivator's companions. **Confused about the bodhi of the Buddhas, he will lose his proper knowledge and understanding.**

K3   He gives it a name and warns us to be aware of it.

Sutra:

"**This is the fourth state, in which he draws an erroneous conclusion based on the idea that there is a universal awareness. He strays far from perfect penetration and turns his** back on the City of Nirvana, thus sowing the seeds of a distorted view of awareness.

Commentary:

This is the fourth state, in which he draws an erroneous conclusion based on the idea that there is a universal awareness. In this fourth kind of attachment, he claims to know everything and thinks there's nothing he does not know. However, that's just his attachment. He really doesn't know anything at all. He realizes a false result. "Erroneous" means that there's no such thing. **He strays far from perfect penetration.** He is way off track, going against the dharma-door of cultivating perfect penetration through the ear. And he **turns his back on the City of Nirvana,** on the principle of non-production and non-destruction. **Thus he is sowing the seeds of a distorted view of awareness,** an upside-down understanding. Take plants – nobody would regard them as sentient beings, yet he does just that. He says that people are just plants, and that plants can also become people.

Someone suggests, "But there are trees endowed with souls. Doesn't that mean they have awareness?"

No. In such cases, there is a spirit inhabiting the tree. It's not that the tree itself has awareness and is a sentient being.

J5 Attachment to birth that is not actually birth.
K1 When formations are gone, consciousness appears.

Sutra:

"Further, the good person has thoroughly seen the formations skandha as empty. He has ended production and destruction, but he has not yet perfected the subtle wonder of ultimate serenity.

Commentary:

Further, the good person who is cultivating samadhi has investigated to the point that he **has thoroughly seen the formations skandha as empty. He has ended production and destruction, but he has not yet perfected the subtle wonder of**

the state of **ultimate serenity**. He still carries the tiny seeds of production and destruction within him.

K2 A wrong understanding leads to a mistake.

Sutra:

"**If he has attained versatility in the perfect fusion and interchangeable functioning of the sense faculties, he may speculate that all things arise from these perfect transformations. He then seeks the light of fire, delights in the purity of water, loves the wind's circuitous flow, and contemplates the accomplishments of the earth. He reveres and serves them all.** He takes these mundane elements to be a fundamental cause and considers them to be everlasting. He will then fall into the error of taking what is not production to be production. Kashyapa and the brahmans who seek to transcend birth and death by diligently serving fire and worshipping water will become his companions. Confused about the bodhi of the Buddhas, he will lose his knowledge and understanding.

Commentary:

If he has attained versatility in the state of **perfect fusion and interchangeable functioning of the** six **sense faculties,** if he can follow his inclinations and do as he wishes, **he may speculate that all things arise from these perfect transformations.** Becoming attached to the perfect transformations from which everything comes forth, **he then seeks the light of fire** and worships fire with extreme devotion. He also **delights in the purity of water,** sincerely revering the pure nature of water, and **loves the wind's circuitous flow,** being inspired by the nature of wind with its continuous movement.

And he **contemplates the accomplishments of the earth. He reveres and serves them all** – the various aspects of earth, water, fire and wind. He bows to fire, prostrates himself before water, worships the wind, and makes obeisance to the earth.

He says, "It is truly inconceivable. How is fire able to emit light? Water is so pure. I really ought to worship it."

From morning to night he bows to water, fire, wind, and earth, worshipping the four elements. He serves them by making offerings to them. Each spirit has spirits connected with it, and soon he is treating the earth spirits, water spirits, fire spirits, and wind spirits as his own ancestors. Mahakashyapa[7] was originally a member of the fire-worshipping religion, and he used to bow in homage to fire.

He takes these mundane elements – earth, water, fire and wind – **to be a fundamental cause** of himself, and he **considers them to be everlasting.** He says they abide forever. Well, it's true that earth, water, fire and wind are just the treasury of the Tathagata. However, you should pay reverence to the treasury of the Tathagata, and not to earth, water, fire, and wind. Otherwise you are putting a head on top of a head. Instead of working on the fundamentals of venerating the treasury of the Tathagata and respecting the Buddha, he is busy worshipping the superficial aspect. **He will then fall into the error of taking what is not production to be production.** He wants to end birth and death, but being unable to do so, he forms such an attachment.

Kashyapa and the brahmans who seek to transcend birth and death by diligently serving fire and worshipping water will become his companions. Kashyapa belongs to the "great turtle clan." The brahmans are those who cultivate pure practices. They exert themselves physically and mentally by engaging in various unbeneficial ascetic practices. They make offerings to fire and bow to water, hoping that by serving the four elements they can end birth and death. The cultivator becomes the friend and comrade of such people. **Confused about the** true nature of **bodhi of the Buddhas, he will lose his knowledge and understanding.** He loses his genuine wisdom.

---

[7]. The Buddha's disciple

K3 He gives it a name and warns us to be aware of it.

Sutra:

"**This is the fifth state, in which he confusedly pursues the elements, setting up a false cause that leads to false aspirations based on speculations about his attachment to worship. He strays far from perfect penetration and turns his back on the City of Nirvana, thus sowing the seeds of a distorted view of transformation.**

Commentary:

This is the fifth state, in which he confusedly pursues the elements, setting up a false cause that leads to false aspirations based on speculations about his attachment to worship. This is the fifth upside-down theory. His speculations about his attachment lead him to worship and make offerings to the four elements. He becomes confused about his own everlasting true mind, the treasury of the Tathagata, and goes running out after the material elements instead. He bases himself on fallacious knowledge and views in his quest to escape birth and death. This is the "false cause." With this wrong cause, he vainly hopes to transcend birth and death. **He strays far from** the dharma door of **perfect penetration and turns his back on the City of Nirvana, thus sowing the seeds of a distorted** and wrong **view of transformation.**

J6 Attachment to a refuge that is not actually a refuge.
K1 After formations are ended, consciousness manifests.

Sutra:

"**Further, the good person has thoroughly seen the formations skandha as empty. He has ended production and destruction, but he has not yet perfected the subtle wonder of ultimate serenity.**

Commentary:

Further, the good person, who is cultivating perfect penetration through the ear by directing the hearing inward to listen to the inherent nature, **has thoroughly seen the formations**

skandha as empty. He has investigated the formations skandha, seen it as empty, and broken through it. **He has already ended** the path of **production and destruction, but he has not yet perfected** the bliss of **the subtle wonder of ultimate serenity.**

K2 A wrong understanding leads to a mistake.

Sutra:

"He may speculate that there is an emptiness within the perfect brightness, and based on that he denies the myriad transformations, taking their eternal cessation as his refuge. If he interprets this as a supreme state, he will fall into the error of taking what is not a refuge to be a refuge. Those abiding in the shunyata of the Heaven of [Neither Thought nor] Non-Thought will become his companions. Confused about the bodhi of the Buddhas, he will lose his knowledge and understanding.

Commentary:

He may speculate that there is an emptiness within the perfect brightness, and based on that he denies the myriad transformations, taking their eternal cessation as his refuge. He speculates that there is an emptiness within the brightness, but that is not the case. Isn't that to deny the existence of all the myriad things? Therefore, it is not a refuge of eternal cessation. However, he makes it his refuge.

If he interprets this as a supreme state, if he has such a crazy understanding, **he will fall into the error of taking what is not a refuge to be a refuge.** He wants to rely on a refuge, but there is no such refuge. It is not eternal production or eternal cessation, so it cannot be a refuge, which is what he takes it to be. There is no refuge.

Those abiding in the shunyata of the Heaven of [Neither Thought nor] Non-Thought become his companions. His attachment is not to the Heaven of No Thought among the heavens of the fourth dhyana, but rather the Heaven of Neither Thought Nor

Non-thought. The spirits of emptiness (*shunyata*) there become his companions. **Confused about the bodhi of the Buddhas, he loses his** proper **knowledge and understanding.**

K3 Giving its name and instructions to awaken.

Sutra:

"This is the sixth state, in which he realizes a state of voidness based on the idea of emptiness within the perfect brightness. He strays far from perfect penetration and turns his back on the City of Nirvana, thus sowing the seeds of annihilationism.

Commentary:

This is the sixth state of crazy understanding, **in which he realizes a state of voidness based on the idea of emptiness within the perfect brightness.** The state he attains doesn't really exist. **He strays far from perfect penetration.** He goes against the practice of that dharma-door. He **turns his back on the City of Nirvana.** What he does is contrary to the wonderful fruition of nirvana, **and he sows the seeds of annihilationism.**

J7 Attachment to an unattainable craving.
K1 After formations are ended, consciousness manifests.

Sutra:

"**Further, the good person has thoroughly seen the formations skandha as empty. He has ended production and destruction, but he has not yet perfected the subtle wonder of ultimate serenity.**

Commentary:

Further, the good person who is cultivating samadhi **has thoroughly seen the formations skandha as empty.** For him, the formations skandha is already empty. **He has ended production and destruction, but he has not yet perfected the subtle wonder of ultimate serenity.** He has yet to perfect the wonderful bliss of nirvana.

K2	A wrong understanding leads to a mistake.

Sutra:

"**In the state of what seems to be perfect permanence, he may bolster his body, hoping to live for a long time in that subtle and perfect condition without dying. If he interprets this as a supreme state, he will fall into the error of being greedy for something unattainable. Asita and those who seek long life will become his companions. Confused about the bodhi of the Buddhas, he will lose his knowledge and understanding.**

Commentary:

In the state of what seems to be perfect permanence, he may bolster his body, hoping to live for a long time in that subtle and perfect condition without dying. He may try to make his body durable because he wishes to dwell in the world forever. He seeks immortality and a life of essential clarity and perfection. **If he interprets this as a supreme state,** if he has such a crazy understanding, **he will fall into the error of being greedy for something unattainable.** He craves immortality but cannot attain it.

Asita and those who seek long life will become his companions. "Asita" is a Sanskrit name that translates as "incomparable," meaning "no one can compare with him." He and his followers are an external sect; they dwell in the heavens and crave immortality. The cultivator joins ranks with them. **Confused about** the dharma-door of **the bodhi of the Buddhas, he will lose his** proper **knowledge and understanding.**

K3	Giving its name and instructions to awaken.

Sutra:

"**This is the seventh state, in which he sets up the false cause of bolstering and aspires to permanent worldly existence, based on his attachment to the life-source. He strays far from perfect penetration and turns his back on the City of Nirvana, thus sowing the seeds for false thoughts of lengthening life.**

Commentary:

This is the seventh state, in which he sets up the false cause of bolstering and aspires to permanent worldly existence, based on his attachment to the life-source. He clings to the source of his own life and bolsters his body in the hope of attaining long life.

He strays far from perfect penetration. He goes against the dharma-door of cultivating the perfect penetration of the ear by directing the hearing inward to listen to his own nature. **And** not only that, **he turns his back on the City of Nirvana, thus sowing the seeds for false thoughts of lengthening life.**

J8 Attachment to truth that is not actually truth.
K1 After formations are ended, consciousness manifests.

Sutra:

"**Further, the good person has thoroughly seen the formations skandha as empty. He has ended production and destruction, but he has not yet perfected the subtle wonder of ultimate serenity.**

Commentary:

Further, the good person who is cultivating samadhi **has thoroughly seen the formations skandha as empty;** he has broken through the formations skandha. **He has ended production and destruction, but he has not yet perfected the subtle wonder** and wonderful bliss **of ultimate serenity.**

K2 A wrong understanding leads to a mistake.

Sutra:

"**As he contemplates the interconnection of all lives, he wants to hang on to worldly enjoyments and is afraid they will come to an end. Caught up in this thought, he will, by the power of transformation, seat himself in a lotus flower palace, conjure up an abundance of the seven precious things, increase his retinue of beautiful women, and indulge his mind. If he interprets this as a supreme state, he will fall into the error of** taking what is not the truth to be the truth. Vignakara will become his companion. Confused about the bodhi of the Buddhas, he will lose his knowledge and understanding.

Commentary:

As he contemplates the interconnection of all lives, this person sees that his own life is interrelated with the lives of all beings, and **he wants to hang on to worldly enjoyments and is afraid they will come to an end.** He fears that his worldly existence will come to an end, and he doesn't want it to end.

Caught up in this thought, he will, by the power of transformation, seat himself in a lotus flower palace, conjure up an abundance of the seven precious things, increase his retinue of beautiful women, and indulge his mind. Within his lotus flower palace, he conjures up all kinds of gems and enlarges his following of concubines and beautiful women. Then he gives free rein to lust and greed.

If he interprets this as a supreme state, he will fall into the error of taking what is not the truth to be the truth. At this point, he again considers this to be supreme. He thinks he has attained what is true, but it is not true. It is merely what he maintains.

Vignakara will become his companion. "Vigna" is Sanskrit and translates as "to tie and to bind." This refers to tying and binding living beings with rope. "Kara" is also Sanskrit and translates as "my doing." This means, "The bondage of all living beings, that is, their lack of freedom, is all my doing. It is because of me that they are not free." That's how the members of this external sect think. This cultivator joins ranks with them. **Confused about the bodhi of the Buddhas, he will lose his** proper **knowledge and understanding** and will only have wrong knowledge and understanding.

K3 Giving its name and instructions to awaken.

Sutra:

"**This is the eighth state, in which he decides to indulge in worldly enjoyments, based on his wrong thinking. He strays far from perfect penetration and turns his back on the City of Nirvana, thus sowing the seeds for becoming a demon of the heavens.**

Commentary:

This is the eighth state, in which he decides to indulge in worldly enjoyments, based on his wrong thinking. Due to his wrong thoughts, he gets caught up in his burning passion for worldly things. **He strays far from perfect penetration.** He goes against the dharma-door of cultivating perfect penetration through the ear. **And** he **turns his back on the City of Nirvana** and the principle it embodies, **thus sowing the seeds for becoming a demon of the heavens.** He will be reborn among the demons in the heavens.

J9 Fixed-nature hearers.
K1 After formations are ended, consciousness manifests.

Sutra:

"**Further, the good person has thoroughly seen the formations skandha as empty. He has ended production and destruction, but he has not yet perfected the subtle wonder of ultimate serenity.**

Commentary:

Further, the good person has investigated and **has thoroughly seen the formations skandha as empty. He has already ended** the nature that is subject to **production and destruction, but he has not yet** fully **perfected the subtle** and **wonder** bliss **of ultimate serenity.**

K2 A wrong understanding leads to a mistake.

Sutra:

"**In his understanding of life, he distinguishes the subtle and the coarse and determines the true and the false.** But he only seeks a response in the mutual repayment of cause and effect, and he turns his back on the way of purity. In the practice of seeing suffering, eliminating accumulation, realizing cessation, and cultivating the Way, he dwells in cessation and stops there, making no further progress. If he interprets this as a supreme state, he will fall and become a fixed-nature hearer. Unlearned sanghans and those of overweening pride will become his companions. Confused about the bodhi of the Buddhas, he will lose his knowledge and understanding.**

Commentary:

In his illusory **understanding of life, he distinguishes the subtle and the coarse.** He differentiates between what is fine and what is coarse, **and determines the true and the false.** He judges what is true and what is false. **But he only seeks a response in the mutual repayment of cause and effect.** He seeks a response through cause and effect. The response also comes from cause and effect. **And he turns his back on the way of purity.**

In the practice of seeing suffering, eliminating accumulation, realizing cessation, and cultivating the Way. To see suffering means to know suffering. The truth of suffering includes the three sufferings, the eight sufferings, and limitless sufferings. The truth of accumulation refers to all our afflictions. Cessation refers to cultivating the Way and realizing cessation, that is, attaining the wonderful bliss of nirvana. The Way refers to the way of cultivation. That's what is meant by knowing suffering, eliminating accumulation, longing for cessation, and cultivating the Way. **He dwells in cessation and stops there, making no further progress.** When he reaches cessation, he stops advancing.

If he interprets this as a supreme state, if he comes up with a crazy rationalization which he considers superior, **he will fall and**

become a fixed-nature hearer. What is a fixed-nature hearer[8]? We've talked about this before. He is a person who refuses to turn from the small and go toward the great. He becomes satisfied prematurely and refuses to advance further. **Unlearned sanghans and those of overweening pride will become his companions.** He is as ignorant as the unlearned bhikshu who thought the fourth dhyana was the fourth fruition of arhatship. Such people become his companions. **Confused about the Buddha's** enlightened **bodhi**-nature, **he will lose his** proper **knowledge and understanding.**

K3 Giving its name and instructions to awaken.

Sutra:

"This is the ninth state, in which he aspires toward the fruition of cessation, based on perfecting the mind that seeks responses. He strays far from perfect penetration and turns his back on the City of Nirvana, thus sowing the seeds for becoming enmeshed in emptiness.

Commentary:

This is the ninth state, in which he aspires toward the fruition of cessation, based on perfecting the mind that seeks responses. He strays far from the dharma-door of **perfect penetration** through the ear. **And** he **turns his back on the City of Nirvana, thus sowing the seeds for becoming enmeshed in emptiness.** He gets stuck in emptiness and stillness. He has no desire to progress and no wish to retreat. Emptiness becomes the most important thing in his life. He gets wrapped up in emptiness. Actually, emptiness means there is nothing at all, but he invents an emptiness within emptiness and becomes attached to it.

---

[8]. Shravaka.

J10 Fixed-nature pratyekas.
K1 After formations are ended, consciousness manifests.

Sutra:

"**Further, the good person has thoroughly seen the formations skandha as empty. He has ended production and destruction, but he has not yet perfected the subtle wonder of ultimate serenity.**

Commentary:

Further, the good person has thoroughly seen the formations skandha as empty. He has thoroughly investigated the states of the formations skandha, and they are empty for him. **He has already ended** the states of **production and destruction, but he has not yet perfected the subtle wonder** and bliss **of ultimate serenity.**

K2 A wrong understanding leads to a mistake.

Sutra:

"**In that perfectly fused, pure, bright enlightenment, as he investigates the profound wonder, he may take it to be nirvana and fail to make further progress. If he interprets this as a supreme state, he will fall and become a fixed-nature pratyeka. Those enlightened by conditions and solitarily enlightened ones who do not turn their minds to the great vehicle will become his companions. Confused about the bodhi of the Buddhas, he will lose his knowledge and understanding.**

Commentary:

In that state of **perfectly fused, pure, bright enlightenment, as he investigates the** principle of **profound wonder, he may take it to be nirvana and fail to make further progress** in his cultivation, even though he has not yet broken through the consciousness skandha. **If he interprets this** wild and false understanding **as a supreme state, he will fall and become a fixed-nature pratyeka** who fails to turn from the small and go toward the great.

Those enlightened by conditions and solitarily enlightened ones who do not turn their minds to the great vehicle, the fixed-nature arhats, **will become his companions.** He will join ranks with them. **Confused about the bodhi of the Buddhas,** the path to enlightenment, **he will lose his** proper **knowledge and understanding.**

K3 Giving its name and instructions to awaken.

Sutra:

"**This is the tenth state, in which he realizes a profound brightness based on fusing the mind with perfect enlightenment. He strays far from perfect penetration and turns his back on the City of Nirvana, thus sowing the seeds for being unable to surpass his attachment to the brightness of perfect enlightenment.**

Commentary:

This is the tenth state, the last of the gates of the consciousness skandha. If you can pass through this gate, then you won't have to worry anymore. There is no further danger. Unfortunately, this final step is not an easy one to take. At this point he's off by just a tiny bit. It is said, "If you are off by a hairsbreadth at the beginning, you will miss by a thousand miles at the end." If you're just a tiny bit off at the start, you'll be way off at the stage of fruition. This state is one **in which he realizes a profound brightness based on fusing the mind with perfect enlightenment.** At this time, the doctrine of perfect enlightenment is about to merge with his permanent true mind, and he attains a purity and brightness.

He strays far from perfect penetration. Nevertheless, he has not meshed with the dharma-door of perfect penetration of the ear, because he still has attachments. **And he turns his back on the City of Nirvana,** going against the wonderful fruition of nirvana, **thus sowing the seeds for being unable to surpass his attachment to the brightness of perfect enlightenment.** He cannot get past his attachment to that state of perfection. There is still that tiny bit which he does not understand before he breaks through the consciousness skandha.

If at this point he can break through without succumbing to crazy interpretations, then he will have broken through all five skandhas. When the five skandhas have been broken through, he will attain the positions of the ten faiths, the ten dwellings, the ten practices, the ten transferences, and the ten grounds. Then he can rest assured that he will attain Buddhahood.

I3 Conclusion on the harm and command to offer protection.
J1 Show how this happens due to interaction.

Sutra:

"**Ananda, these ten states of dhyana are due to crazy explanations on the path of cultivation. Relying on them, the cultivator becomes confused and claims to have attained complete realization before actually having done so. All these states are the result of interactions between the consciousness skandha and his mental efforts.**

Commentary:

Ananda, you should pay special attention to this point and understand it well. You should recognize the demon states that appear in **these ten states of dhyana** – these ten dharma-doors of contemplation in stillness. These ten states which appear in the cultivation of dhyana **are due to crazy explanations on the path of cultivation.**

Relying on them, the cultivator becomes confused and claims to have attained complete realization before actually having done so. At this point, although he has not attained the Way and realized the fruition, he says, "I've realized the fruition." Not having realized the first fruition, he says he has. Not having attained the second, third, or fourth fruitions either, he claims he has. He has not become a Buddha, yet he claims he has. If you ask him how he became a Buddha, he doesn't know. A Buddha who doesn't know how he attained Buddhahood is certainly a muddled Buddha! But Buddhas all have perfect understanding, and there are no muddled Buddhas. If he's muddled, then he is just a ghost, goblin, demon, or weird creature who doesn't understand the truth.

All these states are the result of interactions between the consciousness skandha and his mental efforts. These are tricks of the consciousness skandha. When you work hard, the consciousness skandha battles against your skill. If you have the slightest bit of greed, lust or false thinking, you will enter a demonic state. If you become attached to this state, then you will be possessed by a demon.

You will come up with some crazy theory, and once you do, it will be very hard to smash through it. Even if others point out to the cultivator that he is incorrect, he won't believe them. He will think, "What do you know, anyway? I'm already a Buddha! What you're saying is not right." Even if they tell him, he won't believe them. That is why such states occur.

[January 1983]

Just now, Guo Di said most of us have placed the state of breaking through the five skandhas too high, and he's absolutely right. The *Heart Sutra* says,

> "When Bodhisattva Avalokiteshvara was practicing the profound prajna paramita, he illuminated the five skandhas and saw that they are all empty, and he crossed beyond all suffering and difficulty."

Avalokiteshvara (the "one who contemplates at ease") was sitting there meditating, advancing step by step in his cultivation of dhyana, heading towards the stage of wisdom. He was able to understand that the five skandhas are empty. Once a person sees the skandhas of form, feeling, thinking, formations, and consciousness as empty, he will no longer be obstructed by them. Since they no longer cover him over, his wisdom comes forth.

At this point, he has not by any means realized any fruition or left the triple realm. He has some wisdom, which allows him to leave suffering and attain bliss. Yet he has not really left suffering and attained bliss; he still has a long way to go. He still has to "deeply enter the sutra treasury and have wisdom like the sea," and to not be turned by states. Right now, he is still being turned by the states of the five skandhas. Not only has he not realized the fourth fruition, he hasn't even reached the first fruition. An arhat of the first fruition can walk without his feet having to touch the ground. His feet are about half a centimeter off the ground, so they never get muddy no matter where he goes. That's because he has eradicated the eighty-eight grades of delusion of views.

The delusion of views involves being confused by the state one is faced with and becoming attached to it. When one realizes the fruition, "The eyes see forms, but inside there is nothing. The ears hear sounds, but the mind doesn't know." One sees everything as empty and one has no attachments, so how could one "catch on fire and become possessed by a demon?" There are no demons to encounter and no fires to catch.

Being confused by principles and engaging in discrimination is called the delusion of thoughts. Sages of the second and third fruition must cut off the delusion of thoughts. If someone had already cut off the delusions of thought while cultivating in the realm of the five skandhas, would he be entertaining all kinds of wild thoughts and speculations? Would he make all kinds of discriminations as he investigates the principle? No way. He would be able to decisively resolve any matter which comes up without having to discriminate and speculate about it. Those false thoughts all come from his consciousness. His consciousness is constantly discriminating the subtlest details. Not only has he not realized any fruition, he can't even ascend to the Heaven of Neither Thought nor Non-thought. Why not? Because he hasn't even seen through and put down his body! He's still going around in circles, expending effort on that stinking skinbag!

Do you think that someone who has broken through the five skandhas has realized some fruition? Breaking through the five skandhas is a path that has to be walked, and he is walking on that path. All of you should clearly recognize this state. Don't be like the unlearned bhikshu, who mistakenly thought that the fourth dhyana heaven was the fourth fruition. A person who has broken through the five skandhas is only at the level of the first or second dhyana. He is still in the very early stages of cultivation. He has only just begun. You shouldn't mistake an elementary school student who has just begun his studies for a college graduate. Child prodigies who advance very quickly in their studies are not that common. In fact, they are extremely rare. You should be very clear about the dharma. I didn't say this earlier, because I wanted to see how much wisdom you all had. If a person hasn't cut off the delusion of views and the delusion of thought, how can he have realized any fruition? It would be impossible.

[January 1983]

He hasn't realized any fruition yet. Those are all false states. Even if he has broken through form, feeling, thinking, formations, and consciousness, he still hasn't realized any fruition. He's just traveling on the path of cultivation, that's all. If he had realized any fruition, he would become irreversible; how could a demon possess him? Even a person who has realized the first fruition cannot be possessed by a demon.

[March 1983]

The *Heart Sutra* says, "He illuminated the five skandhas and saw that they are all empty, and he crossed beyond all suffering and difficulty." One who has broken through the five skandhas has merely understood the principle of emptiness; he certainly hasn't ended birth and death or attained any fruition. He is still walking on the path (of cultivation) and has not reached his destination yet, so he can't be said to have ended birth and death. He has understood the principle of emptiness, which is a partial view, and at this point he feels that there isn't any suffering and there isn't any happiness. If he were to stop at this point, he would fall into an external path. If he continues to progress, then it will be possible for him to become enlightened and to realize the fruition – but he must be vigorous. Therefore, in cultivation, no matter what level you reach, if you become satisfied with what little you have attained and feel you've gone far enough, then you are simply limiting yourself and quitting when you're only halfway there. That will be as far as your understanding goes, and you will make no further progress.

J2 Confusion will bring harm.

Sutra:

"Dull and confused living beings do not evaluate themselves. Encountering such situations, their minds are confused by their individual likings and past habits, so they stop to rest in what they take to be the ultimate refuge. They claim to have perfected unsurpassed bodhi, thus uttering a great lie. After their karmic retribution as externalists and deviant demons comes to an end, they will fall into the Relentless Hells. The sound-hearers and those enlightened by conditions cannot make further progress.

Commentary:

Dull and confused living beings do not evaluate themselves. Living beings are obstinate and intractable in their delusion. They do not stop to consider just what they are. They haven't shed their dog hides and pig skins, yet they claim to be Buddhas. They really overestimate themselves.

Encountering such situations, their minds are confused by their individual likings and past habits. "Individual likings" refers to their personal desires and greedy attachments, which have confused and stupefied their minds in life after life. **So they stop to rest in what they take to be the ultimate refuge.** They figure they have reached a treasure trove. But in fact, they are abiding in a transformed city. That transformed city is not the treasure trove. These people were on a quest for treasures, but after going halfway, they grew weary and decided to give up. At that point, a person with spiritual powers conjured up a city and told them, "The treasure trove is just up ahead. We can go there and collect all the treasures. We can bring back all sorts of precious and rare jewels." The idea was that after they got there and took a rest, they could continue onwards. But all the people went to the transformed city, and thinking it was the treasure trove, they rested and did not go further. They say this is their final place of refuge, the place they want to go to.

They claim to have perfected unsurpassed bodhi. They claim they have realized unsurpassed bodhi and become Buddhas already, **thus uttering a great lie.** They haven't attained Buddhahood, but they say they have. Would any intelligent person say such a stupid thing? To say you've reached a position that you haven't reached is just being stupid. In a democratic country, we say everyone can become president. True, everyone has the potential to become president, but that doesn't mean everyone is the president. You have to be elected to office before you actually are the president. You can't just say that everyone is a president. Then who is the real president? Who is the vice-president? It's the same principle here. If you've never gone to school or studied anything, and you don't even know how to sign your own name, could you really become the president? It's the same with becoming a Buddha. If you haven't cultivated, and you don't have what it takes to spend six years in the Himalayas or forty-nine days under the bodhi tree – if you haven't put in even one day of such effort, how could you become a Buddha? That would be too easy. That's crazy.

After their karmic retribution as externalists and deviant demons comes to an end – after the demonic karma they incurred has come to an end, **they will fall into the Relentless Hells.** Their lives as demons will also come to an end at some point. When that happens, they will fall into the Relentless Hells. **The sound-hearers and those enlightened by conditions cannot make further progress.** If fixed-nature sound-hearers or fixed-nature pratyekabuddhas utter a great lie, they will not fall into the hells. However, they won't be able to advance either. They cannot make further progress.

J3 Command to offer protection.

Sutra:

"All of you should cherish the resolve to sustain the Way of the Tathagata. After my nirvana, transmit this dharma-door to those in the Dharma-ending Age, universally causing living beings to awaken to its meaning. Do not let the demons of views cause them to create their own grave offenses and fall. Protect, comfort, and compassionately rescue them and dispel evil conditions. Enable them to enter the Buddhas' knowledge and understanding with body and mind so that from the beginning to the final accomplishment they never go astray.

Commentary:

All of you, Ananda, and all the great bodhisattvas, great arhats, great bhikshus, great elders, and others in this assembly, **should cherish the resolve to sustain the Way of the Tathagata.** You should honor the principles spoken by the Tathagata. **After my nirvana, transmit this dharma-door** of the *Shurangama Sutra*, that of "directing the hearing inward to listen to the inherent nature, until the nature attains the Unsurpassed Way." Transmit this dharma-door of perfect penetration **to those in the Dharma-ending Age.** You should transmit this every day to those in the Dharma-ending Age, **universally causing living beings to awaken to its meaning.** Let all living beings understand these principles clearly.

Do not let the demons of views cause them to create their own grave offenses and fall. There are demons of views and demons of views and love. When people see states, demons of views cause them to be moved by the states. Sometimes people see things, give rise to love, and get turned by those states. That's the demons of views and the demons of views and love. Don't let them cause people to create offenses and fall.

Protect, comfort, and compassionately rescue them – all living beings – **and dispel evil** and improper **conditions.** Subdue the crazy mind and wild nature. Put an end to wrong knowledge and views.

Enable them to enter the Buddhas' knowledge and understanding with body and mind so that from the beginning to the final accomplishment they never go astray. Do not allow them to be sidetracked as they walk on the proper path.

CHAPTER 7

Concluding Instructions

G3 Concluding instructions.
H1 First instructs to transcend and certify.
I1 All Buddhas' former certification.

Sutra:

"It is by relying on this dharma-door that the Tathagatas of the past, as many as fine motes of dust in eons as many as the Ganges' sands, have enlightened their minds and attained the Unsurpassed Way.

Commentary:

It is by relying on this dharma-door of the *Shurangama Sutra* **that the Tathagatas of the past, as many as fine motes of dust in eons as many as the Ganges' sands, have enlightened their minds and attained the Unsurpassed Way.** By following this dharma-door of the great Shurangama Samadhi, their minds became enlightened and they realized the fruition of the Unsurpassed Way. This is the path they traveled. Now we also want to investigate this path. Only by cultivating this Way to perfection can we become Buddhas. It's not the case that we can reach Buddhahood without even taking the first step. Not to mention Buddhahood, even in the world, how many years of effort does it take to get a Bachelor's, a Master's, or a doctoral degree? How much more must you work to attain a transcendental Buddhahood! If you were to claim to be a Buddha without even having taken the first step, that would be even more incredible than a dream! Even in a dream, you wouldn't say such an outrageous thing. Becoming a Buddha is not that simple.

I2 The end of consciousness is transcendence.

Sutra:

"**When the consciousness skandha ends, your present sense faculties will function interchangeably. Within that interchangeable functioning, you will be able to enter the bodhisattvas' vajra dry wisdom. In your perfect, bright, pure mind, there will be a transformation.**"

Commentary:

When the consciousness skandha ends. When the formations skandha came to an end, you were in the consciousness skandha. If you had reached the position of the eighth consciousness, at that point you would be able to see the worlds of the ten directions as clearly as crystal. Nothing would obstruct your vision. However, before the consciousness skandha completely become the eighth consciousness, and the very subtle process of production and destruction is still going on in the seventh consciousness. Once those subtle movements of the seventh consciousness are gone and only the eighth consciousness remains, you will see everything in the universe as clearly as crystal. At that time, the eighth consciousness is transformed into the Buddhas' great perfect mirror wisdom. That state cannot be obtained, however, before you completely smash through the seventh consciousness. That is what it means to put an end to the consciousness skandha.

If the subtle movements of the seventh consciousness are gone, **your present** six **sense faculties will function interchangeably.** The interchangeable functioning of the six sense faculties was discussed above. Each faculty has the functions of all six. For example, the eyes, which could only see things before, can now hear, smell, taste, eat, touch, and think as well. One opens and unites the faculties so they can function interchangeably.

Within that interchangeable functioning, you will be able to enter the bodhisattva's vajra dry wisdom. "Vajra" means indestructible, which means non-retreating. You attain the three kinds of non-retreat: non-retreating position, non-retreating thought, and non-retreating practice. "Dry wisdom" refers to the stage of dry wisdom. **In your perfect, bright, pure mind, there will be a transformation.**

Sutra:

"**It will be like pure vaidurya that contains a precious moon, and in that way you will transcend the ten faiths, the ten dwellings, the ten practices, the ten transferences, the four additional practices, the vajra-like ten grounds of a bodhisattva's practice, and the perfect brightness of equal enlightenment.**

Commentary:

What will the transformation be like? **It will be like** a **pure,** undefiled piece of **vaidurya that contains a precious moon, and in that way you will transcend** the positions of **the ten faiths, the ten dwellings, the ten practices, the ten transferences,** and **the four additional practices,** which were discussed earlier. The four additional practices are heat, summit, patience, and foremost in the world. You will also transcend the states and levels of skill represented by **the vajra-like ten grounds of a bodhisattva's practice and the perfect brightness of equal enlightenment.**

---

13   Perfect realization of the ultimate fruition.

Sutra:

"**You will enter the Tathagata's sea of wondrous adornments, perfect the cultivation of bodhi, and return to the state of non-attainment.**

Commentary:

In this state, **you will enter the Tathagata's sea of wondrous adornments, perfect the cultivation of bodhi, and return to the state of non-attainment.** Ultimately, there is nothing to be attained. Why? Because bodhi is inherent in you and is not obtained from outside. The treasury of the Tathagata is not something obtained externally. Rather, it is inherently yours. Thus, you "return to the state of non-attainment."

H2 He then instructs us to protect and uphold it.
I1 He first explains how it accords with the honored ones of the past.

Sutra:

"**These are subtle demonic states that all Buddhas, World Honored Ones, of the past, discerned with their enlightened clarity while in the state of shamatha and vipashyana.**

Commentary:

These ten states discussed above, which occur in the consciousness skandha, **are subtle demonic states that all Buddhas, World Honored Ones, of the past, discerned with their enlightened clarity while in the state of shamatha and vipashyana.** Shamatha is a kind of samadhi, in this case the wonderful Shurangama Samadhi.

Vipashyana refers to the skill of subtle and refined contemplation. Because of their enlightened understanding, they could discern those demonic states, which are extremely subtle and very difficult to detect.

[December 2, 1992]

Disciple: Here the wonderful Shurangama Samadhi is explained as shamatha, but earlier shamatha referred to the three stoppings and three contemplations.

Venerable Master: The three stoppings and three contemplations are just an analogy. The principle is about the same.

Disciple: But it still isn't the wonderful Shurangama Samadhi.

Venerable Master: He may realize and enter the wonderful Shurangama Samadhi later on. This is explained differently in different places; it depends on the context. It's explained at a deeper level here. It is as when a child grows up, he does things differently, even though he has the same name and is the same person. There are changes, but it's pretty much the same thing. It's explained one way here, and another way there. If you insist on clinging to one way, then you don't understand.

Disciple: But only someone with the Venerable Master's wisdom can do this.

Venerable Master: For example, let me ask you about a quote from the Chan school, "With empty hands grasping a hoe, I walk and ride an ox. I walk across a bridge; the bridge flows, but not the water." What does this mean? Have you heard me say this before? There's nothing special about it! Of course your hands have to be empty to grasp a hoe. If your hands are holding something, how can they grasp the hoe? Most people ask, "How can empty hands grasp a hoe?" They don't understand, because they can't turn it around. That's how the Chan school is.

Disciple: Chan masters usually talk in such a bizarre way, so even when they say something logical, people still can't figure out what they're saying.

Venerable Master: They were speaking to the conditions of the time, so if you talk about their words now, it's like trying to sketch something that changes over time – it will be off the mark. The Chan masters deliberately spoke that way so you wouldn't understand and you wouldn't know what their real meaning was.

Disciple: Their words were aimed at a specific person or event, and not directed at other people.

Venerable Master: When those of later generations quote their words, they are simply "talking about food instead of eating it, and counting others' wealth instead of their own" – not getting any real benefit.

Disciple: For example, if a person is on the brink of enlightenment, then a Chan master may hit him and cause him to be enlightened. Yet if those of later generations casually hit people, they won't get any results.

Venerable Master: As soon as you hit them, they get mad. When your cultivation has reached maturity, you can bump into something or touch something and get enlightened. When the time hasn't come, then even if you want to get enlightened, it won't happen. The more you want to, the less you'll be able to get enlightened, because your wishes are only false thoughts. You don't recognize your false thoughts, and so you follow along with your human mind, thinking, thinking, thinking... you can think to the end of the world and you still won't get anywhere.

I2   Orders him to recognize the demonic states, and to protect and uphold the samadhi.

Sutra:

"**If you can recognize a demonic state when it appears and wash away the filth in your mind, you will not develop wrong views.**"

Commentary:

If you can recognize a demonic state when it appears before you and be able to tell whether it is a demon or a Buddha, **and** you can **wash away the filth in your mind, you will not develop wrong views.** Some states come from demons external to you and some come from your own mind. The external demons are easy to subdue. The internal demons of the mind are very difficult to subdue, because once you have wrong knowledge and views, it's very difficult to free yourself from them. After you have recognized the external demons, you have to cleanse away the filth of your own mind. What filth? The most important kind of filth in the mind is greed. We keep talking around it, and it always comes back to that. Greed, to be more specific, is lust. If you don't have any thoughts of lust, you have washed away the filth of the mind, and you will not develop wrong views. If you do not cleanse the mind of lust, then a lot of problems will come your way. All these problems arise because of greed. All kinds of trouble, afflictions, and ignorance then arise; and when they do, you get caught up in wrong views. If you can wash away these faults, you will also be rid of wrong views.

Sutra:

"**The demons of the skandhas will melt away, and the demons from the heavens will be destroyed. The mighty ghosts and spirits will lose their wits and flee. And the li, mei, and wang liang will not dare to show themselves again.**

Commentary:

The demons of the five **skandhas,** which have been discussed, **will melt away, and the demons from the heavens will be destroyed.** If you have genuine wisdom and don't get caught up in wrong views, the demons of the heavens will be obliterated. You will strike fear into their hearts. **The mighty ghosts and spirits will lose their wits and flee.** These beings are so strong that they can knock over Mount Sumeru single-handedly. But if you have proper knowledge and views and you have the great Shurangama Samadhi, these powerful ghosts and spirits will lose their wits and flee in terror when they see you. **And the li, mei, and wang liang will not dare to show themselves again.** *Li*, *mei*, and *wang liang* are types of ghosts that were discussed earlier. They will also be gone for good.

Sutra:

"**You will directly arrive at bodhi without the slightest weariness, progressing from lower positions to great nirvana without becoming confused or discouraged.**

Commentary:

You will directly arrive at bodhi, the state of the Buddha, **without the slightest weariness.** You won't have any difficulty or trouble **progressing from lower positions to great nirvana without becoming confused or discouraged.** Even those with inferior roots will be able to progress. You will head straight for the wonderful fruition of nirvana, and your mind will not experience those earlier kinds of confusion and ignorance.

Sutra:

"**If there are beings in the Dharma-ending Age who delight in cultivating samadhi, but who are stupid and dull, who fail to recognize the importance of dhyana, or who have not heard the dharma spoken, you should be concerned lest they get caught up in deviant ways. You should single-mindedly exhort them to uphold the Dharani Mantra of the Buddha's Summit. If they cannot recite it from memory, they should have it written out and place it in the meditation hall or wear it on their person. Then none of the demons will be able to disturb them.**

Commentary:

If there are beings in the Dharma-ending Age who delight in cultivating samadhi, but who are stupid and dull. No matter how much you teach living beings about being good, they still insist on going down bad roads. You don't teach them how to be bad, but they go down bad roads all by themselves. Learning to be good is as difficult as ascending to the heavens. Learning to be bad is as easy as sliding downhill. Why? The habits of living beings are very strong, and they have too much greed and desire. Those old habits, old problems, old karmic hindrances, and debts from offenses created in past lives are so numerous that they drag one down when one wants to go up. Learning to be good is as hard as climbing to the heavens, but learning to be bad is as easy as going downhill. Why? Because living beings have no wisdom and are stupid and dull.

They are ones **who fail to recognize the importance of dhyana.** They do not realize the vital importance of cultivating the Way. They do not know how necessary the practice of still contemplation is. **Or** they are those **who have not heard the dharma spoken.** They don't know about the dharma. Although they have not heard dharma lectures and they don't know how to meditate and practice still contemplation, they nonetheless delight in cultivating samadhi. Those who wish to cultivate samadhi have to understand the Way and be clear about the dharma. So **you should be concerned lest they get caught up in deviant ways.** If you fear that such people will come to have wrong knowledge and views, then you must warn them.

You should single-mindedly exhort them to uphold the Dharani Mantra of the Buddha's Summit. Urge them to recite the most supreme dharani, the Shurangama Mantra. **If they cannot recite it from memory, they should have it written out and place it in the meditation hall.** If they keep reciting the mantra but cannot memorize it and have to look at the book, you can tell them to write it out and place it in the room where they sit in meditation. That's because, "Wherever the sutra is kept the Buddha is present." How much the more is this the case for the mantra. Wherever this mantra is found, there will be Vajra Treasury Bodhisattvas and their retinues, and all the dharma-protecting good spirits. **Or** you can tell these cultivators to **wear it on their person. Then none of the demons will be able to disturb them.** If you wear the mantra on your body, the demons cannot get to you.

[January 1983]

If a person who has been possessed by a demon recites the Shurangama Mantra, will the demon leave? If you recite the Shurangama Mantra, whatever demon you have will leave, provided you recite with single-minded concentration. If you recite with a concentrated mind, without any extraneous false thoughts or any greed, then the demon will go far away. It's only to be feared that you'll recite the mantra on the one hand, but entertain false thoughts on the other, and that you won't be able to get rid of thoughts of killing, stealing, sexual misconduct, lying, and taking intoxicants. If that's the case, then no mantra that you recite will be efficacious.

I3   Advises him to revere this teaching as an example from the past.

Sutra:

"You should revere this final paradigm of ultimate cultivation and progress of the Tathagatas of the ten directions."

Commentary:

With utmost sincerity and concern, Shakyamuni Buddha makes a final entreaty. He says to Ananda, **"You should revere this final paradigm of ultimate cultivation and progress of the Tathagatas of the ten directions."** You should respect and honor the wonderful Shurangama Samadhi, the dharma-door of the "perfect penetration of the ear through directing the hearing inward to listen to the inherent nature," and also the dharma-door of the spiritual Shurangama Mantra – the Supreme Honored Dharani Mantra of the Buddha's Summit which unites all aspects of the dharmas and holds limitless meanings. This is the mind and nature of all the Tathagatas of the ten directions. It is the mother of all Tathagatas. It is the most ultimate, most thorough, and most subtly wonderful dharma-door of cultivation and progress. It is the final paradigm of all the Tathagatas of the ten directions. It is the most important dharma-door, which has been explained at the very end. It is the most important paradigm, method, and instruction concerning the road you should take to attain the Buddhas' knowledge and understanding.

CHAPTER 8

The Arising and Cessation of the Five Skandhas

E2 Request for further explanation of the arising and cessation of the five skandhas.
F1 Ananda repeats the former teaching and makes a request.

Sutra:

Ananda then arose from his seat. Having heard the Buddha's instruction, he bowed and respectfully upheld it, remembering every word and forgetting none. Then once more in the great assembly he spoke to the Buddha, "The Buddha has told us that in the manifestation of the five skandhas, there are five kinds of falseness that come from our own thinking minds. We have never before been blessed with such subtle and wonderful instructions as the Tathagata has now given.

Commentary:

Ananda then arose from his seat. Having heard the Buddha's instruction, he bowed and respectfully upheld it, remembering every word and forgetting none. Hearing Shakyamuni Buddha's teaching, Ananda bows to the Buddha, but this time he does not cry. He cried so many times in the past, but now he does not cry, because he has eaten his fill. He's been like a child drinking milk. Now that he's full, he doesn't cry anymore. Or again, he's like a child that wants candy; once he gets his fill of sweets, he stops crying. Ananda has also obtained some candy to eat, so he does not cry anymore. He prostrated himself and upheld the dharma-door of the great Shurangama Samadhi with extreme reverence. He had memorized the spiritual Shurangama Mantra without getting a single syllable wrong or leaving any out and every word and phrase was very clear. As he recited the mantra with his mouth, he contemplated it in his mind and did not create any evil karma with his body. Thus the three karmas of body, mouth, and mind were all pure as he recited the spiritual Shurangama Mantra.

Then once more in the great assembly he spoke to the Buddha. People should not get the wrong idea here. When Ananda speaks out again in the assembly, it's certainly not the case that he is showing off. It's not that he wants everyone to notice him. What is he doing, then? He is seeking the dharma on behalf of living beings. He is doing it not for his own sake, but for you and me – his fellow cultivators in the present time. He thinks, "Oh, in the future there will be a dharma assembly in America. Someone will lecture on the *Shurangama Sutra* there, and those people may not have totally understood it to this point, so I will ask for some more dharma on their behalf." We should really be grateful to Ananda.

He said, **"The Buddha has told us that in the manifestation of the five skandhas** of form, feeling, thinking, formations, and consciousness, **there are five kinds of falseness that come from our own thinking minds."** Each of these five kinds of falseness further divides into ten kinds of demonic states. **"We have never before been blessed with such subtle and wonderful instructions as the Tathagata has now given.** Those of us in this great assembly have never before, in our ordinary, daily lives, heard the Buddha speak such wonderful doctrines. We have truly gained what we never had before, and we are peaceful and content in body and mind."

Sutra:

"**Further, are these five skandhas destroyed all at the same time, or are they extinguished in sequence? What are the boundaries of these five layers?**

Commentary:

Further, are these five skandhas of form, feeling, thinking, formations and consciousness **destroyed all at the same time** – can we get rid of them all at once – **or are they extinguished in sequence?** Do they go away little by little, in a certain order, one layer after another? **What are the boundaries of these five layers?** What are their limits?

Sutra:

"**We only hope the Tathagata, out of great compassion, will explain this in order to purify the eyes and illuminate the minds of those in the great assembly, and in order to serve as eyes for living beings of the future.**"

Commentary:

We only hope the Tathagata, out of great compassion, will explain this. Our only wish is that the Tathagata will let the great compassion issue forth from his heart and explain this for us, **in order to purify the eyes and illuminate the minds of those in the great assembly.** Clear up our eyes and minds. If your mind does not understand, you will not cultivate. If your eyes are clouded by defilements, they will not be able to see clearly. So Ananda asks that the eyes and minds of those in the great assembly be purified. Not only does he want their eyes and minds to be purified, he also requests that the Buddha **serve as eyes for living beings of the future** – that is, for you, me, and all other living beings of the present. We are all included in the definition of living beings. You cannot exclude yourself even if you want to.

If you say, "I don't count. I am not part of the definition of living beings," then let me ask you, what are you? Speak up. Even if you wanted to, you can't run away. Even if you put on wings, you can't fly off. Even if you went to the moon, you would still be a living being. You can't be anything else. So be good and admit that you're part of our group. Don't run away. Being good means you shouldn't lose your temper or act up. Your mind shouldn't feel like a pancake that sizzles and sticks to the pan. That's very hard to bear.

Ananda says, "Be eyes for us and for those of the future." The mission does not end here. "Eyes for the future" continues on into the future, and by definition that is a time that hasn't arrived yet.

When you hear this, don't you think it's wonderful? Does it make sense? When you laugh, all the people who don't understand Chinese are confused and want to know what you're laughing about, so let's translate this quickly!

F2   The Buddha answers three questions.
G1   He first answers that they arise from falseness.
H1   He shows the reasons for false thinking.
I1   Pursuing the source and finding it empty.

Sutra:

The Buddha told Ananda, "The essential, true, wonderful brightness and perfect purity of basic enlightenment does not admit birth and death, nor any mundane defilements, nor even empty space itself. All these are brought forth because of false thinking.

Commentary:

The Buddha told Ananda, "The essential, true, wonderful brightness and perfect purity of basic enlightenment does not admit birth and death. What is this state like? It is just the essential, true, wonderfully bright and perfectly pure state of basic enlightenment. Birth and death cannot exist in that state, **nor any mundane defilements, nor even empty space itself."** What is being described is the treasury of the Tathagata. It is the basic substance of true suchness, the Buddha-nature inherent in us all. It's not that you have it and I don't, or that I have it and you don't. We are all endowed with the essential, true, wonderful brightness and perfect purity of basic enlightenment. Within it there is not a single defilement. Within it there is not a single thing which is established. There isn't anything at all. If you can return to the origin, then you will be free of ignorance, lust, greed, stupidity and false thinking – you will have none of them. It is an absolute and total purity. That is the aim of our cultivation: to return to that place inherent in us all. If this place did not exist, there would be no reason for anyone to cultivate.

We can all see empty space, but do you know where it comes from? **All these are brought forth because of false thinking.** Empty space comes from our false thoughts. False thinking brings into being the five skandhas, the five turbidities, and the six knots. It creates all kinds of troublesome things. This is just a case of looking for something to do when there isn't anything to do. Why do you do it? Because you have no work to do, and you want to look for some. That's okay if you can reap a reward. Unfortunately, though, the more you work, the more you lose. If you work for others, the more work you do, the more money you lose. It's also like running a business – the longer you run it, the more money you lose. You keep taking losses until eventually the treasury of the Tathagata is pressed flat beneath the mountain of the five skandhas. Once that happens, the bandits of the six sense faculties and the six sense objects occupy the mountain of the five skandhas as their hideout. They go all over it robbing and plundering. See how all the time until today you have been attracting thieves and sheltering bandits. At the beginning you were doing business, but then you began to lose capital, and now it's cost you your life. The thieves go about looting and stealing, and they go right ahead and kill people as well. Therefore, your inherent nature is squashed underneath the mountain of the five skandhas, and the six sense faculties and six sense objects are bandits that go around looting everywhere. Do you understand now? If you understand this principle, then I have not lectured on the sutra in vain. If you don't understand, then you will have to study it gradually.

Sutra:

"The source of basic enlightenment, which is wonderfully bright, true, and pure, falsely gives rise to the material world,

just as Yajnadatta became confused about his head when he saw his own reflection.

Commentary:
The source of basic enlightenment, in which not a single thing abides – his essential, true, wonderful brightness and perfect purity of basic enlightenment – **which is wonderfully bright, true, and pure, falsely gives rise to the material world.** When that happens, falseness arises based on truth. In the treasury of the Tathagata, falseness arises. The "sentient world" refers to all living beings while the "material world" refers to the mountains, rivers, buildings, and the earth itself.

It is **just as Yajnadatta became confused about his head when he saw his own reflection.** One morning he got up, looked in the mirror, and saw that the person in the mirror had eyes, ears, lips, and a nose, and he exclaimed, "Why don't I have a head like that? That person in the mirror has one, why don't I?" He went running all over the place trying to find his head. Do you think his head was actually lost though? Do you remember that I mentioned Yajnadatta earlier? If not, try to think back. What kind of person was Yajnadatta? Was he an intelligent person or a foolish one? Did he have a head, or was he headless? If you reply that he had no head, would you think he was a freak if you saw him? Think about it.

Today is the beginning of a new life for all of us here, so we must wash our bodies and minds clean. Put aside all the unclean things you were involved with in the past, and be sure that from now on the things you pick up are clean. By "clean" we mean being free of the five dull servants: greed, hatred, stupidity, pride, and doubt. Today's precept transmission was the first of its kind in America, and so you are the first initiates into Buddhism in this country. But you should know that there aren't any advantages for the people who come first. You will have to endure bitterness. Why is that? Because there is no model to follow. There are no precedents, and so you don't know how to go about what you have to do. Sometimes you'll get disoriented. You'll make mistakes without even realizing they are mistakes. Why? Because you basically don't understand what you're going about doing, and there is nowhere you can go to learn.

Although Japanese Buddhism has been in America for a long time, it is a very synthetic Buddhadharma. By that I mean it tends to be abstract and lacking in substance. You may call what they practice the Buddhadharma, but it really isn't like the Buddhadharma. But if you say it's a secular practice, they will tell you it's the Buddhadharma. It's impossible to tell what it really is. It doesn't fit the mold. Why not? Because it doesn't have a genuine foundation. For instance, there's a Korean monk now who claims to be of the Cao Creek Sect. It's hard to figure out how Cao Creek got to Korea. It is a case of "Hanging out a sheep's head, but selling dog's meat."[9] He hangs out a sign that says "the waters of Cao Creek," but what he sells is the mud and silt of Korea. There's no water in it, so how can it be Cao Creek? I really don't like to talk this way, but I see that these kinds of people are simply too pitiful. It's a case of the blind leading the blind. He claims to be of the Cao Creek Sect, and a lot of intelligent Americans follow him and become part of the Cao Creek Sect, too, but just exactly what is the origin of Cao Creek? They don't know. Where is Cao Creek located? What does that place look like? They don't know. This is truly a ridiculous sham.

Now you have received the precepts of orthodox Buddhism. This is the proper Buddhadharma, and it's different from those heretical sects that cheat people of their money in the name of the Way. For example, they say, "Give me sixty-five dollars, and I will transmit the dharma to you." This isn't that. Now you have been given a precept sash. The money you paid does not come to me. It is used to purchase your sash. Whenever you attend a dharma assembly, you should wear the sash. It shows reverence for the Buddha, the Dharma, and the Sangha. This dharma assembly will conclude tomorrow. From now on, whenever there is a dharma assembly, the people wearing sashes should stand in the front and

---

[9]. False advertising.

those wearing only the robe, but not the sash, should stand in the back. Also, those who have held the precepts for a longer time should stand in front, and those who have newly received the precepts should stand in the back. This is the order we follow in Buddhism.

Today I congratulate you all for completing your three-month course of study. Although your study has concluded, your work is just starting. What is your work? You must help all human beings in the world to end their suffering. Their suffering can be ended only if someone lends a helping hand. The suffering of humanity is not limited to a single country. Throughout the whole world, humanity is suffering. Therefore, people of great wisdom are needed to remind humanity of its suffering. Only then will human beings know to seek for true happiness. What is the greatest suffering? The greatest source of suffering is our greed. Greed is one of the greatest afflictions. Anger is also one of the biggest afflictions. And stupidity is also one of the greatest afflictions. Greed, anger, and stupidity are the three poison. Yet people feel that these three are their best friends, and so they are reluctant to part with them. Due to their lack of understanding, people don't renounce these poisons. If they understood, the suffering of humanity would come to an end.

In this Shurangama dharma assembly, which began on July 16, we cultivated and studied non-stop from six o'clock in the morning until nine o'clock in the evening every day. This period of a little over three months has been tremendously valuable. Now, this valuable time has already passed, and you have learned this precious knowledge and made it a part of yourselves. You must tell the whole world about the Buddhadharma that you have learned, so the whole world will know how to leave suffering, attain bliss, and realize great wisdom. Don't do any more foolish things or things that don't benefit people.

This dharma assembly could be considered the first of its kind in Buddhism throughout the entire world. It's absolutely unprecedented. Although there are many sutra lectures in other places, they don't study from morning till night without rest like we've done. Now you should take the principles of Buddhism you've learned and use them to help all the world's people who are adrift in the sea of suffering. Help them to depart from suffering, find happiness, and quickly attain the Buddha Way. This is my hope.

---

12   Judges the upside-down speculations to be wrong.

Sutra:

"**The falseness basically has no cause, but in your false thinking, you set up causes and conditions. But those who are confused about the principle of causes and conditions call it spontaneity. Even empty space is an illusory creation; how much the more so are causes and conditions and spontaneity, which are mere speculations made by the false minds of living beings.**"

Commentary:

This passage discusses the causes and conditions of our false thoughts. What is meant by "causes and conditions?" When a person does not understand the principle of causes and conditions, in his confusion he will regard it as spontaneity and thus fall among the externalists. Therefore the text says: **The falseness basically has no cause.** There is no basis for a source of false thinking. Without any basis, there is no substance to it.

Someone asked me, "What is false thinking?"

My reply was, "What you're asking right now about false thinking is just false thinking. Your question itself is false thinking." Where do you go to find false thoughts? They don't have any root. Once they pass, they are gone. Being false, they are without substance. To speak of false thinking as a "thing" is already inappropriate, because fundamentally, there isn't any "thing." **But in your false thinking, you set up causes and conditions.** In your false thinking, without any basis, you say that there are causes and conditions.

But those who are confused about the principle of causes and conditions call it spontaneity. If you understand causes and conditions, there's no problem. But those who are confused about the principle of causes and conditions do not have any understanding of it.

"Dharma master, ultimately, what are these causes and conditions you've been talking about?" you may ask.

Causes and conditions were discussed at length earlier in the sutra. It is a teaching used for refuting the teachings of external teachings. It is a teaching for the initial vehicle, and thus is basically not a particularly deep doctrine. It basically says that whatever the cause, so will be the conditions. People who do not understand the doctrine of causes and conditions will call it spontaneity instead. That's a case of "swallowing the date whole."[10] What is meant by swallowing the date whole? Maybe you aren't familiar with dates. You could say it's "swallowing an apple whole," without biting or chewing it first. What does it taste like? You don't know. Those who are confused about the principle of causes and conditions, those who misunderstand it, call it spontaneity, which is a doctrine of external sects.

Even empty space is an illusory creation. Now this does not refer to causes and conditions or spontaneity. This refers to empty space. What is empty space? It comes from your false thinking. As the verse spoken earlier by Manjushri Bodhisattva says: "The space created within great enlightenment / Is like a single bubble in all the sea." The empty space in the nature of great enlightenment is just like a bubble in the ocean; it comes from false thinking.

How much the more so are causes and conditions and spontaneity, which are mere speculations made by the false minds of living beings. What are causes and conditions? What is spontaneity? Causes and conditions and spontaneity – these two theories – are just speculations dreamed up by the false-thinking minds of

---

[10.] Jumping to conclusions.

living beings. I don't know if my explanation is correct, but you can all think about it.

Sutra:

"Ananda, if you perceive the arising of falseness, you can speak of the causes and conditions of that falseness. But if the falseness has no source, you will have to say that the causes and conditions of that falseness basically have no source. How much the more is this the case for those who fail to understand this and advocate spontaneity.

Commentary:

Ananda, if you perceive the arising of falseness, you can speak of the causes and conditions of that falseness. Do you know how false thinking comes into being? If you know where false thinking comes from, then you can talk about its causes and conditions. **But if the falseness has no source, you will have to say that the causes and conditions of that falseness basically have no source.** Since there is no falseness to begin with, what basis do you have for a discussion of the causes and conditions of false thinking? Since the falseness has no substance, it has no source. There is nothing at all. All phenomena are empty of characteristics. There is no source or foundation for the falseness. **How much the more is this the case for those who fail to understand this and advocate spontaneity.** If you don't even understand causes and conditions and you further advocate the principle of spontaneity, you will fall among the externalists. That won't do at all.

---
13 Concluding with reiteration that the cause is false thinking.

Sutra:

"Therefore, the Tathagata has explained to you that the fundamental cause of all five skandhas is false thinking.

Commentary:

Therefore, because of the principles explained above, **the Tathagata has explained to you** very clearly **that the**

fundamental cause of all five skandhas – form, feeling, thinking, formations, and consciousness – **is false thinking.** What is the basic cause of the five skandhas? False thinking. If you investigate false thinking, you will find that it has no substance of its own. In fact its mother is the five skandhas, and that is where it comes from. The five skandhas come from false thinking, and false thinking comes from the five skandhas. Based on the truth, falseness arises. Didn't I tell you this earlier? The mountain of the five skandhas is squashing you. And there are also six thieves on the mountain gathering their troops, horses, and supplies and going on looting raids. They will stop at nothing. The mountain of the five skandhas covers over the treasury of the Tathagata, so that it cannot reveal itself. If there were only the mountain of the five skandhas, that wouldn't be so bad, but then six thieves come along and indulge in wanton robbery and theft. Buried under it all is the treasury of the Tathagata. If you can subdue the six thieves and the five skandhas, then your treasury of the Tathagata will reveal itself.

[January 1983]

We are now here investigating the Buddhadharma every day, and we should apply ourselves to it in the morning and in the evening; that's how it should be, day after day. If we fail to do this one day, then we'll have missed an opportunity. In the very second that you think of not continuing to do this, you lose the benefit you have gained. It's like a cat waiting to catch a mouse. It stays there waiting for a few days, and then goes off, because it's not patient enough. As soon as it leaves, the mouse comes out and doesn't get caught. That's how strange it is. It is also like when someone has been fishing for a few days, but no fish have snapped the bait because all the small fish have been devoured by a big fish. The big fish, having eaten its fill of little fish, doesn't want to eat anything else, so it's just there sleeping. It doesn't eat for several days, but when it finally starts getting hungry, the fisherman runs out of patience and leaves, without having caught a single fish.

Basically, fishing and catching mice are both acts of killing. We cultivators are also engaged in killing. Our targets are the six thieves – our eyes, ears, nose, tongue, body and mind. We've been keeping watch over these six thieves for a few days, and so they haven't been able to have their way. But as soon as we become lax, the six thieves act up and rebel. That's how fierce they are. That's why we must be devoted in thought after thought. We must not slack off for even one second, or else the demons come. The demons bothered cultivators even when the Buddha was in the world, so they also had to be very cautious and to constantly work hard at cultivation.

What proof is there that demons were around when the Buddha was in the world? When the sutras were being compiled after the Buddha had entered nirvana, Ananda took the seat of the dharma host in the dharma assembly. At that time, his appearance became inconceivably adorned and perfect. The arhats in the assembly wondered what was going on:

"What? Has Ananda become a Buddha?"

"Has a Buddha come from another world?"

"Is this a demon?"

Now, if there were no demons during the Buddha's time, why did those great arhats entertain such doubts right after the Buddha had entered nirvana? Demons must have frequently showed themselves even in the Buddha's day. All of you should reflect on this. When we apply ourselves to cultivation, we must not be careless even for an instant. At all times, we must plant our feet on solid ground and seriously cultivate. We are pursuing the truth, and if we slack off even the slightest bit our karmic obstacles will appear.

H2　Detailed examination of the fivefold false thinking.
I1　The false thinking of the form skandha.
J1　Explains that one's body is because of thinking.

Sutra:

"Your body's initial cause was a thought on the part of your parents. But if you had not entertained any thought in your own

mind, you would not have been born. Life is perpetuated by means of thought.

Commentary:

Shakyamuni Buddha says, "Ananda, **your body's initial cause was a thought on the part of your parents.**" How did you get your present body? Where did it come from? It was due to this kind of thought on the part of your parents. Although the text says "thought" here, it is actually an emotion. To put it more clearly, the "thought" is a kind of emotion. Why is it said to be an emotion? Because egg-born beings come from thought, and womb-born beings come from emotion. Ananda is womb-born, not egg-born, so in his case the "thought" that caused his birth was emotion. Generally speaking, it's false thinking. At a deeper level, it's thought. And to go even deeper, it's emotion. The initial cause is the emotion of the parents. Because parents have the thought of emotional desire, they engage in sexual activity. As a result, a child is born. So isn't the child born from emotion?

But if you had not entertained any thought in your own mind, you would not have been born. Because your parents had emotional thoughts, sexual activity took place. However, when you were in the "body while in between skandhas," if you didn't have the emotion of either loving your father and hating your mother, or loving your mother and hating your father, then your body would not have come into existence. You, too, in that period between skandhas, had thoughts of emotion. Because of that thought of emotion, your "body while in between skandhas" entered the womb. If you hadn't had that emotional thought, you wouldn't have entered the womb and you wouldn't have this body. That is a definite fact. There's no way you can disagree with it. The text very decisively states that if you didn't have that thought of emotion, your body would absolutely not have come into being. How did it come into being?

Life is perpetuated by means of thought. The thought of emotion transmitted your life to you. The reason you have life is because of your emotional involvement with others. "Life is perpetuated by means of thought" means that your thoughts cause your lives to continue. If you didn't have any thought, your births and deaths would be ended. When the thinking skandha comes to an end, you leave distorted dream-thinking far behind. All dream-thinking will be gone. If your false thoughts are gone, your births and deaths will come to an end. Why do you undergo births and deaths? Simply because you have too many false thoughts. When one thought ceases, the next one arises. When that thought ceases, another one arises. Like waves on water, thoughts arise in endless succession and cause life to continue.

J2 Provides an analogy to explain in detail.

Sutra:

"As I have said before, when you call to mind the taste of vinegar, your mouth waters. When you think of walking along a precipice, the soles of your feet tingle. Since the precipice doesn't exist and there isn't any vinegar, how could your mouth water at the mere mention of vinegar, if it were not the case that your body originated from falseness?"

Commentary:

The philosophical doctrines discussed in the *Shurangama Sutra* are ultimate. This is the summit of philosophy, the ultimate truth. But of course, the ultimate truth is also just the ultimate false thought. The sutra is "true" in that it describes real situations. But where do these situations originate? In false thinking. The principle is ultimate, but its source is in false thinking. If false thoughts arise, the principle comes into existence. Without false thinking, the principle doesn't exist, either.

Ananda, **as I have said before.** Do you remember what I told you before, about what happens **when you call to mind the taste of vinegar?** You think, "Ooh, that vinegar is really sour. Ugh! Those sour plums are really tart. One bite makes my teeth go weak." As soon as you think about this, **your mouth waters.** Your mouth secretes saliva, not because you're hungry, but because you're thinking of something sour. In Chinese, the expression "drinking vinegar" is used to describe jealousy. Don't be jealous of others; jealousy leaves a sour taste in your mouth. **When you think of walking along a precipice, the soles of your feet tingle** and become weak. You might lose your footing and plummet over the edge into the gorge thousands of feet below. Pretty dangerous, huh?

Since the precipice doesn't exist and there isn't any vinegar, how could your mouth water at the mere mention of vinegar? The precipice isn't really there; you are just thinking about it. But at the mere thought, your feet tingle – literally "go sour," in Chinese. Above, your mouth goes sour at the thought of sour plums or vinegar, and here, your legs and feet "go sour" at the thought of a precipice. How can your feet go sour? You tell me.

Someone says, "Dharma master, you don't have to explain it. I already understand. I'm already enlightened, in fact. What did I enlighten to? Well, you were explaining earlier how each of the six sense faculties has the functions of all six. It must be that the feet go sour because they can eat."

Is that really how it is? I don't believe in your enlightenment. How come I haven't been enlightened to this yet, and you have already done so? There is no such principle. I cannot accept such a principle, because it is nothing but false thinking. The feet cannot eat, hear, or see things. The six faculties that function interchangeably are the eyes, ears, nose, tongue, body, and mind. The feet are not included. That's why I absolutely refuse to acknowledge your so-called enlightenment.

There really isn't any precipice and there isn't any vinegar. Your false thoughts are all it takes to make your mouth water and your feet tingle and go weak. **If it were not the case that your body originate from falseness,** if your body did not come from illusory false thought, if it did not befriend false thinking, if it did not join false thinking, then why would your mouth water at the mention of vinegar? If your body did not come about because of false thought – emotional thought, why would saliva form in your mouth when I talk about vinegar? The vinegar is only being talked about; it is not really there. Since it is hypothetical, why is there a sour taste in your mouth? Can you still argue that the sourness in your mouth and the tingling in your feet do not come from false thinking? No, because they do come from false thinking.

J3 Concludes by naming it false thinking.

Sutra:

"Therefore, you should know that your present physical body is brought about by the first kind of false thinking, which is characterized by solidity.

Commentary:

Therefore, because of the principles explained above, **you should know that your present physical body is brought about by the first kind of false thinking, which is characterized by solidity.** You call it "solid," but this is just a name. In fact, your body is created by the first kind of false thought, by the skandha of form.

I2 The false thinking of the feeling skandha.
J1 Thinking results in feeling.

Sutra:

"As described earlier, merely thinking about a high place can cause your body to tingle and ache.

Commentary:

Then, **as** was **described earlier** in the section above, **merely thinking about a high place can cause your body to tingle and ache.** Imagine yourself standing at the edge of a high precipice. Just talking and thinking about it makes your feet start to tingle and ache. You feel very uncomfortable, as if your legs won't support you and you are going to fall. If you actually do walk to the edge of a deep abyss and look down into that bottomless void, the soles of your feet will turn to jelly. Even though you are not in danger of falling, you feel as if you are about to fall. This feeling is brought about by your false thinking.

For example, you can walk for miles on level ground without your feet ever turning to jelly or tingling from false thinking. But if you have to walk across a single plank bridge above a gorge with a mighty river racing below, you start thinking things like, "Wow, if I fell from here, it'd be all over. I'd drown and lose my life for sure." Everything was fine until you had that false thought but now all of a sudden your feet turn to jelly and you cannot take another step. As a result you do fall. It all happened because you had such a thought. If you had not had that false thought but, say, had just walked with your eyes closed, without knowing when you were crossing a single plank bridge, nothing would have happened. So you decide you'll try to cross the bridge with your eyes closed next time. But then you'll fall just the same, because you cannot see where you are going. If you cross the bridge with your eyes open, you have false thoughts about the churning water below, and you get scared. If you cross the bridge with your eyes shut, you'll walk off the bridge and fall as well.

Therefore, don't have false thoughts with your eyes open, and don't close your eyes and try to kill off your false thoughts that way. It won't work. This is the crux of the dilemma: If you have false thinking, your feet will turn to jelly; if you close your eyes, you will also fall into the gorge. Closing your eyes will not solve the problem. The greatest difficulty is right here. It would be best not to have any false thoughts; then nothing at all would happen.

J2 Discussing its extent and concluding with the name.

Sutra:

"Due to that cause, feelings arise and affect your body, so that at present you pursue pleasant feelings and are repelled by unpleasant feelings. These two kinds of feelings that compel you are brought about by the second kind of false thinking, which is characterized by illusory clarity.

Commentary:

Due to that cause, feelings arise and affect your body. When you were born, you received your physical body, which has shape and form, **so that at present you pursue pleasant feelings and are repelled by unpleasant feelings.** You like what is favorable and beneficial to you, but you dislike what is harmful to you. **These two kinds of feelings** – these two false thoughts **that compel you** – **are brought about by the second kind of false thinking, which is characterized by illusory clarity.** "Illusory" means unreal, so this clarity is not real. This is the second kind of false thinking that you have.

I3   The false thinking of the thinking skandha.
J1   Body and mind in mutual response.

Sutra:

"**Once your thoughts arise, they can control your body. Since your body is not the same as your thoughts, why is it that your body follows your thoughts and engages in every sort of grasping at objects? A thought arises, and the body grasps at things in response to the thought.**

Commentary:

Once your thoughts arise, they can control your body. These false thoughts that you have drive your body, but your body is not your thoughts. **Since your body is not the same as your thoughts,** since the body and the mind are not the same sort of thing, why are they aware of each other? **Why is it that your body follows your thoughts and engages in every sort of grasping at objects?** Why is it that when you give rise to a thought, your body acts accordingly? **A thought arises, and the body grasps at things in response to the thought.** Why is your body controlled by your thoughts? As soon as you have a thought your body wants to grasp at the object you are thinking about. Why does your body function in unison with your thoughts? What is a thought? You can have one, two, three, four, five, six, seven, eight, nine, ten thoughts... but here the text refers to just one thought. The *Prajna Sutra of the Humane King Who Protects His Country* says that there are ninety *kshanas* in a single thought. A kshana is an extremely short period of time. And yet within one kshana there are nine hundred births and deaths, that is, nine hundred productions and destructions. Thus it is said,

> When not a single thought arises,
> the entire substance manifests.
> When the six sense faculties suddenly move,
> one is covered by clouds.

If you could keep from having a single thought, the entire substance would manifest. What entire substance? The great function of the entire substance, the treasury of the Tathagata. It is your inherent family treasure; it is the scenery of your homeland; it is your original face. Upon the slightest movement of the six sense faculties, you become obscured by a covering of clouds. If a cultivator reaches the point where he does not have a single thought then the ghosts and spirits have no way to get at him. If not a single thought arises, then not a single thought passes away. If you cannot prevent thoughts from arising, then you cannot prevent them from passing away. This is an important point. If you can understand it then when you do not have a single thought the entire substance will manifest. But if your six faculties move again, you will be obscured by the dark clouds.

J2 Discussing its extent and concluding with the name.

Sutra:

"When you are awake, your mind thinks. When you are asleep, you dream. Thus your thinking is stirred to perceive false situations. This is the third kind of false thinking, which is characterized by interconnectedness.

Commentary:

When you are awake, your mind thinks. A few days ago, I talked about Lord Zhuang who was born as his mother was waking up. Because of this, his mother resented him and favored her second son, Gong Shuduan. She wanted the second son to inherit his father's throne and become the king. Therefore, she repeatedly asked King Wu to pass the throne to his younger son rather than to his older son. But King Wu would not allow it, and so Lord Zhuang still became the king. When Lord Zhuang became king, his mother told Gong Shuduan to instigate a rebellion. But that also failed. So that is the story of Lord Zhuang. When you are awake, the thinking skandha is in control.

When you are asleep, you dream. When you are asleep, you dream. Your thinking skandha produces dreams. Previously, we mentioned how the thinking skandha could make one perceive things incorrectly in one's sleep. For example, if you are asleep and people are beating on clothes or pounding rice nearby, you may hear it as bells and drums being played. **Thus your thinking is stirred to perceive false situations.** When you dream, your thinking skandha makes you perceive the false situation of bells and drums being played.

This is the third kind of false thinking, which is characterized by interconnectedness. "Interconnectedness" means working together. The thinking skandha functions whether you are awake or asleep, so we call this "interconnection," which means mutual cooperation. This is the third kind of false thinking, and it is associated with the thinking skandha.

I4   The false thinking of the formations skandha.
J1   Lack of awareness of bodily changes.

Sutra:

"The metabolic processes never stop; they progress through subtle changes: your nails and hair grow, your energy wanes, and your skin becomes wrinkled. These processes continue day and night, and yet you never wake up to them.

Commentary:

The metabolic processes never stop; day and night they continue. This is the formations skandha, which flows on unceasingly like waves. As one thought ceases, the next one arises. As that thought passes by, the next one comes up. They arise and cease one after another. These metabolic and transformational processes never end. They just go on working, never stopping to rest. **They progress through subtle changes** which you cannot perceive because they are so minute. Without your realizing it, the house is moved out from under you, and everything looks different. What are these subtle changes?

Your nails and hair grow. If you don't cut your nails for two days, they grow a little bit. After three days, they are a bit longer. After four days, they are longer still. Each day, they are longer than the day before. But do you know how much they grow in each second and each minute? Do you know how they grow longer? If you don't trim your hair for a month, it may grow almost half an inch. But how much does it grow each day? You don't know. You say, "Well, I'll calculate it." Sure, but will it be accurate? You can try using a computer to calculate it and see if the computer knows.

Your energy wanes. Your energy decreases from day to day. People are full of energy and zest in their youth, and they also have a lot of vitality in their prime. However, as they get older they start losing their energy. Although it's not totally gone, it's on the decline. **And your skin becomes wrinkled.** Your skin gets lined like a chicken's skin, and your hair turns as white as crane feathers. Your features become terribly aged, and you can no longer pass yourself off as a young person. No amount of makeup can transform your eighty-year-old face into that of a twenty-year-old.

These processes continue day and night. This work goes on day and night – your nails grow, your hair gets longer, your energy wanes, and your skin gets wrinkled. It's more reliable than a clock. If you don't wind up your clock, it will stop. But you don't have to wind up your metabolism; it does its work just the same, unless you die. When you're dead, it stops working. **And yet you never wake up to them.** They pursue you day and night – through your youth, your prime, and your old age, right up to your death. After you die, you get reborn, and then you have to die again. You undergo endless rounds of birth and death, without ever waking up. You go right on being confused through it all. You're muddled when you come and muddled when you go. That's what the false thinking of the formations skandha is all about.

Sutra:

"If these things aren't part of you, Ananda, then why does your body keep changing? And if they are really part of you, then why aren't you aware of them?

Commentary:

If these things aren't part of you, Ananda, then why does your body keep changing? Your body goes through all these transformations – the nails and hair grow longer, the energy wanes, and the skin gets wrinkled. You say your fingernails aren't yours? Then why do they continually grow long? You say the hair isn't yours? Then why does it keep growing on your head? You say the energy isn't yours, but why do you sometimes feel weak when your energy is insufficient? If your face isn't yours, how is it possible for it to become wrinkled? If you say the wrinkles don't have anything to do with you, why does your face get wrinkled? Why do those changes occur to your own body? If this isn't you, then why does your body keep changing? From your youth, you are transported into middle age. From middle age you move on to old age. From old age you go right on to death. You cannot say these things are not yours. If this isn't your body, then you are not real. **And if you insist that they are really part of you, then why aren't you aware of them?** Why can't you sense them at all? Your nails and your hair are growing, but you do not perceive it happening. Your energy is waning, but you do not feel it. Your face is getting wrinkled, but you cannot detect it, nor do you know when the change took place. This is a double refutation: If you say they belong to you, that's incorrect; but if you say they do not belong to you, that's also incorrect. And so, what is it, you ask? It's false thinking! That's their source. They are all creations of false thinking.

J2 Discusses its extent and concludes with the name.

Sutra:

"Your formations skandha continues in thought after thought without cease. It is the fourth kind of false thinking, which is subtle and hidden.

Commentary:

Your formations skandha functions continuously, but its subtle movements are not at all easy to perceive. They are secret and obscure, and you are not aware of them at all. This is the fourth kind of false thinking, which is associated with the formations skandha.

I5 The false thinking of the consciousness skandha.
J1 Directly destroying the duality of true and false.

Sutra:

"Finally, if your pure, bright, clear, and unmoving state is permanent, then there should be no seeing, hearing, awareness, or knowing in your body. If it is genuinely pure and true, it should not contain habits or falseness.

Commentary:

Finally, if your pure, bright, clear, and unmoving state is permanent, then there should be no seeing, hearing, awareness, or knowing in your body. At this point, when you experience a pure brilliance and your state is clear and imperturbable, if you say this is a permanent state, then the functions of seeing, hearing, awareness, and knowing should not occur in your body. **If it is genuinely pure and true, it should not contain habits or falseness.** Habits and false thinking should not arise.

Sutra:

"How does it happen, then, that having seen some unusual thing in the past, you eventually forget it over time, until neither memory nor forgetfulness of it remain; but then later, upon suddenly seeing that unusual thing again, you remember it clearly from before without forgetting a single detail? How can you keep track of the permeation that goes on in thought after thought in this pure, clear, and unmoving consciousness?

Commentary:

How does it happen, then, that having seen some unusual thing in the past, you eventually forget it over time, until neither memory nor forgetfulness of it remain. What is the reason for this? You may have seen something very peculiar, but after many years, you have no memory of it and you have no forgetfulness of it either. If you're able to say that you've forgotten something, that means you still have some recollection of its occurrence. However, now there is neither memory nor forgetfulness of it.

But then later, upon suddenly seeing that unusual thing again, you remember it clearly from before without forgetting a single detail. If you suddenly see that strange thing again, you will recall how you remembered it, how you encountered it in the past and how it appeared to you then. You will not forget a single detail.

How can you keep track of the permeation that goes on in thought after thought in this pure, clear, and unmoving consciousness? In that clear and unmoving state, a kind of permeation is going on in thought after thought. How does one keep track of this? How does one recollect it? How do you explain the situation of having put something completely out of mind, only to remember it again when you encounter it again? Before seeing it again, you cannot recall it. But once you encounter it, you automatically recall it. How can this be reckoned? Who could keep these books straight? Who keeps track of this? This proves that although you have temporarily forgotten about it, your eighth consciousness remembers. That's why when you see the thing, you remember. There isn't really anyone keeping track. It's naturally stored in the eighth consciousness.

J2 Uses an analogy to explain.

Sutra:

"Ananda, you should know that this state of clarity is not real. It is like rapidly flowing water that appears to be still on the surface. Due to its speed you cannot perceive the flow, but that does not mean it is not flowing. If this were not the source of thinking, then how could one be subject to false habits?

Commentary:

Ananda, you should know that this state of clarity is not real. That still and unmoving place described above is not really still after all. Why not? **It is like rapidly flowing water that appears to be still on the surface.** When you look at it, it seems to have no waves and no current. **Due to its speed you cannot perceive the flow, but that does not mean it is not flowing.** Since there are no waves, you cannot see that the water is flowing. But that doesn't mean that there's no flow. It's flowing, but you cannot see it because there are no waves. Earlier, we discussed the formations skandha; now we are discussing the consciousness skandha. **If this were not the source of thinking, then how could one be subject to false habits?** If there were no false thoughts in the consciousness skandha, then it would not be influenced and permeated by false habits.

J3   Indicates accurately its time of cessation.

Sutra:

"**If you do not open and unite your six sense faculties so that they function interchangeably, this false thinking will never cease.**

Commentary:

If you do not achieve the state where you can **open and unite your six sense faculties so that they function interchangeably** – if you have not reached that level of cultivation, **this false thinking will never cease.** Unless you attain the state in which you can use your six sense faculties interchangeably, this false thinking will not go away.

J4   Discussing its extent and concluding with the name.

Sutra:

"**That's why your seeing, hearing, awareness, and knowing are presently strung together by subtle habits, so that within the profound clarity, existence and nonexistence are both** unreal. This is the fifth kind of upside-down, minutely subtle thinking.

Commentary:

That's why your seeing, hearing, awareness, and knowing are presently strung together by subtle habits. The functions of your six sense faculties – seeing, hearing, smelling, tasting, tactile awareness, and knowing – are strung together by subtle habits, like beads on a string. These habits are extremely subtle and hard to detect. **So that within the still, profound clarity of your nature, existence and nonexistence are both unreal.** You may maintain that they exist, but they do not really exist. You may claim they don't exist, yet they do exist. **This** kind of intangible situation **is** the state of **the fifth kind of upside-down, minutely subtle thinking.** This kind of false thinking is also very subtle and difficult to detect.

H3 General conclusion of what false thinking brings into being.

Sutra:

"**Ananda, these five skandhas of reception develop with five kinds of false thinking.**

Commentary:

Ananda, these five kinds of **skandhas of reception** – form, feeling, thinking, formations, and consciousness – **develop with five kinds of false thinking.** So these five kinds of false thinking are also produced.

G2 Answers about the depth of the realms of the skandhas.

Sutra:

"**You also wanted to know the depth and scope of each realm. Form and emptiness are the boundaries of form. Contact and separation are the boundaries of feeling. Remembering and forgetting are the boundaries of thinking. Destruction and production are the boundaries of formations. Deep purity entering to unite with deep purity belongs to the boundaries of consciousness.**

Commentary:

You also wanted to know the depth and scope of each realm. You wanted to know whether the realm of each skandha was shallow or deep. What are they like? Where are their boundaries? I will tell you now. **Form and emptiness are the boundaries of form.** Form and emptiness are relative to each other, and they are the boundaries of form. **Contact** with **and separation** from the objects of touch **are the boundaries of feeling. Remembering and forgetting are the boundaries of thinking. Destruction and production are the boundaries of formations. Deep purity entering to unite with deep purity belongs to the boundaries of consciousness.** Purity unites with purity, and that forms the realm of the eighth consciousness.

G3 Answers about the suddenness or gradualness of cessation.

Sutra:

"At their source, these five skandhas arise in layers. Their arising is due to consciousness, while their cessation begins with the elimination of form.

Commentary:

At their source, these five skandhas arise in layers. The five skandhas are produced in layers. There is a mutual cycle, and they aid one another. **Their arising is due to consciousness, while their cessation begins with the elimination of form.** How does cessation happen? Once form is gone, then the skandhas will become empty. They arise from consciousness, and their cessation begins when form is eliminated.

Sutra:

"You may have a sudden awakening to the principle, at which point they all simultaneously vanish. But in terms of the specifics, they are eliminated not all at once, but in sequence.

Commentary:

You may have a sudden awakening to the principle, at which point they all simultaneously vanish. You understand the principle very clearly. Once you have awakened, the methods of cultivation you have used cease to exist, and the notion of awakening is also gone. If you understand the principle, then even the idea of awakening is gone. **But in terms of the specifics, they are eliminated not all at once, but in sequence.** On the noumenal level, you have become enlightened. But at the level of phenomena, elimination takes place in sequence. It's like taking off clothing. You have to first take off the first layer, and then the second layer, the third layer, the fourth layer, the fifth layer. In terms of specifics, you have to eliminate them in sequence. Having understood the principle, you still have to cultivate at a practical level. Only through actual cultivation can you break through all five skandhas.

[January 1983]

Earlier one of my disciples commented that five layers of clothing is not a very apt analogy for the five skandhas, because the *Heart Sutra* says, "He illuminated the five skandhas and saw that they are all empty, and he crossed beyond all suffering and difficulty." If they were like five layers of clothing, then when all the layers were peeled away, the person would be naked. So his comment that this would cause people to have false thoughts is true enough.

Before the five skandhas have been broken through, the person is still covered by the five layers of clothing, and people don't have so many false thoughts. Once the skandhas are broken through and the person is naked – oh no! So the analogy is slightly problematic. No wonder you said it caused you to have false thoughts. What do you think should be done? Can you offer another explanation? The five layers of clothing are visible, while the five skandhas are invisible. The visible and the invisible are different.

The five skandhas are merely a kind of *yin* energy, and it can also become *yang* energy. *Yin* demons can become *yang* demons; it all depends on whether or not you know how to use them. If you know, then you won't be turned by them, and the state isn't a bad one. But if you are greedy for spiritual powers, advantages, or states, then you've been turned by them.

The five skandhas, also known as the five *yin*, are five kinds of *yin* energy. It's because of the *yin* energy that you come under demonic possession. *Yang* energy makes a person a bodhisattva. However, the important thing is not to get attached. When you have no attachments, then

> You wear clothes all day,
> and yet you haven't put on a thread.
> You eat all day,
> and yet you haven't consumed a gain of rice.

You aren't attached to whether you are wearing clothes or not. People who truly cultivate have no attachments to such matters. It's not necessarily a matter of taking off five layers of clothing, because what will you do when you're not wearing anything? This is just a very simple analogy that I gave because I was worried that you might not understand.

In reality, it's just a mass of energy acting up. This energy can be proper or deviant. Deviant energy means *yin* energy, and proper energy means *yang* energy. If you don't know how to use it, then it turns into a *yin* demon. If you do know how to use it, then it becomes a *yang* demon. At this point you should neither think of good nor think of bad. Don't crave good states, and don't be afraid of bad states. When you encounter a state, just act as if it didn't exist. Don't get attached to it. I know that my disciple doesn't want to take off his five layers of clothing, because he'd feel embarrassed if he did.

Sutra:

"I have already shown you the knots tied in the karpasa cloth. What is it that you do not understand, that causes you to ask about it again?"

Commentary:

I have already shown you the knots tied in the karpasa cloth. I tied six knots in the cloth. **What is it that you do not understand, that causes you to ask about it again?** Why is it that you still don't understand? Why are you asking me about it all over again? You're belaboring the point.

F3 Concluding exhortation to transmit this teaching.

Sutra:

"You should gain a thorough understanding of the origin of this false thinking and then transmit your understanding to cultivators in the future Dharma-ending Age. Let them recognize this falseness and naturally give rise to deep disdain for it. Let them know of nirvana so that they will not linger in the triple realm.

Commentary:

Ananda, **you should** find and **gain a thorough understanding of the origin of this false thinking and then transmit your understanding to cultivators in the future Dharma-ending Age.** Enable all living beings to thoroughly understand this principle. Transmit this principle to those in the Dharma-ending Age. **Let them recognize this falseness and naturally give rise to deep disdain for it.** Cause all those cultivators to know that the falseness of false thinking comes from themselves. Let them clearly understand its source and pattern, so that they become disgusted with it. **Let them know of nirvana.** When living beings know that they are capable of realizing nirvana, **they will not** want to **linger in the triple realm.** They will not wish to remain in the burning house of the three realms – the desire realm, the form realm, and the formless realm.

"There is no peace in the three realms. They are like a house on fire." Great Master Lian Chi ("Lotus Pond") was an eminent dharma master in China. After he had left the home-life, he was always thinking about going home to see his wife. He did, in fact go back again and again to see her. His wife was a very intelligent person, however, and she thought over the situation. Her husband had left home, but he wasn't cultivating. He still held on to emotional love and could not put it down. He kept coming home, and that really wasn't the way to do it. So she dug a big pit right in front of the door to her house, and covered it with a mat. Inside the pit she built a small fire. The next time Great Master Lian Chi came back home, he stepped into the trap and fell into the burning pit. "What are you doing – building a pit of fire right here?" he cried.

His wife replied, "If you know it's a pit of fire, why do you keep coming back?"

Hearing that one sentence, he became enlightened and never went home again. That illustrates the saying, "There is no peace in the three realms. They are like a house on fire." The desire realm, the form realm, and the formless realm are not pleasant or safe places. Rather, they are like a burning house.

CHAPTER 9

Exhortation to Propagate the Sutra

B3 Propagation section.
C1 Compares to blessings of offering to Buddhas.

Sutra:

"**Ananda, suppose someone were to fill up all the space in the ten directions with the seven precious things and then present them as an offering to Buddhas as numerous as motes of dust, with his mind set on serving and making offerings to them in thought after thought. Do you think this person would reap many blessings from making such an offering to the Buddhas?**"

Commentary:

Ananda, suppose someone were to fill up all the space in the worlds of the **ten directions with the seven precious things and then present them as an offering to Buddhas as numerous as motes of dust, with his mind set on serving and making offerings to them in thought after thought.** There would be gold, silver, vaidurya, crystal, mother-of-pearl, red pearls, and carnelian everywhere. He would then very respectfully hold them up as an offering to limitless, boundless Buddhas. He would be bowing and making offerings in every thought, without letting a moment go by in vain.

Do you think this person would reap many blessings from making such an offering to the Buddhas? What do you think? This person has given such a tremendous quantity of the seven precious things as an offering to the Buddhas. Under these circumstances, will he obtain a great reward of blessings? What do you say?

Sutra:

Ananda answered, "Since space is limitless, the precious things would be boundless. In the past, someone gave the Buddha seven coins and consequently was reborn as a wheel-turning king in his next life. As to this person who now fills up all of space and all the Buddhalands with an offering of precious things that could not be reckoned through endless eons, how could there be a limit to his blessings?"

Commentary:

Ananda answered, "Since space is limitless, the precious things would be boundless. In the past, someone gave the Buddha seven coins and consequently was reborn as a wheel-turning king in his next life." A wheel-turning sage king has a thousand sons. It is not known how many wives he has. A wheel-turning sage king has awesome virtue. He has a vehicle that can take him around the four great continents in just a couple of hours. His vehicle is probably faster than any modern-day rocket. That is one of the treasures he owns.

As to this person who now fills up all of space and all the Buddhalands with an offering of precious things that could not be reckoned through endless eons, how could there be a limit to his blessings? The person who offered seven coins to the Buddha attained the position of a wheel-turning sage king. Now this person gives an offering not of a mere seven coins, but of a quantity of the seven precious things that fills empty space and the dharma realm. Even if one spent a limitless and inconceivable number of eons, one could never finish calculating his blessings and virtue. How could you say that his blessings have a limit? They have no limit.

C3 Praising the merit of extinguishing evil.

Sutra:

The Buddha told Ananda, "All Buddhas, Tathagatas, speak words which are not false. There might be another person who had personally committed the four major offenses and the ten parajikas so that, in an instant he would have to pass through the Avichi Hells in this world and other worlds, until he had passed through all the Relentless Hells in the ten directions without exception.

Commentary:

The Buddha told Ananda, "All Buddhas, Tathagatas, speak words which are not false. The Buddhas do not tell lies. There might be another person who had personally committed the four major offenses and the ten parajikas." The four major offenses are killing, stealing, sexual misconduct, and lying. In the *Shurangama Sutra*, they are known as the "four clear instructions on purity," which you heard about earlier. The ten parajikas are the ten major bodhisattva precepts. Parajika means cast out, for someone who commits these offenses is cast out of the sea of the Buddhadharma. These ten offenses cannot be repented of. If you want to understand them in detail, you can look up the first ten bodhisattva precepts. So that, in an instant, he would have to pass through the Avichi Hells in this world and other worlds, until he had passed through all the Relentless Hells in all the worlds throughout the ten directions – he would have undergone suffering for his offenses in every single hell without exception.

Sutra:

"And yet if he could explain this dharma-door for just the space of a thought to those in the Dharma-ending Age who have not yet studied it, his obstacles from offenses would be eradicated in response to that thought, and all the hells where he was to undergo suffering would become lands of peace and bliss.

Commentary:

And yet if he could explain this dharma-door of the great Shurangama Samadhi **for just the space of a thought to those in the Dharma-ending Age who have not yet studied it, his obstacles from offenses would be eradicated in response to that thought.** If in the Dharma-ending Age, for as short a time as the space of a single thought, this person could teach the dharma-door of the *Shurangama Sutra* to people who have not yet studied the Buddhadharma, his offenses would swiftly be eradicated. **And all the hells where he was to undergo suffering would become lands of peace and bliss.** All the suffering he was due to undergo in the various hells would become peace and happiness that he gets to enjoy. He would not experience any suffering at all.

Sutra:

"The blessings he would obtain would surpass those of the person previously mentioned by hundreds of thousands of millions of billions of times, indeed by so many times that no calculations or analogies could express it.

Commentary:

The blessings he would obtain would surpass those of the person previously mentioned. The blessings obtained by the person who explains the *Shurangama Sutra* surpass those gained by the person who fills empty space and the dharma realm with the seven precious things and offers them to as many Tathagatas as there are motes of dust, respectfully serving and making offerings to them. If you can explain the *Shurangama Sutra* for people who don't understand the Buddhadharma, the blessings you obtain surpass those of the other person **by hundreds of thousands of millions of billions of times, indeed by so many times that no calculations or analogies could express it.** Your reward of blessings is so much greater that there is no way to figure out just how great it is.

C4 Brings up the supremacy of two benefits.

Sutra:

"Ananda, if living beings are able to recite this sutra and uphold this mantra, I could not describe in endless eons how great the benefits will be. Rely on the teaching I have spoken. Cultivate in accord with it, and you will directly realize bodhi without encountering demonic karma."

Commentary:

Ananda, if living beings in the future **are able to recite this sutra and uphold this mantra, I could not describe in endless eons how great the benefits will be.** If I were to speak in detail about the benefits of reading and reciting the *Shurangama Sutra* and reciting the Shurangama Mantra, I still wouldn't finish no matter how many great eons had passed.

All of you should **rely on the teaching I have spoken. Cultivate in accord with it, and you will directly realize bodhi without encountering any demonic karma.** Follow this method to cultivate, and you will straightaway be able to accomplish the unsurpassed fruition of bodhi, without undergoing any further demonic karma.

[January 1983]

The *Shurangama Sutra* is a sutra that acts like a demon-spotting mirror in Buddhism. All the celestial demons, externalists, and the *li, mei,* and *wang liang* ghosts reveal their true appearance when they see the *Shurangama Sutra*. They have no way to hide and no place to which they can flee. And so in the past, when Great Master Zhi Zhe heard of the existence of this sutra, he bowed in the direction of India for eighteen years. For eighteen years, he used this spirit of utmost sincerity to pray for this sutra to be brought to China.

Of all the greatly virtuous and eminent monks of the past, all the wise and lofty Sanghans, there was not a single one who did not praise the *Shurangama Sutra*. Therefore, as long as the

Shurangama Sutra exists, the Buddhadharma exists. If the *Shurangama Sutra* is destroyed, then the Buddhadharma will also become extinct. How will the decline of the dharma come about? It will begin with the destruction of the *Shurangama Sutra*. Who will destroy it? The celestial demons and externalists will. They see the *Shurangama Sutra* as being like a nail in their eyes and a thorn in their flesh. They can't sit still and they can't stand steady; they are compelled to invent a deviant theory that says the *Shurangama Sutra* is false.

As Buddhist disciples, we should recognize true principle. Every word of the doctrines in the *Shurangama Sutra* is the absolute truth. There isn't one word that does not express the truth. So now that we are studying the fifty skandha demons, we should realize even more just how important the *Shurangama Sutra* is. The *Shurangama Sutra* is what the deviant demons, ghosts, and goblins fear most.

The Venerable Master Hsu Yun lived to be a hundred and twenty years old, and during his whole life, he didn't write a commentary for any sutra other than the *Shurangama Sutra*. He took special care to preserve the manuscript of his commentary on the *Shurangama Sutra*. He preserved it for several decades, but it was later lost during the Yunmen incident. This was the Elder Hsu's greatest regret in his life. He proposed that, as left-home people, we should study the *Shurangama Sutra* to the point that we can recite it by memory, from the beginning to the end, and from the end to the beginning, forwards and backwards. That was his proposal. I know that, throughout his whole life, the Elder Hsu regarded the *Shurangama Sutra* as being especially important.

When someone informed the Elder Hsu that there were people who said the *Shurangama Sutra* was false, he explained that the decline of the dharma occurs just because these people try to pass fish eyes off as pearls, confusing people so that they cannot distinguish right from wrong. They make people blind so that they can no longer recognize the Buddhadharma. They take the true as false, and the false as true. Look at these people: This one writes a book, and people all read it. That one writes a book, and they read it too. The real sutras spoken by the Buddha himself are put up on the shelf, where no one ever reads them. From this, we can see that living beings' karmic obstacles are very heavy. If they hear deviant knowledge and deviant views, they readily believe them. If you speak dharma based on proper knowledge and proper views, they won't believe it. Speak it again, and they still won't believe it. Why? Because they don't have sufficient good roots and foundations. That's why they have doubts about the proper dharma. They are skeptical and unwilling to believe.

Here at the City of Ten Thousand Buddhas, we will be setting up the Shurangama Platform, so it will be ideal if some of you bring forth the resolve to read the *Shurangama Sutra* every day for one or two hours. You can study it daily just as if you were studying in school and memorize it so that you can recite it by heart. If you can recite the *Shurangama Sutra*, the *Dharma Flower Sutra*, and even the *Avatamsaka Sutra* from memory, that will be the very best. If someone is able to recite the *Shurangama Sutra*, the *Dharma Flower Sutra*, and the *Avatamsaka Sutra* from memory, then it will mean that this is still a time when the proper dharma exists in the world. Therefore, in such a wonderful place as the City of Ten Thousand Buddhas, everyone should bring forth a great bodhi resolve to do these things. It's not that we are competing with others. We should be outstanding, rise above the crowd, and do these things.

In the past, I had a wish: I wanted to be able to recite the *Dharma Flower Sutra* and the *Shurangama Sutra* from memory. In Hong Kong, I have a disciple who can recite the *Shurangama Sutra* from memory. I taught him to study the *Dharma Flower Sutra*, but in the end he probably didn't finish memorizing it which is very regrettable. In such a fine place as we have here, each of you should bring forth a great resolve to study the Buddhist sutras and precepts – the *Shurangama Sutra*, the *Dharma Flower Sutra*, the vinaya in four divisions, and the *Brahma Net Sutra* – until you can recite them from memory. That would be the best, for then the proper dharma would surely remain here for a long time.

C5 Concludes with the dharma bliss experienced by the great assembly.

Sutra:

When the Buddha finished speaking this sutra, the bhikshus, bhikshunis, upasakas, upasikas, and all the gods, humans, and asuras in this world, as well as all the bodhisattvas, those of the two vehicles, sages, immortals, and pure youths in other directions, and the mighty ghosts and spirits of initial resolve all felt elated, made obeisance, and withdrew.

Commentary:

When the Buddha finished speaking this sutra, all the great **bhikshus;** all the **bhikshunis; upasakas,** a Sanskrit word that means "men who serve closely," that is, laymen who draw near to and serve the Buddha; **upasikas,** women who serve closely; **and all the gods, humans, and asuras in this world** (By now you all know what asuras are; they have the biggest tempers and they love to fight. One of my disciples says his dog is an asura. Well, maybe he himself is an asura as well! But I believe that after you all have heard the *Shurangama Sutra,* you will become bodhisattvas, and no longer have the temper of asuras); **As well as all the bodhisattvas of other lands; those of the two vehicles,** the sound-hearers and those enlightened by conditions; **sages, immortals, and pure youths,** who enter the path of cultivation in their youthful innocence, **in other directions, and the mighty ghosts and spirits of initial resolve all felt elated, made obeisance, and withdrew.**

Now that we have finished hearing this sutra, no matter what kind of beings we are, whether we are gods, humans, asuras, hell-beings, hungry ghosts, or animals, we must bring forth the bodhi resolve. We must all practice the bodhisattva path. We must all be bodhisattvas. Do not continue to create the causes for becoming other kinds of beings. We must create the causes for becoming Buddhas and Bodhisattvas, and we must realize the fruitions of bodhisattvahood and Buddhahood. Shakyamuni Buddha made predictions for us and for all living beings long ago. It is said, "People who recite 'Namo Buddha' just once will all accomplish Buddhahood." Not to mention reciting it many times, if we simply say "Namo Buddha" once, in the future we will definitely become Buddhas, although we do not know when.

By listening to the *Shurangama Sutra*, we have come to understand a lot of Buddhadharma. There is inconceivable merit and virtue in this. That's why it was said that the merit and virtue of filling the space of the ten directions with the seven precious things and making an offering of them to the Buddhas is not as great as that of explaining the *Shurangama Sutra*. Now that we have finished explaining the *Shurangama Sutra*, your suffering has come to an end and my toil has also ended. Why? Because we don't have to work so hard. In the future when you practice the bodhisattva path, there may be more suffering, but you will endure it willingly; it will not be forced upon you by others. You yourself are willing to accept those troubles.

Therefore, we should make the bodhisattva resolve and practice the bodhisattva path. I hope that everyone who has heard the *Shurangama Sutra* lectured will make a bodhisattva resolve. I'll say it again: no matter whether you are a god, a human being, an asura, a hell-being, a hungry ghost, or an animal, you must all resolve to become enlightened. Don't be confused anymore. One who is enlightened is a Buddha, and one who is confused is a living being. Now we all hope to become enlightened a little sooner.

General Index

A

American Patriarch 169
Ananda
    should be thanked 281—282
Asita 256
Avalokiteshvara Bodhisattva 265
Avatamsaka Sutra 164

B

Bodhisattva
    genuine or phony 95, 103, 110, 126
Brahma Net Sutra 98
Buddha
    characteristics of 56
    genuine or phony 126
Buddha eye 39—40

C

Cao Creek Sect 287
causes and conditions
    refutes externalists 290
chamunda, ghost 156
Chan Masters
    and their bizarre methods 275—276
Chang Ren, Great Master 64—66
Chang Ti, Great Master 65
City of Ten Thousand Buddhas 163, 164
computers 162
Confucius
    on ghosts and spirits 85
    stopped dreaming 173
consciousness skandha

the tricks of 265
consciousness skandha, ten states of
    attachment to a refuge that is not actually a refuge 253—255
    attachment to a wrong idea of permanence 245—247
    attachment to an ability that is not actually an ability 241—245
    attachment to an awareness that is not actually awareness 247—250
    attachment to an unattainable craving 255—257
    attachment to birth that is not actually birth 250—253
    attachment to causes and that which is caused 237—241
    attachment to truth that is not actually truth 257—259
    fixed-nature hearers 259—261
    fixed-nature pratyekas 262—264
cultivation
    being diligent 225—226, 267—268
    being patient 292—293

D

delusion
    of thought 266
    of view 266
demons 151—152
    can aid one's cultivation 85
    can convert true cultivators 165
    disturbs one's cultivation 3—4, 18—20
    during the Buddha's time 293

General Index

gathering instead of subduing 158
getting rid off 279
in Taiwan 136—139
internal and external 276—277
spotting one 95, 121, 164—165
the older, the more powerful 150
dharma
   meaning of 5—6
Dharma Flower Sutra 164
dharma of great compassion
   and the Buddha eye 40
dharma of the thousand hands and thousand eyes
   and the Buddha eye 40
Dharma-ending Age 162
dreams
   and the thinking-skandha 173—174

E

eagle spirit 160
eighth consciousness
   ending the seventh 272
   joined consciousness 242
enlightenment 276

F

false states 182—183
false thinking 289, 292, 296—297
   attracts demons 64
   perils of 285
   the dilemma 297—298
false thinking, of the skandha of
   consciousness 304—307
   feeling 297—299
   form 293—297
   formations 301—304
   thinking 299—301
fear
   of demons 85—86

feeling skandha, ten states of
   attached to emptiness and slandering precepts 73—76
   attached to existence and indulging in lust 76—79
   experiencing ease leads to joy 66—68
   passing through danger leads to anxiety 62—66
   praises himself as being equal to the Buddhas 54—57
   samadhi out of balance brings much reverie 57—59
   seeing the sublime and becoming proud 68—70
   suppression of the self leads to sadness 52—53
   wisdom comes lightness and ease 71—72
   wisdom out of balance brings much arrogance 60—62
Five Great Heart Mantras 16
five signs of decay 8
five skandhas 266—267, 292, 309
   and the five layers 309—310
   are empty 265
form skandha, ten states of
   body becomes like grass or wood 40—41
   body can transcend obstructions 27—29
   can see everywhere without obstruction 41—43
   can see things in the dark 38—40
   essence and souls alternately separate and unite 32—35
   false visions and false words 44—46
   light pervades and he can extract intestinal worms 30—32
   sees and hears distant things 43—44
   space takes on the color of precious

things 37—38
state changes and Buddhas appear
  35—37
formations skandha, ten states of
  eight ideas about the non-existence of
    form 216—219
  eight kinds of negation 220—223
  five kinds of immediate nirvana 227—
    230
  four kinds of sophistry 201—213
  four theories regarding finiteness
    196—201
  four theories regarding pervasive permanence 187—191
  four upside-down theories 191—196
  seven theories on the cessation of existence 223—227
  sixteen ways in which form can exist after death 213—216
  two theories on the absence of cause 178—187
four kinds of offerings 119

G

ghosts
  and anger 64
  and suicides 63
  becoming demons 104
  possessing others 4, 65
  should be respected 85
goblin 18
Gong Shuduan 300
good and evil
  difficult to climb, easy to slip 278
gossip
  see talking
Great Sovereign God
  see Maheshvara, god
greed 95—96

  danger of 93

H

Heart Sutra 75, 265, 267, 309
Hsu Yun, Venerable Master
  on the Shurangama Sutra 318—319
Hsuan Hua, Tripitaka Master
  and a deviant disciple 61—62
  and his disciple who got trapped in the heavens 16
  and Liu Jintong 53—54
  and money 129
  and the "as-you-wish" demon 150—151
  and the fierce demon woman 157—158
  and the snakes 89—90
  and Xu Guilan 158—160

I

infatuation 11—12
investigation of "who?" 202—204

J

Japanese Buddhism 287
Journey to the West 149
  Monkey 149—150

K

Kapila, religion 240
killing 47—48

L

Lian Chi, Great Master
  and the pit of fire 311—312
life
  is perpetuated by thought 294—295
Liu Jintong 53, 76, 122

love
    lovesick, loneliness 58

M

Maheshvara, god 243—244
Manjushri, Bodhisattva 290
marriage 15
Matangi 23
mind
    is telegraphic 14—15
money 5

N

natures, three kinds of
    speculative, dependent and perfect 212—213
New Buddhism 128
Nishyanda, Buddha 60

O

one-word Chan 207—208
outflows
    freedom from 17—18

P

pishacha, ghost 156
polygamy 78
possession
    by demons 88, 141
    by fox spirits 107—108
    by ghosts 65
Prajna Sutra of the Humane King Who Protects His Country 299
precepts 172—173
    should not be too rigid 48—49
    violating 74—76
propriety 172

R

reciting
    from memory 319—320
religions
    identifying the false 97—98
    new and trendy 129

S

Sainika 249
samadhi 172—173
sexual misconduct 48
Shakyamuni Buddha
    and the dharma-ending age 161—162
    and the old man 185—186
shamatha 274
Shurangama Sutra
    the importance of 317—319
six sense organs 292
    uniting 236—237, 239, 272—273
skandha
    see consciousness skandha
    see feeling skandha
    see form skandha
    see formations skandha
    see thinking skandha
skandha-demon 21
sleeping
    and the thinking skandha 174
snakes 89
sophistry
    of "no" 207
    of "yes" 208
souls and spirits, of a person 32—34
space
    is like a wisp of clouds 12—14
spirits 252
    possessing others 4
    should be respected 85

see souls and spirits, of a person
stealing 48
suffering
　causes for 288
suicide
　see ghosts, and suicides

T

talking
　should be reduced 6–7
television 162
thinking skandha, ten states of
　greed for clever skill 84–99
　greed for immortality 152–160
　greed for peace and quiet 124–132
　greed for profound emptiness 145–152
　greed for spiritual powers 141–145
　greed for spiritual responses 117–123
　greed for union 105–111
　greed to analyze things 111–117
　greed to know past lives 132–140
　greedy for adventure 99–105
time
　cannot be obtained 197
　waits for no man 225

V

Vairochana Buddha 36
Vaishali, prince 249
Vajra Sutra 65
Vasishtha 249
Vignakara 258
vipashyana 274

W

walnuts
　are filling 135
wheel-turning sage king 314

wife-swapping 78
wisdom 172–173
　to discern right and wrong 183–184
wonderful contemplative wisdom 149
worms 31
Wu, King 300
Wuda, National Master 91

X

Xu Guilan, and the demon 158–159
Xuan Zang, Great Master 18

Y

Yongjia, Great Master 162

Z

Zhi Zhe, Great Master 317
Zhou, Dynasty 150
Zhuang Zi 176
Zhuang, lord 300

The Dharma Realm Buddhist Association

Mission

The Dharma Realm Buddhist Association (formerly the Sino-American Buddhist Association) was founded by the Venerable Master Hsuan Hua in the United States of America in 1959. Taking the Dharma Realm as its scope, the Association aims to disseminate the genuine teachings of the Buddha throughout the world. The Association is dedicated to translating the Buddhist canon, propagating the Orthodox Dharma, promoting ethical education, and bringing benefit and happiness to all beings. Its hope is that individuals, families, the society, the nation, and the entire world will, under the transforming influence of the Buddhadharma, gradually reach the state of ultimate truth and goodness.

The Founder

The Venerable Master, whose names were An Tse and To Lun, received the Dharma name Hsuan Hua and the transmission of Dharma from Venerable Master Hsu Yun in the lineage of the Wei Yang Sect. He was born in Manchuria, China, at the beginning of the century. At nineteen, he entered the monastic order and dwelt in a hut by his mother's grave to practice filial piety. He meditated, studied the teachings, ate only one meal a day, and slept sitting up. In 1948 he went to Hong Kong, where he established the Buddhist Lecture Hall and other Way-places. In 1962 he brought the Proper Dharma to the West, lecturing on several dozen Mahayana Sutras in the United States. Over the years, the Master established more than twenty monasteries of Proper Dharma under the auspices of the Dharma Realm Buddhist Association and the City of Ten Thousand Buddhas. He also founded centers for the translation of the Buddhist canon and for education to spread the influence of the Dharma in the East and West. The Master manifested the stillness in the United States in 1995. Through his lifelong, selfless dedication to teaching living beings with wisdom and compassion, he influenced countless people to change their faults and to walk upon the pure, bright path to enlightenment.

Dharma Propagation, Buddhist Text Translation, and Education

The Venerable Master Hua's three great vows after leaving the home-life were (1) to propagate the Dharma, (2) to translate the Buddhist Canon, and (3) to promote education. In order to make these vows a reality, the Venerable Master based himself on the Three Principles and the Six Guidelines. Courageously facing every hardship, he founded monasteries, schools, and centers in the West, drawing in living beings and teaching them on a vast scale. Over the years, he founded the following institutions:

The City of Ten Thousand Buddhas and Its Branches

In propagating the Proper Dharma, the Venerable Master not only trained people but also founded Way-places where the Dharma wheel could turn and living beings could be saved. He wanted to provide cultivators with pure places to practice in accord with the Buddha's regulations. Over the years, he founded many Way-places of Proper Dharma. In the United States and Canada, these include the City of Ten Thousand Buddhas; Gold Mountain Monastery; Gold Sage Monastery; Gold Wheel Monastery; Gold Summit Monastery; Gold Buddha Monastery; Avatamsaka Monastery; Long Beach Monastery; the City of the Dharma Realm; Berkeley Buddhist Monastery; Avatamsaka Hermitage; and Blessings, Prosperity, and Longevity Monastery. In Taiwan, there are the Dharma Realm Buddhist Books Distribution Association, Dharma Realm Monastery, and Amitabha Monastery. In Malaysia, there are the Prajna Guanyin Sagely Monastery (formerly Tze Yun Tung Temple), Deng Bi An Monastery, and Lotus Vihara. In Hong Kong, there are the Buddhist Lecture Hall and Cixing Monastery.

Purchased in 1974, the City of Ten Thousand Buddhas is the hub of the Dharma Realm Buddhist Association. The City is located in Talmage, Mendocino County, California, 110 miles north of San Francisco. Eighty of the 488 acres of land are in active use. The remaining acreage consists of meadows, orchards, and woods. With over seventy large buildings containing over 2,000 rooms, blessed with serenity and fresh, clean air, it is the first large Buddhist monastic community in the United States. It is also an international center for the Proper Dharma.

Although the Venerable Master Hua was the Ninth Patriarch in the Wei Yang Sect of the Chan School, the monasteries he founded emphasize all of the five main practices of Mahayana Buddhism (Chan meditation, Pure Land, esoteric, Vinaya (moral discipline), and doctrinal studies). This accords with the Buddha's words: "The Dharma is level and equal, with no high or low." At the City of Ten Thousand Buddhas, the rules of purity are rigorously observed. Residents of the City strive to regulate their own conduct and to cultivate with vigor. Taking refuge in the Proper Dharma, they lead pure and selfless lives, and attain peace in body and mind. The Sutras are expounded and the Dharma wheel is turned daily. Residents dedicate themselves wholeheartedly to making Buddhism flourish. Monks and nuns in all the monasteries take one meal a day, always wear their precept sash, and follow the Three Principles:

> *Freezing, we do not scheme.*
> *Starving, we do not beg.*
> *Dying of poverty, we ask for nothing.*
> *According with conditions, we do not change.*
> *Not changing, we accord with conditions.*
> *We adhere firmly to our three great principles.*
> *We renounce our lives to do the Buddha's work.*
> *We take the responsibility to mold our own destinies.*
> *We rectify our lives to fulfill the Sanghan's role.*
> *Encountering specific matters,*
> *   we understand the principles.*
> *Understanding the principles,*
> *   we apply them in specific matters.*
> *We carry on the single pulse of*
> *   the Patriarchs' mind-transmission.*

The monasteries also follow the Six Guidelines: not contending, not being greedy, not seeking, not being selfish, not pursuing personal advantage, and not lying.

International Translation Institute

The Venerable Master vowed to translate the Buddhist Canon (Tripitaka) into Western languages so that it would be widely accessible throughout the world. In 1973, he founded the International Translation Institute on Washington Street in San Francisco for the purpose of translating Buddhist scriptures into English and other languages. In 1977, the Institute was merged into Dharma Realm Buddhist University as the Institute for the Translation of Buddhist Texts. In 1991, the Venerable Master purchased a large building in Burlingame (south of San Francisco) and established the International Translation Institute there for the purpose of translating and publishing Buddhist texts. To date, in addition to publishing over one hundred volumes of Buddhist texts in Chinese, the Association has published more than one hundred volumes of English, French, Spanish, Vietnamese, and Japanese translations of Buddhist texts, as well as bilingual (Chinese and English) editions. Audio and video tapes also continue to be produced. The monthly journal Vajra Bodhi Sea, which has been in circulation for nearly thirty years, has been published in bilingual (Chinese and English) format in recent years.

In the past, the difficult and vast mission of translating the Buddhist canon in China was sponsored and supported by the emperors and kings themselves. In our time, the Venerable Master encouraged his disciples to cooperatively shoulder this heavy responsibility, producing books and audio tapes and using the medium of language to turn the wheel of Proper Dharma and do the great work of the Buddha. All those who aspire to devote themselves to this work of sages should uphold the Eight Guidelines of the International Translation Institute:

1. One must free oneself from the motives of personal fame and profit.
2. One must cultivate a respectful and sincere attitude free from arrogance and conceit.
3. One must refrain from aggrandizing one's work and denigrating that of others.
4. One must not establish oneself as the standard of correctness and suppress the work of others with one's fault-finding.
5. One must take the Buddha-mind as one's own mind.
6. One must use the wisdom of Dharma-Selecting Vision to determine true principles.
7. One must request Virtuous Elders of the ten directions to certify one's translations.
8. One must endeavor to propagate the teachings by printing Sutras, Shastra texts, and Vinaya texts when the translations are certified as being correct.

These are the Venerable Master's vows, and participants in the work of translation should strive to realize them.

Instilling Goodness Elementary School, Developing Virtue Secondary School, Dharma Realm Buddhist University

"Education is the best national defense." The Venerable Master Hua saw clearly that in order to save the world, it is essential to promote good education. If we want to save the world, we have to bring about a complete change in people's minds and guide them to cast out unwholesomeness and to pursue goodness. To this end the Master founded Instilling Goodness Elementary School in 1974, and Developing Virtue Secondary School and Dharma Realm Buddhist University in 1976.

In an education embodying the spirit of Buddhism, the elementary school teaches students to be filial to parents, the secondary school teaches students to be good citizens, and the university teaches such virtues as humaneness and righteousness. Instilling Goodness Elementary School and Developing Virtue Secondary School combine the best of contemporary and traditional methods and of Western and Eastern cultures. They emphasize moral virtue and spiritual development, and aim to guide students to become good and capable citizens who will benefit humankind. The schools offer a bilingual (Chinese/English) program where boys and girls study separately. In addition to standard academic courses, the curriculum includes ethics, meditation, Buddhist studies, and so on, giving students a foundation in virtue and guiding them to understand themselves and explore the truths of the universe. Branches of the schools (Sunday schools) have been established at branch monasteries with the aim of propagating filial piety and ethical education.

Dharma Realm Buddhist University, whose curriculum focuses on the Proper Dharma, does not merely transmit academic knowledge. It emphasizes a foundation in virtue, which expands into the study of how to help all living beings discover their inherent nature. Thus, Dharma Realm Buddhist University advocates a spirit of shared inquiry and free exchange of ideas, encouraging students to study various canonical texts and use different experiences and learning styles to tap their inherent wisdom and fathom the meanings of those texts. Students are encouraged to practice the principles they have understood and apply the Buddhadharma in their lives, thereby nurturing their wisdom and virtue. The University aims to produce outstanding individuals of high moral character who will be able to bring benefit to all sentient beings.

Sangha and Laity Training Programs

In the Dharma-ending Age, in both Eastern and Western societies there are very few monasteries that actually practice the Buddha's regulations and strictly uphold the precepts. Teachers with genuine wisdom and understanding, capable of guiding those who aspire to pursue careers in Buddhism, are very rare. The Venerable Master founded the Sangha and Laity Training Programs in 1982 with the goals of raising the caliber of the Sangha, perpetuating the Proper Dharma, providing professional training for Buddhists around the world on both practical and theoretical levels, and transmitting the wisdom of the Buddha.

The Sangha Training Program gives monastics a solid foundation in Buddhist studies and practice, training them in the practical affairs of Buddhism and Sangha management. After graduation, students will be able to assume various responsibilities related to Buddhism in monasteries, institutions, and other settings. The program emphasizes a thorough knowledge of Buddhism, understanding of the scriptures, earnest cultivation, strict observance of precepts, and the development of a virtuous character, so that students will be able to propagate the Proper Dharma and perpetuate the Buddha's wisdom. The Laity Training Program offers courses to help laypeople develop correct views, study and practice the teachings, and understand monastic regulations and ceremonies, so that they will be able to contribute their abilities in Buddhist organizations.

Let Us Go Forward Together

In this Dharma-ending Age when the world is becoming increasingly dangerous and evil, the Dharma Realm Buddhist Association, in consonance with its guiding principles, opens the doors of its monasteries and centers to those of all religions and nationalities. Anyone who is devoted to humaneness, righteousness, virtue, and the pursuit of truth, and who wishes to understand him or herself and help humankind, is welcome to come study and practice with us. May we together bring benefit and happiness to all living beings.

Dharma Realm Buddhist Association Branches

The City of Ten Thousand Buddhas
P.O. Box 217, Talmage, CA 95481-0217 USA
Tel: (707) 462-0939 Fax: (707) 462-0949
Home Page: http://www.drba.org

Institute for World Religions (Berkeley Buddhist Monastery)
2304 McKinley Avenue, Berkeley, CA 94703 USA
Tel: (510) 848-3440

Dharma Realm Buddhist Books Distribution Society
11th Floor, 85 Chung-hsiao E. Road, Sec. 6, Taipei, Taiwan R.O.C.
Tel: (02) 2786-3022 Fax: (02) 2786-2674

The City of the Dharma Realm
1029 West Capitol Avenue, West Sacramento, CA 95691 USA
Tel: (916) 374-8268

Gold Mountain Monastery
800 Sacramento Street, San Francisco, CA 94108 USA
Tel: (415) 421-6117 Fax: (415) 788-6001

Gold Wheel Monastery
235 North Avenue 58, Los Angeles, CA 90042 USA
Tel: (323) 258-6668

Gold Buddha Monastery
248 East 11th Avenue, Vancouver, B.C. V5T 2C3 Canada
Tel: (604) 709-0248 Fax: (604) 684-3754

Gold Summit Monastery
233 1st Avenue, West Seattle, WA 98119 USA
Tel: (206) 284-6690 Fax: (206) 284-6918

Gold Sage Monastery
11455 Clayton Road, San Jose, CA 95127 USA
Tel: (408) 923-7243 Fax: (408) 923-1064

The International Translation Institute
1777 Murchison Drive, Burlingame, CA 94010-4504 USA
Tel: (650) 692-5912 Fax: (650) 692-5056

Long Beach Monastery
3361 East Ocean Boulevard, Long Beach, CA 90803 USA
Tel: (562) 438-8902

Blessings, Prosperity, & Longevity Monastery
4140 Long Beach Boulevard, Long Beach, CA 90807 USA
Tel: (562) 595-4966

Avatamsaka Hermitage
11721 Beall Mountain Road, Potomac, MD 20854-1128 USA
Tel: (301) 299-3693

Avatamsaka Monastery
1009 4th Avenue, S.W. Calgary, AB T2P OK8 Canada
Tel: (403) 234-0644

Kun Yam Thong Temple
161, Jalan Ampang, 50450 Kuala Lumpur, Malaysia
Tel: (03) 2164-8055 Fax: (03) 2163-7118

Prajna Guanyin Sagely Monastery (formerly Tze Yun Tung)
Batu 5½, Jalan Sungai Besi,
Salak Selatan, 57100 Kuala Lumpur, Malaysia
Tel: (03) 7982-6560 Fax: (03) 7980-1272

Lotus Vihara
136, Jalan Sekolah, 45600 Batang Berjuntai,
Selangor Darul Ehsan, Malaysia
Tel: (03) 3271-9439

Buddhist Lecture Hall
31 Wong Nei Chong Road, Top Floor, Happy Valley, Hong Kong, China
Tel: (02) 2572-7644

Dharma Realm Sagely Monastery
20, Tong-hsi Shan-chuang, Hsing-lung Village, Liu-kuei
Kaohsiung County, Taiwan, R.O.C.
Tel: (07) 689-3717 Fax: (07) 689-3870

Amitabha Monastery
7, Su-chien-hui, Chih-nan Village, Shou-feng,
Hualien County, Taiwan, R.O.C.
Tel: (07) 865-1956 Fax: (07) 865-3426

Verse of Transference

May the merit and virtue accrued from this work,
Adorn the Buddhas' Pure Lands,
Repaying four kinds of kindness above,
And aiding those suffering in the paths below.

May those who see and hear of this,
All bring forth the resolve for Bodhi,
And when this retribution body is over,
Be born together in the Land of Ultimate Bliss.

Dharma Protector Wei Tuo Bodhisattva